NET | **MARKETS**

DRIVING SUCCESS IN THE
B2B NETWORKED ECONOMY

TOM DAGENAIS & DAVID GAUTSCHI

McGraw-Hill
Ryerson

Toronto Montréal Boston Burr Ridge, IL Dubuque, IA Madison, WI New York
San Francisco St. Louis Bangkok Bogotá Caracas Kuala Lumpur Lisbon
London Madrid Mexico City Milan New Delhi Santiago Seoul
Singapore Sydney Taipei

McGraw-Hill
Ryerson Limited

A Subsidiary of The **McGraw·Hill** Companies

ISBN: 0-07-089308-X

1234567890 GTC 098765432
Printed and bound in Canada.

National Library of Canada Cataloguing in Publication Data

Dagenais, Tom A.
    Net markets : driving success in the B2B networked economy

ISBN 0-07-089308-X

1. Electronic commerce. 2. Business enterprises—Computer networks.
I. Gautschi, David II. Title.

HF5548.32.D33 2001   658.8'4   C2001-903892-5

Publisher: **Joan Homewood**
Editorial Co-ordinator: **Catherine Leek**
Production Co-ordinator: **Sandra Deak**
Editor: **Lynn Schellenberg**
Interior Design and Electronic Page Composition: **Heidy Lawrance & Associates**
Cover Design and Imaging: **Brian Boucher**

Table of Contents

Acknowledgements

Writing this book has been a challenge. During the course of the past year, the B2B domain has experienced a dramatic rise and fall of participants. This fluctuation has been more than matched by a rise and fall of sentiment on the part of various onlookers—journalists, investment analysts, academics, and others. We are grateful to an extraordinary collection of people who have helped us to stay the course, to focus on the fundamentals, and to see this project through to its completion.

We are both especially indebted to the fine research support of Marc MacKinnon from the D&T Toronto office and to Mike Russell from the D&T Seattle office. These two gentlemen went well beyond the call of duty to find sources, synthesize research findings, and provide us inspiration and critique. In short, without their undaunted dedication this book would not have found closure.

A number of our Deloitte and Touche colleagues have contributed to our thinking and have offered us the gift of encouragement even when we might have been thinking twice about what we had embarked on. Anne Taylor, Deborah Wells, Mike Wien, Kenny Smith, Steve Wagner provided us key support and encouragement. Mimi Cremer, Nat D'Ercole, Dennis Kushner and a legion of staff consultants worked closely with us on projects applying many of the concepts and methodologies in the book and provided critique and feedback that helped us both to clarify our thinking and to refine our delivery of value to our clients.

We are also grateful to the following individuals who provided us valuable perspective from the market: Marc Cameron and Susan Little,

Transcore DAT Services; Louise Kitchen and George Wood, Enron OnLine (now UBS Warburg); Mark Skoda (Executive VP of the Global Logistics Practice at i2); Tim Bradshaw, TD MarketSite; and Darius Sabavala, Janus Enterprise International.

Our perspectives and thinking have been significantly influenced by the work of various thinkers and practitioners. We have extended the early work of Louis P. Bucklin on distribution channel structure in our discussion of primitive economic flows in Chapter 4. In Chapters 2 through 4 our treatment of the product and costs of Net Markets applies and extends work that Roger Betancourt has conducted in collaboration with David Gautschi on the economics of services and distribution. The discussion throughout the book of market efficiency and the characteristics of capital market microstructure draws upon the contemporary field of finance, especially upon the work of Maureen O'Hara. As we discuss in Chapters 3 and 4, Net Markets are subject to the dimensions of both competitive strategy as framed by Michael Porter and by co-opetition as framed by Adam Brandenburger and Barry Nalebuff. The discussion of institutions, at various points in the book, draws upon the provocative work of Douglass North, and the specific reference to property rights is an adaptation of classic arguments of Ronald Coase and more contemporary work of Yoram Barzel. We absolve these individuals of any errors in our interpreting their contributions to the expanding body of knowledge that relates to the understanding of Net Markets. Our colleagues at Deloitte Research also have been extremely helpful in providing us current analysis and perspective on the expanding domain of B2B models in the contemporary networked economy.

Our publisher, Joan Homewood and our editors Cathy Leek and Lynn Schellenberg, of McGraw-Hill Ryerson, have suffered with gracious patience as we violated deadlines and as events, such as the tragedy of September 11, interrupted the best laid plans for this book. Their counsel and their poise have enriched the efforts we put into completing this project.

Finally, we express a great debt of gratitude to our families who tried to look the other way as we found ourselves contaminating vacations and other family time with activities relating to 'the book.' To Mara, Micheal and Steve Dagenais and to Dee, Heidi, and Lisa Gautschi, we thank you and love you for loving us in spite of this project!

Introduction

"B2B is Dead"… will go down in history as one of those quotes that clearly shows the human race's inaccuracy in predicting the future. It will sit alongside the famous quotes from Thomas J. Watson, CEO of IBM in 1958, who stated "I think there is a market for about five computers" and from Ken Olson, then President, Chairman and Founder of Digital Equipment Corporation, who said in 1977, "There is no reason anyone would want a computer in their home." Along with "B2C is dead," "the Internet is a fad," and "Everything that can be invented has been invented," the concept of B2B being dead only a few years after the phrase was coined in the popular press is preposterous.

The statement "B2B is dead" was made by Tom Siebel, President of Siebel Software in response to the difficulties many B2B software companies were facing with falling stock prices in the market. It reflected the fact that most software vendors were having profitability problems because of lackluster sales. More importantly, their profitability problems arose because B2B software vendors had based future revenue projections partly on transaction revenues from Net Market makers, who were having trouble creating "liquidity." A very interesting word, liquidity, meaning many different things to many different people. Liquidity, or lack of it, will be a topic deeply explored in this book.

In writing this book, we clearly understand that we are flying in the face of some of the most prestigious technology leaders, business writers and analysts on the planet. And we intend to prove that

B2B, while not being a roaring success up to this point, is far from dead. Indeed, it is just at the embryonic stages of what will be a very long life.

When we talk about concepts such as Business to Business (B2B), Business to Consumer (B2C), electronic procurement, electronic marketplaces (Net Markets), or any other electronic business concept, we need to understand that the focus on these initiatives must always be to provide unique value to a business, its customers, its suppliers or any other stakeholder who will use the technology. The concept of *value*, as we will explain later, is often nebulous, with numerous definitions. Creating value is very dependent on circumstances and therefore the value of B2B is circumstantial to your organization. No one can define value for your business, or redefine it without a corresponding impact on your organization and the part you play in the demand or supply chain of your industry.

Concepts such as supply chain, procurement, inventory management are old concepts changed by the Internet.

The real underlying opportunity of B2B commerce lies in the ability to bind organizations together. Much like nuclear fusion, which fuses atoms to create energy far in excess of the individual atoms, B2B is about the binding of businesses together to create energy, in the form of increased revenue and profits, where the sum of the whole is greater than the sum of the parts alone. The whole in this case is the chain of supply and demand that exists in all business models today. The Internet allows this fusion to happen on a global scale through concepts such as public, private and vertical Net Markets. It brings together both the buying and selling of goods and services, and as such, B2B must be viewed in an integrated manner. Understanding the concepts of selling or buying on the Internet in isolation is not enough to ensure appreciation of the true power of the Internet, B2B commerce or Net Marketplaces.

Some Definitions

We should start with some basic definitions that will apply throughout this book.

Business-to-business commerce (B2B) is defined as a commercial transaction (exchange of money for goods or services) conducted by any two business entities for profit.

Business-to-consumer commerce (B2C) is defined as a commercial transaction (exchange of money for goods or services) conducted by a business with the end consumer of the good or service for profit using the Internet as the means for facilitating the communications and execution of the transaction.

Net Markets are entities that facilitate B2B or B2C commercial transactions using the Internet as the means for facilitating the communication and execution of the transaction.

Most books on B2B have tended to focus on the revolutionary nature of the technology or the doom and gloom awaiting those businesses that do not immediately adopt some form of electronic commerce. Some books have also focused on the rags-to-riches opportunity that every business will miss if they don't get in the game.

This book is not like the others. We have taken a business executive's perspective on the implications of B2B Net Markets on your business and the overall business environment globally. The book leads you through the options and challenges of implementing real, valuable B2B tools and technologies. More importantly, it identifies and articulates the day-to-day business implications of B2B. Every executive needs to understand not only the various concepts of B2B, but how each of these will directly impact the organization. The real impact of B2B comes in the functional areas of the business: finance and taxation, people, processes, organizational design, security and control. Each B2B initiative can have very different and profound impacts on each of these functional areas. In addition, each of these various technologies provides different value and return on investments and therefore not all B2B initiatives are created equal.

We believe that business executives need to know how their business enterprises will get the job done, knowing that the train has left the station in terms of digital communications and the network economy. This book will help explain a few things:

- what is out there in terms of B2B technologies and business solutions
- what drives these technologies and the major trends in business to business
- how these tools and technologies can provide value

What the CEO needs to know is how to adapt to these technologies and how to exploit these technologies and the changes they represent to business advantage.

This book is about two key concepts:

- the *business drivers* of B2B, which make its future success inevitable
- the *business value* that B2B can deliver to any business, which can be derived only if the CEO understands the process by which that value is harnessed by an organization

We also discuss:

- how and why current B2B failures in the market have occurred
- how and why current B2B successes in the market have occurred
- how to identify the drivers of B2B success in any industry or business
- the evolution of B2B technologies and that there is no one technology solution that delivers value in all circumstances, necessitating a "portfolio approach"
- how value is created by B2B
- how the seven key trends in B2B will shape and change both the drivers of success and the value proposition of B2B
- where the phenomenon is going and what that means to any business

We have written this book to assist the senior executive team who may not have the internal technology or business skills readily available in their organization to assess the strategic and practical implications of new customer demands and electronic marketplace competition.

The implications of these new Net Market business models on most businesses are extensive and complex. They raise questions which most senior executives should be able to answer including:

- How will we capitalize on these new Net Market business opportunities?
- Which Net Market business model or models work in our industry?
- Can we create new and unique value for our customer that does not exist in our industry today?

- What are our competitors doing?
- Who are our new competitors now?
- What is the impact on our traditional people, processes and technologies should we decide to embark on any B2B initiative?

Business Drivers of B2B Commerce

The business drivers of B2B commerce require that a more holistic view of B2B be taken. The success of B2B initiatives is not just about technology. On the contrary, the most significant aspect of B2B failure has not been technology failure. The truly successful B2B initiatives have been able to influence, react to, and co-exist with, a number of cultural, market and institutional dimensions that exist in their industries. These dimensions are powerful forces that must be reckoned with in every industry. In many cases, B2B has taken the view that just because technology can allow a business to never see or meet a trading partner, that most organizations prefer that mode of business relationship. In this case, the assumption is that the convenience provided by the technology (not having to speak to a trading partner) is of more value than the inherent risk created by not having an interpersonal relationship with that trading partner. The "institution" of interpersonal business communication is discarded for the technological value provided by "anonymous" trading. In a world where interpersonal communication in business has existed for thousands of years, sometimes culture and tradition are much stronger in business than the "value" inherent in efficient, anonymous trading. In many industries, simple institutions such as knowing your trading partner or passing pieces of paper on the stock exchange trading floor are very difficult to change, even when the inherent value of doing so is obvious. Therefore, a successful B2B initiative cannot make any assumptions about "value" or about the ease of influencing, changing or creating new institutions in an industry. The drivers of success are based on the complex inter-relationship of market needs, institutions, demand, technology, and in some cases, state or government regulations.

In the chapters that follow we explore and illustrate these drivers and their dimensions and provide a framework with which to define B2B initiatives in a manner that will consider the drivers and bring them closer to B2B success.

Some Historical Perspective

Catastrophic failures in business are not new and certainly not constrained to any one industry or era. The herd mentality displayed by the capital market that drove billions of dollars of investment into ideas that had no basis in economic reality has been seen before. The electric power industry and the railroad industry at the turn of the 20th century show remarkably similar characteristics to the B2B and B2C technology industries of the late 1990s. The historic gold rushes of the Yukon, California, and Australia showed the same characteristics. In all cases, the industries flourished, in time, after the euphoria had worn off, and the profits began to accrue to those businesses that determined how to create value by playing a key part in the new industry. In the early days of the electric power industry, most "experts" did not see a use for electric power outside of the light bulb. Many experts predicted that with this limited use, the only viable means of creating power would be through small generators that would be a part of every household. The concept of hydroelectric generating stations, a nationwide power grid and the central generation and distribution of power with state regulatory controls was not even conceivable until many, many years after the great discovery by Ben Franklin. It required a maturing of the technology from direct current to alternating current thus permitting the long-distance transmission of electricity. By that time in the late 1890s, a myriad of small power plants, built by different firms whose systems were incompatible, had sprung up everywhere. Had the electrical industry itself not quickly centralized, the U.S. could have developed a confusion of different currents, voltages, and wiring systems, a reality which existed in London, England, in 1900.

Sound familiar? There are parallels with that scenario in the B2B space and the Internet space today: many different standards, many incompatibilities, many providers. As with the electric industry, we see the maturing of B2B and the standardization of transactions along with free and ubiquitous access to the Internet as being a foregone conclusion. With those evolutions, the foundation for highly cost-effective B2B transaction processing will exist. A consolidation of the market will take place and the number of vertical, horizontal and industry Net Markets will reduce to a number that is supportable by the economic benefit these organizations create.

In the early days of the automobile industry, over 240 companies competed in the ten years from 1900 to 1910. Now there are only 40 worldwide. It is predicted that only five will exist by 2010.

The issues are the same today for B2B purveyors. There have been a great number of failures in B2B and B2C. We will talk about them in this book, to provide an understanding and a framework for our readers to ensure your endeavor avoids these mistakes and that you are able to understand how to create value and actually have wealth accrue to your business.

The Stereotyping of Failure

If you are an avid reader of the popular press, you would have surmised that the failures of most B2C and B2B initiatives were caused by the following:

- poor or non-existent business management skills among the founders of those dotcom businesses, who were technical geeks fresh out of school
- wealth-crazy, marketing-savvy midlife crisis types who had no interest in creating a business that made money, but only an interest in creating a stock that had a huge valuation
- technology problems suffered by visionaries who could think up great ideas but not get the hardware and software to work to deliver on the vision
- poorly designed and marketed Web sites, causing the classic "liquidity problem," the term used to explain failure when not enough buyers or sellers transact business through the Web site

In fact, during our research of the underlying causes of failure (or, for that matter, of success) it became evident that these causes are red herrings that do not lead to what went wrong and how to avoid failure in the future. This book will provide a framework for understanding the drivers of success and the causes of failure. It will provide a compelling argument for the long-term success of B2B initiatives.

What Is Value?

In order to determine value, we must define what we mean. While there are many definitions of value in a business context, we have settled on one definition that we will use throughout this book. Simply stated value can be defined as:

> Value for the business entity is the price a customer is willing to pay for the product the business supplies to the market or reduction in cost to an entity created through new, unique and desired efficiencies in the way in which it creates and delivers goods or services to the market or by which it acquires goods and services from the market.

Accounting profit equals revenue minus costs; economic profit is accounting profit net of the cost of capital the business must employ.

Revenue derives from the prices customers pay for the quantities of goods and services they buy from the business entity.

Cost is a complex combination of scale, input prices and production technologies.

In using this definition of value, it is important to note that efficiency plays a major role in the definition. The efficiencies must be new, unique and desired by the participants in the business transaction. They must result in direct economic benefit to the participants in the transaction through increased revenue or reduced costs.

A market can be said to be more efficient if prices for a good or service do not fluctuate as widely as when the market did not exist.

The value of the enterprise is based on the expectation of discounted net cash flows of a business over time.

Efficiencies are gained in four key areas in business.

There are *market efficiencies* that allow businesses to trade in a manner that provides benefits from allowing each trading partner to buy and sell their goods and services at a point in time when they need to do so. In a perfect market, all goods produced would be sold at time of manufacture, and all goods and services demanded would be provided exactly at the time they are needed. In addition, in a perfect market, the cost paid for the goods and services is such that the buyer can obtain them at a cost less than what it would take to produce them him- or herself. Cost is defined not only as the cost of the actual goods, but as the total cost of creating the goods, including transaction processing costs, risk costs and opportunity costs. The seller would be able to make a profit on the transaction, in fact, maximize that profit, while producing the goods or services at a cost lower than the buyer would incur making the goods.

Perfect markets do not exist in any industry, and the challenges of supply, demand and pricing are apparent everywhere. Businesses are overstocked or short-stocked; they are liquidating merchandise, charging premiums and vertically integrating in order to survive, all because of imperfect markets. Any B2B initiative that can move an industry or market closer to perfection will assist in creating market efficiencies and so have value to the trading partners. The stock exchange is one market that has moved much closer to perfection, although many investors would say it is still quite a distance away.

Efficiencies can also be created in managing transaction *risks*. Risks that are associated with any business transaction are wide ranging. There is the risk that payment will not be made by the buyer. There is the risk that the goods will not be delivered on time, or at all or in the desired quantity. There is also the risk that the goods will not be of the quality or specification required. All of these risks create uncertainty in both the buyer and seller and require businesses to undertake a variety of risk mitigation processes to manage the risk. Most of the ancillary services provided by financial institutions and insurance companies today are a result of companies looking for ways to mitigate risk. The concept of factoring receivables (selling receivables balances at a discount to a third party) was created out of the need for businesses to manage payment risk. Performance bonds and escrow accounts are other concepts created to manage risk. On a broader basis, many businesses have acquired their suppliers and begun the process of vertically integrating their business to ensure that they can control the availability and price of raw materials to their core business. All of these instruments and strategies are designed to manage risk. Value can be created in B2B initiatives through providing efficiencies to trading partners in reducing or eliminating these risks. Value can also be created by reducing the costs associated with managing these risks.

Value is also created through providing *time efficiencies*. Reducing the time to perform a required task in the trading process is of value to both parties. Time efficiency can be split into time to process a transaction, time to produce a good or service, or time to deliver a good or service. The time dimension has become an exceedingly important factor in business as a competitive advantage. In industries characterized by a large number of potential providers that are relatively homogeneous (for example, cellular phone providers), time to deliver or time to process an order could provide the unique value proposition for competitive advantage. Where the time necessary to process a business transaction is a significant component of the overall exchange of value (as in insurance claims processing) any efficiency in reducing the time associated with processing a claim could provide significant value to both the insurance company and the claimant. Time efficiency is often touted as a key value of B2B. It is also the dimension which is the most difficult to quantify in terms of benefit. The time efficiency dimension should not be confused with the cost efficiency dimension. The value of the time efficiency dimension is in reducing the actual time to perform a task. The ancillary benefits derived in reducing overall costs associated with performing a task are a separate dimension. It is important to understand that in many industries time efficiencies provide significant value and, in some cases, may actually increase overall costs.

Finally, efficiencies can be created by reducing the cost of acquiring goods and services. The ability for a business to source goods and services at a lower cost than in the previous trade exchange has a value. *Cost efficiencies* can be garnered through access to greater amounts of knowledge about the current market for raw materials. Cost efficiencies can also come from expanding the number of trading partners, thus increasing competition for the business. Efficiencies can also come from cost reductions in the production of goods and services. These efficiencies are generally created through the application of different production techniques or through the elimination of steps in the process. By eliminating a distributor or reseller, a business might achieve cost efficiencies by going direct to the customer. This disintermediation of the middleman is only efficient if the overall costs of going direct to the customer in fact go down. Many B2B failures have occurred because this assumption was incorrect and the manufacturer experienced cost increases by eliminating the middleman.

These four efficiencies, *Markets, Risk, Cost* and *Time,* are the foundation of value in the B2B Networked Economy. We will explore and apply this framework throughout the book in order to illustrate how value is created in B2B initiatives.

B2B Net Market Participants

In the Net Markets world, there are a number of key stakeholders. Each stakeholder has a part to play and a particular value to derive from the relationship. In this book we will refer to three specific stakeholders:

1. Net Market participants
2. Net Market makers
3. Net Market ancillary service providers

Net Market participants are those buyers and sellers who choose to connect to a Net Market. These primary organizations transact business through the marketplace. In most industries, these participants will extend from the raw materials providers all the way through to the end consumer of the final product, whatever that may be. In the automobile industry, participants could be everyone from the buyer of the car through to the iron ore mine that digs the raw ore to produce the steel that goes into the car. In most cases, participants in the supply chain are defined as those who can obtain value from participating in the exchange and obtain one or more of the four key efficiencies of B2B.

Net Market makers are those organizations that own and operate the electronic marketplace. These owners and operators may be companies that are fully independent of the market (that is, are not also buyers or sellers) or could be major and dominant participants in the exchange as both buyers and sellers. Net Market makers have a unique place in B2B, as they must clearly understand the value created by the exchange for each participant. They must also ensure that their business model of operation allows them to operate the exchange and make a profit from doing so. In that regard, they must clearly understand the drivers of value and ensure that value accrues to the participants and ancillary service provider.

Net Market ancillary service providers are all of those organizations that provide services through the Net Market to participants that increase the value proposition of the Net Market. By definition, they must provide services that create or increase the efficiencies in markets, risk, cost or time.

As an example, companies that provide financial services to allow for the automatic payment and deposit of funds from a transaction into the seller's account would be ancillary service providers that provide risk efficiencies around the payment process.

Whether you are a participant, market maker or ancillary service provider, you should read this book in its entirety.

Participants must clearly understand their needs and must be able to determine whether a Net Market and its ancillary service providers provide value. Net Market makers must clearly understand the drivers of value in order to ensure that their market adequately addresses the needs of the participants. They must also understand which ancillary services are required to increase value.

Finally, ancillary service providers who possess a clear understanding of the drivers of value can tailor their offerings to the specific industry and improve the value equation of the marketplace.

How This Book Is Structured

The first part of this book provides the business executive with a backdrop on the B2B and B2C market and lays the foundation for understanding the business drivers and the value creation opportunities of B2B.

In Chapter 1 we review why many current B2B business models are flawed through the analysis of a variety of B2B and B2C failures and success stories. Through this analysis, we can identify the key themes and common drivers that seem to be omnipresent in most B2B initiatives.

In Chapter 2 we introduce the MIDST Success Framework which identifies the five key dimensions of B2B Success:

- the Markets Dimension
- the Institutional Dimension
- the Demand Dimension

- the State Policy Dimension
- the Technology Dimension

In Chapter 3, we introduce the spectrum of B2B technology solutions from e-procurement through to private Net Markets. In doing so, we explore the differences between these technologies and identify how value is derived from each. In order to clearly understand value, we introduce the MaRCoT Value Framework. This framework has been created to provide the reader with a simple model for understanding value. The MaRCoT framework discusses value in terms of four key efficiencies:

- Market efficiencies
- Risk efficiencies
- Cost efficiencies
- Time efficiencies

Using real-life company case studies, we will frame the value proposition of B2B and work with the MaRCoT Value Framework to demonstrate its application.

With a clear understanding of both the drivers and the value models, we explore in Chapter 4 the concept of how value is created and how it is impacted throughout the value chain through the interjection of various B2B business models and technologies. By exploring the concept of the five primitive business flows, the ways in which value is created and shifted in the supply and demand chain by B2B commerce, we complete our review of the key tools through which any B2B initiative should be delivered. The primitive flows include:

- Product flow
- Payment flow
- Information flow
- Property Rights flow
- Risk flow

Finally, Chapter 5 provides an overview of the seven key trends in B2B that are reshaping B2B as it evolves to meet the existing challenges. We discuss the seven key trends both in terms of their impact on the MaRCoT Value Framework and how they are influenced by the MIDST Success Drivers.

The next part of the book, The Seven Key Trends in B2B Commerce, is designed to provide the reader with a clear understanding of the direction of B2B and further insights into the seven trends.

Chapters 6 through 11 explore the impact of the Success Drivers on the seven trends and use the MIDST Success Drivers and MaRCoT Value frameworks to support or refute the drivers and value of the trend.

Chapter 12 discusses the business implications on Net Market stakeholders, focusing on the key stakeholders in B2B—participants (buyers and suppliers), Net Market makers and Net Market ancillary service providers.

Finally, in our Conclusion, we look at the impact of the events of September 11, 2001, on B2B and attempt to put forward a view of the ongoing evolution of B2B commerce. In looking forward we are hoping to provide you with some ideas on the possibilities for the B2B.

By writing the book we hope to provide an alternative view to the notion that B2B is dead. Indeed, we hope that you, the reader, will conclude that B2B is alive and well, in embryonic form with a long promising future ahead.

1

Watch Your Step: B2B Traps Ahead!

OVERVIEW AND GOAL OF THE CHAPTER

The promise of electronic business and the predictions of the demise of the bricks-and-mortar way of doing business have been well publicized and well documented. Only months ago heady predictions were commonplace, among them, that there would be $7 trillion per year in trading on B2B exchanges by 2005 (a major information service provider) over 50 percent of all business transactions would be conducted over the Internet also by 2005 (a different major information service provider), and B2B would be reducing the cost of doing business by 20 to 50 percent (a major investment bank).

CEOs all over the world have lived through the dotcom crash and read reports of ex-dotcom executives and erstwhile Internet millionaires now looking for "real" work.

With the extensive press surrounding so many failures of B2B businesses, it would be easy to dismiss the predictions made by almost every industry analyst who covered *technology* at the turn of the 21st century that B2B would dramatically and permanently change the face of business in the next five years. The reality of the

B2B *space* is that failures have occurred. But so have successes. While it is quite easy to point to a failure and attribute it to the unrealistic pressures and expectations of overzealous investors or far-fetched ideas born in the minds of starry-eyed dotcommers, we think the reasons for failure can be identified and explained in business and economic terms. If one learns best from mistakes, then we are now standing on a bonanza in the B2B world. Success stories have much to offer us as well. In this chapter we hope to provide a perspective that will stimulate your thinking as you progress on your own B2B journey. We will explore some real-life case studies of failure and success in the B2B market. These case studies review various types of business models, most of which are new and different. Before we begin exploring the cases, we will first take the opportunity to define a business model in its simplest terms.

Defining a Business Model

A *business model* is an idea, a concept of how one can earn an economic return from an activity that provides value for someone else.

Knowing how to provide value to someone else is a human challenge extending well beyond the confines of business enterprise. Knowing how to provide value to someone else and earning an economic return from doing so adds to the complexity of the challenge and is the key problem that all business enterprise attempts to address.

Often business success is determined by the clarity of the business model. The business model affords its creator a reference point that enables the planning and execution of a set of business processes to deliver value. In no case does a technology dictate a business model, and in few cases, if any, does technology determine the success of the enterprise or its business model. This last point is important to acknowledge because there are countless examples of business successes and failures in technologically advanced domains where the business model failed or succeeded without reference to the technology used to deliver unique value.

Often the success of a business enterprise and the distinctiveness of its underlying business model derive from factors beyond the control of its owners and managers. For example:

- states enact laws and policies that render a mode of realizing economic return more or less difficult (for instance, choosing not to enforce sales tax collection has abetted the growth of catalog retailers)
- as customers and users learn, their demands evolve either to increase or reduce their use of resources of a third-party enterprise (for example, certain value added resellers (VARs) specializing in providing computer support to small businesses may find that their user base erodes as users become more skilled)
- the activities of suppliers and the suppliers' suppliers to earn their own economic returns may reinforce or undercut the plans and methods of the downstream agent to earn a return for himself (for example, Taiwanese producers of microchips restrict production, thus delaying the shipment of a newly designed microprocessor announced by Intel and of PCs using the microprocessor announced by Dell and Compaq)
- similarly, the pursuits of agents or resellers who serve customers on behalf of an organization may reinforce or undercut the business plans and methods for earning an economic return (for example, Wal-Mart installs state-of-the-art electronic inventory management systems, increases the typical store scale of operations, and requires branded goods manufacturers to accelerate deliveries and bear inventory holding costs)

There are many reasons why a *business model* may succeed or fail, and only some of those reasons relate directly to the thinking and acting of its creator.

Failures everywhere...

For purposes of our discussion, we shall designate a ***business failure*** as:

> Evidence that the enterprise has not delivered on the intended *value proposition* in a way that produces the originally intended economic return.

Consider the four classic reasons ventures fail:

1. Poor financing—the venture does not have enough capital to see it through start-up and through the early years of product development or customer acquisition;
2. Insufficient customer base—too few customers are attracted because the company lacks effective marketing and sales to generate sufficient sales volume;
3. Undifferentiated offering—the company has a good or service which is the same or similar to its competitors and so loses its way in a sea of "me-too" companies trying to compete with a small number of larger, more established competitors in the space;
4. Poor leadership—the management of the company lacks general business know-how or has little relevant experience and expertise in the industry.

This list of potential factors to explain a *business failure* could be much longer. It is probably sufficient to say that the fundamental reasons for business failure have typically reduced to money, market or management. So we shall begin by looking at several failures in the B2B and B2C space and seek to determine the role money, market and management played in their demise.

BIZBUYER.COM

BizBuyer.com of Santa Monica, California, was founded in 1998 with a goal to provide small- and medium-sized businesses with customized price quotes for a variety of goods and services. By matching buyers with sellers via a "buyer profile" and a "vendor profile," BizBuyer.com would provide the buyer with a means of obtaining several quotes online that could meet the buyer's specifications. BizBuyer offered its service free to buyers. In doing so, it eliminated or reduced the typical buyer's need to shop the whole market for prices. BizBuyer's value proposition for buyers was to simplify and accelerate the purchasing process at a low cost.

The vendors who listed on BizBuyer.com paid a fee for submitting a quote. BizBuyer.com's value proposition for vendors was to provide them access to a large market at a low cost of marketing.

BizBuyer.com successfully attracted some very large partners, including Qwest, UUNET and PSINet, all major players in their respective markets. In total, BizBuyer.com raised over $44.5 million in funds from a variety of investors over an 18-month period. In June 1999 the site was launched with much fanfare and with industry analysts espousing the BizBuyer concept as a strong example of *aggregation of demand* that allowed suppliers to reach out to smaller buyers. Within four months of its launch, BizBuyer.com had attracted over 6,000 vendors.

An especially interesting aspect of the original business model was that BizBuyer, while charging the vendor a small fee for the quote, did not charge a transaction fee. BizBuyer did not generate any advertising revenue on the site either. According to Bernard Louvat, BizBuyer.com CEO and founder, BizBuyer would ensure lightening-fast download speeds by never allowing paid advertising on the site to slow down access. Gradually BizBuyer began to charge a listing fee between three and ten dollars depending on the type of good or service and the type of Internet connection the participants used. Generating money for the business appears to have been an evolving concern of management.

Significant outside money did support the business. BizBuyer.com attracted well-heeled backers and board members. CEO Meg Whitman was one of the original angel investors and also a member of the BizBuyer.com board. "I thought there was an opportunity to take on a very fragmented market and create a forum that could be more efficient," she said. "They are on the one-yard line of a 100-yard football field and have a long way to go. But these things tend to grow organically."

One would have to conclude that the football field to which Ms. Whitman was referring was much longer than regulation length, because in December 2000, BizBuyer.com shut down the site. Against various common business performance measures BizBuyer appeared to be doing reasonably well. Not only did BizBuyer.com have $35 million in cash in the bank, it reportedly had over 1.3 million unique visitors to its site each month. BizBuyer also had over 25,000 suppliers responding to customer requests for quotations.

In a retrospective statement, Bernard Louvat summed up the Net Markets problems of BizBuyer.com: "Unfortunately, we could not build the liquidity and transaction volume necessary to support an ongoing market-place, as well as create acceptable returns for our investors in today's financial market environment." The funds left were returned to investors.

So what really was going on here? BizBuyer.com was a well-financed business, with strong management, providing a service unique at the time to an apparently huge market, as measured by the millions of visitors to the site and millions of small businesses looking to save a buck. BizBuyer.com appeared to have all of the pieces one would consider fundamental to success.

Louvat used the word *liquidity* to explain the failure. Liquidity is widely regarded as a key to Net Market success.

Liquidity Defined

To define *liquidity*, first consider a context in which one party—the first party—holds rights to some property, and another party—the counter party—has an interest in acquiring some rights to that property. Liquidity gauges the ease with which prices can be established for rights to the property such that the first party and the counter party may engage in an exchange of property rights. Formally, a market is *liquid* whenever any given first party would be willing to accept a *fungible* asset (usually cash or some money instrument) or a promise to such an asset in exchange for relinquishing some or all rights to the services that the property can generate.

An example might help demonstrate what this definition is all about.

The Story of the Baker and the Truck Driver

Once there was a baker who wanted to acquire a panel truck so she could make deliveries to shops that sold her bread. A friend told the baker about a fellow who had bought a panel truck some months earlier for $25,000. The baker exclaimed that that price was a little less than the total she had paid for one of her ovens and a dough-mixing machine. Because she assumed that everything would depreciate in value at more or less an equal rate, she asked her friend to find the fellow so she could offer him her oven and dough-mixing machine in exchange for the panel truck.

The friend contacted the truck driver and conveyed the baker's offer. The truck driver laughed. "I don't want to work in a hot bakery—I'd rather be sailing! I wouldn't know what to do with baking equipment, but I wouldn't mind raising some dough to buy a small fishing boat. If your friend would like to buy my truck for $20,000, maybe we can do business."

The moral of the story: Both parties in this case valued the assets considered for exchange, but there was no coincidence of needs between them. In order for them to exchange successfully:

- the baker would have to sell her baking equipment to another party for $20,000 and then pay the truck driver for the truck so the truck driver could satisfy himself by buying a small fishing boat or
- the truck driver would have to accept the baking equipment in exchange for the panel truck, and then find another party willing to pay him $20,000 for the equipment so he could buy the boat.

Complicated! The assets in question (baking equipment and the panel truck) could not be bought and sold easily. They were not liquid in the context of the story, with only two parties of divergent needs transacting. One could make these assets potentially liquid, though, by posting them for sale on a site like BizBuyer.com, assuming that a sufficiently large number of people with diverse needs and the ability to pay with fungible assets (that is, money instruments) were paying attention to the BizBuyer.com site.

We measure the degree of market liquidity using what we call the "PTR index." Liquidity results from the interaction of three basic market components at a point in time, and liquidity may wax and wane as the levels of these three components change. **P** is the population of potential exchange **p**artners, **T** is the propensity of the potential exchange partners to **t**ransact, and **R** is the **r**ate or intensity of the transactions of the transacting parties.

$$\textit{Index of liquidity} = P \times T \times R$$

Since these three components interact multiplicatively, liquidity can be achieved with various combinations of PTR. Generally, liquidity is greater the larger the population of potential users (P), the more frequent or the greater the propensity to transact (T), and the greater the average size of a transaction (R). A simple "Rule of Two" applies to the interpretation and use of the index: liquidity can be achieved when two of the components are at high levels, and illiquidity is assured when two of the components are at low levels. There is a range of ambiguous cases in which the components are at medium levels and liquidity may or may not be achieved.

Returning to the situation of BizBuyer.com, we now can articulate the challenge as building at least two of the components to high levels. We know that P was relatively high because there were 25,000 vendors placing profiles on the site and there were over 1.3 million unique visitors to the site each month. But as Bernard Louvat explained, there was insufficient transaction volume. BizBuyer.com had successfully attracted many potential customers, but their propensities to transact were too low, and when they did transact, the lot sizes were too small.

The level of liquidity required to support BizBuyer.com followed from that aspect of the business model that produced the revenues: the pricing model. BizBuyer.com charged vendors a small fee to list a profile on the site, but at start-up BizBuyer.com did not charge prospective buyers entry fees or buyers or sellers fees for executing a transaction. Moreover, Louvat precluded revenues from such ancillary value-creating activities as advertising so as to assure high speeds of Web access for all participants. The only source of revenue for BizBuyer.com was in building up P, and initially only on the vendor side. For BizBuyer to be successful, P would have to be quite large.

The BizBuyer experience illustrates that whether liquidity is "high" or "low" depends on what the venture's business model envisions as requirements to sustain the business. Prices are among the many factors that influence P, T and R. Setting low prices for entry, the right to transact and the scale for the transaction should increase the levels of P, T and R. The relationships between prices and the levels of the liquidity components should look like this:

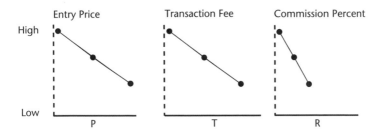

So, setting low prices for any of the components noted in the graph should produce correspondingly high levels of those components. However, setting prices to zero for two components means that the conceivably high resulting levels of those components have no influence on the total revenues generated for the business. Imagine, T (the volume of participants transacting) could approach 100 and R (the average size of the transaction) could be enormous, and BizBuyer.com would still be stuck with the anemic revenues generated from the entry fees charged to participants irrespective of the level of their participation. The unhappy conclusion on BizBuyer.com is this: it didn't matter what the liquidity was; all BizBuyer.com needed to make millions of dollars was millions and millions of participants who would pay an entry or listing fee. In fact, since there were no prices associated with T or R, then there really didn't have to be any transaction volume!

A simple comparison of possible revenues might help to illustrate this. Let's say that BizBuyer charged an average of five dollars for each listed vendor. There were 25,000 vendors, so $5 x 25,000 = $125,000. Let's suppose that a competing Net Market, Dagenais and Gautschi Enterprises, charges a one-dollar listing fee for its 25,000 vendors, or $25,000, and one dollar for each transaction. If D&G Enterprises attract only half of the buyers that BizBuyer had, or 650,000 unique visitors per month (P), and only 25 percent of these visitors transacted (T), then that would constitute $325,000 revenues *per month* plus $25,000 transaction-insensitive revenues to pay for the fixed costs of the operations.

Liquidity was not the problem for BizBuyer.com. The business model was the problem.

There were probably other significant issues as well. Bringing buyers and sellers to a site on the Web requires the articulation of a compelling value proposition. For BizBuyer.com, the value proposition was to simplify and accelerate the purchasing process. The prospective buyer would have evaluated the value in terms of reduced time, lower out-of-pocket cost or enhanced convenience in using the site as compared to conventional ways of accomplishing the same purchasing tasks. The target buyers for BizBuyer.com were small businesses. Traditionally, typical small-business owners look at their suppliers as partners in their businesses and establish relationships with them on the basis of three factors:

1. Proximity to their business and the ability to order and receive goods on a timely basis, as needed to meet demand. They need to stock materials to adequately meet short-term demand yet rarely plan for spikes in demand, so require quick access to these goods from reliable suppliers.
2. Reliability of the supplier and the supplier's trustworthiness in delivering the right goods within specification when needed.
3. Price, generally the lowest price given the specifications and the supplier's ability to meet the needs of the small business on a "spot basis."

Spot buying is important in the small business market. Spot buying occurs when a business needs to meet unexpected spikes in demand, or when the business needs items that are not high-volume or core to the ongoing operation.

A challenge of a Net Market such as BizBuyer.com is not only to provide a way for the small-business owner to get a better price but to do so with suppliers whom the small-business owner can trust and who can deliver, on a spot basis, the right product to the right location, within the specification. These practices are central in determining the demand that small-business users might have had for the Net Market's goods and services; the demand was couched in the context of the traditions of the industry, namely the buying habits and operating customs of small businesses. We refer to such traditions and conventions as *institutions*.

Considering the mix of habits, customs, traditions and quirks of millions of small businesses in hundreds of specialized industries, it would have been a daunting task for a Net Market like BizBuyer.com to understand and then address or change these institutions. Offering the ability to find something quickly at a price that may be lower than the price the potential user currently pays, or even the lowest price in the market, may not be sufficient to change an institution in an industry or a small business.

There were institutional issues among the suppliers, too, who posted quotes on the BizBuyer.com site. The steps entailed in a quoting process typically cannot be accomplished without verbal interaction and the exchange of information to ensure proper specification of the good or service the buyer is seeking. Demand among vendors to post quotes may have been restricted to only those kinds of goods and services that required little negotiation.

Interestingly, technology did not appear to factor into the failure of BizBuyer.com. The software required to operate the site and to manage the business was built and implemented successfully. While some B2C failures in the early days of the e-commerce boom may have been attributed to poorly designed Web sites and service interruptions caused by use of inappropriate hardware or poorly designed software, there is no evidence that technology caused the BizBuyer.com demise.

Was BizBuyer.com a bad idea? Not necessarily, but it was an idea with bad economics. It was well run (securing 25,000 vendors to list and attracting over a million unique visits each month), and it was well financed. In terms of the traditional triumvirate of reasons for failure—money, market and management—it would seem to have overcome the hurdles of success. Yet it did not succeed in capturing any of the value it was creating through appropriately set prices, and it was perhaps not quick enough in responding to the larger-than-life institutional issues of small businesses that might have slowed their adoption of new ways of conducting business.

ENCRYPTIX.COM

EncrypTix.com was founded in 1999 to develop software that enabled the storage, transportation and authentication of tickets, legal documents and other value-bearing instruments in a secure way. EncrypTix.com envisioned a world where movie and theater tickets, gift certificates, airline tickets, vouchers and boarding passes could be delivered over the Internet to users who could then print their own documents on their own printers.

The underlying technology was developed and applied by a company called Stamps.com who had been awarded the right by the U.S. government to distribute postage stamps electronically. Backed by such marquee firms as American Express Travel Related Services Company Inc., Mitsubishi International Corp., Sabre Holdings (American Airlines' reservation and ticketing divisions), and Walt Disney Co., EncrypTix.com could not have had a firmer foundation.

The disposition of the management of the firm was revealed in such pronouncements as "People will have to learn to trust the technology" and "Our technology is approved by the U.S. government" and "If it's good enough for the U.S. government, isn't it good enough for you?" The CEO of EncrypTix.com thought he had a sure winner.

In March 2001, EncrypTix.com was closed by its parent company, reportedly due to delays in the development of the specific technology that would deliver the value proposition. The challenges of creating a technology that could securely deliver a document over a public infrastructure like the Internet to its rightful owner had been daunting enough. Getting the typical business executive to accept an airline ticket in an electronic form, not looking anything like the airline ticket of old, proved also to be a challenge.

Imagine the thousands of conventional business professionals who have spent many years operating with Rolodexes, notepads, daily agendas and airline tickets as a part of their normal routine. While companies such as Palm Inc. have achieved some success in selling their products for the electronic management of calendars and e-mail, the penetration of this technology is still relatively small in relation to the total potential market. Getting people to change the institution of holding a paper airline ticket that represents hundreds or even thousands of dollars and appears to be the only piece of paper the airline industry would trade for a seat on an airplane involves re-imagining a system that has been in place for the past 50 years. Changing this with some magical piece of technology in a matter of 12 months would be a big leap, but not soon enough to generate revenues and profits that could sustain the ongoing investment required to change an institution. That is what Encryptix.com did not consider. Not only was the technology difficult to develop, changing the behavior of a huge market to use the technology was undoubtedly even more difficult.

It is uncertain whether the demise of EncrypTix.com was a result of the inability to deliver the technology on a timely basis, or whether the investors realized that getting the mass market to accept and trust electronic documents was a very long-term venture. The combination of factors has ensured, at least for now, that widespread use of electronic documents for movies and airlines will be farther out on the horizon than the investors expected. As of the fourth quarter of 2001, the electronic airline ticket appears to have taken root in the market, but not in the manner that the principals of Encryptix.com would have imagined. In most cases, passengers receive from the airlines an itinerary that references a secure file that remains within the secure network of the airline. The itinerary is a non-secure file that can be transmitted via the postal service or over the Internet. That is, unlike the Encryptix.com assumption that tickets would be transmitted electronically, the airlines have realized that all a passenger needs to do to gain access to a reserved seat on a flight is to arrive at the airport with a reference code and proper personal identification. The airlines have solved the problem that Encryptix.com sought to solve, but they have done so by exploiting the secure storage afforded by their own IT systems and authenticating by the dual checks of a reference or confirmation code and personal identification produced by the passenger. There is little that the Encryptix.com technology could have added to the capabilities of the airlines to deliver value with their own forms of electronic tickets.

CHEMDEX.COM

The case of Chemdex.com is a particularly interesting one. Formed in 1997, Chemdex.com was established to provide buyers and suppliers of a wide variety of chemicals with the ability to source and sell electronically through a single industry hub. Chemdex.com was an independently owned public vertical market exchange. One rather significant aspect of its business model was that Chemdex.com would take responsibility and title to the goods and ensure delivery. In fact, while many B2B exchanges seek to cut out the middleman and allow manufacturers to deal directly with the end customer, Chemdex.com sought to be the largest aggregator of both demand and supply in a specific vertical market. Chemdex, just as any distributor, would sign agreements with manufacturers to purchase goods from them at substantial discounts. The value to the manufacturer in using Chemdex.com was that it could consolidate orders, payments and processes with one major distributor, namely Chemdex.com. Chemdex.com would then market to the large chemical users to become their key supplier. Promising substantial cost savings by offering its customers one-stop shopping with consolidated ordering and payments, Chemdex.com was hoping to attract a significant share of chemical buyers.

With quick wins in signing Dupont and Genentech, huge chemical purchasers, it looked as though Chemdex.com had the right formula for success. With substantial backing from Ventro Capital group, Chemdex.com poured millions into developing the technology to address all of the unique purchasing needs of the chemical industry.

From 1997 to 2001, Chemdex was able to grow the business from zero to over $150 million in revenue. It had managed to sign agreements with manufacturers, allowing it to represent over 1.7 million products from over 2,400 suppliers. It had over 37,000 registered users. Great story, great success, huge market, strong financial backing, apparently strong demand and an operational technology that did the job.

On March 31, 2001, Chemdex.com ceased operations.

How could this happen?

The business model of Chemdex.com required it to attract buyers—but at a cost. Large buyers expected special discounts and loyalty incentives. Chemdex.com obliged them because it wanted to create strong brand recognition and increase its volume. Because of these practices Chemdex.com was only able to generate a gross margin of just under 6 percent. In addition, 97 percent of its revenue came from the two showcase customers, Dupont and Genentech. Without a broader base of customer demand, it could not increase gross margin, proving that a key component of liquidity is not only volume of transactions, but the breadth of customers and suppliers. In the words of CEO John Thorpe, "The key issue was we could not reach liquidity fast enough." The aspect of liquidity that failed them was what one might call "liquidity of the assortment." That is, even if the market was liquid for the Dupont and Genentech users and their suppliers, there were many users among the 37,000 users registered on the site and many suppliers among the 2,400 attracted to the site who were not finding it easy to trade. The Chemdex Net Market did not perform equally efficiently for all possible traders who visited the site.

Consider what most chemical business executives might view as a key value proposition: lowest cost and widest selection for all their chemical needs. It would seem that Chemdex should have been able to attract significant activity for a large number of chemical buyers. After all, Chemdex had attracted an impressive number of chemical suppliers with a broad and deep assortment of products. So why was the proposition of lowest cost not compelling enough to generate sufficient revenue volume?

A part of the explanation may be found in Thorpe's comment that "the leap from EDI [electronic data interchange] has been too great. We spent $50 million on technology for Chemdex. We were trying to integrate about 20 different applications." In meeting the challenges of any B2B transaction, a large part of the potential value lies in the cost efficiencies and transaction efficiencies that could be achieved by electronically exchanging such documents as purchase orders, shipping reports, receiving reports and invoices. The time and costs associated with processing this paper are substantial. EDI was a technology that allowed for the standardization and electronic conduction of these transactions. The problem with EDI, as with any B2B initiative that promises time and cost savings from reduced paper-processing, is the need to move information seamlessly from supplier to customer and back. The example of Chemdex with over 2,400 suppliers and 37,000 users, many with unique financial and order management systems, illustrates the scale of this undertaking. "Tradenet [an EDI-based trading exchange] was based on a simple standard. The bulk of the revenue came from one document—the order. To jump suddenly from that to the complex many-to-many model of e-marketplaces is everybody's dream, but that's miles away."

Without the value that would be derived from this level of integrated transaction flow between suppliers, Chemdex and buyers, convincing any buyer to use the system for price-saving alone would have been improbable.

Thorpe adds, "We had this vision of added value services, but we were struggling just to get end-to-end transactions through." In a market where customers did not attach sufficient value to "lowest price for chemicals," there was little or no demand because customers did not perceive value in the services provided by Chemdex. A part of the value could have been delivered by the seamless integration of transaction-processing if Chemdex could have achieved that objective.

The challenges of integration and standards for passing transactions between trading partners will be discussed more fully in Chapter 9. At this juncture we simply observe that it is an enormous task for a single organization to attempt to create standardized transaction-processing for an entire industry, as Chemdex endeavored to do within the chemical industry.

Successes can be found...

While the popular press might have us believe that B2B is a failure and cannot possibly be successful, our research has shown that, by any business standard, there are many examples of successful Net Market initiatives. What has driven these initiatives to reach success? What have the leaders in these organizations done to move from concept to success? How have they dealt with building liquidity in the context of their business models?

We will explore some interesting examples of successful Net Market companies and attempt to identify the key drivers that have created their success.

DAT SERVICES

DAT Services of Portland, Oregon, has been in business since 1978. Beginning as an off-line company, it has successfully moved on-line. It started as a truck stop that posted on a bulletin board and announced over a public address system the availability of loads for truckers who were passing through the area with empty trucks. The service was called "Dial A Truck." Over time the system matured to a series of overhead TV monitors that scrolled through the various available load data, much like the displays of flight information at a modern airport.

In the late seventies, as many as 15 percent of all trucks were on the road empty after having delivered their loads to their destinations. The return trip, known as a deadhead, was expensive because truckers paid for fuel but had no load to deliver on the way home. After building a much larger, low-tech approach with over 1,200 truck stops in the United States using the system, DAT began to offer the service over the Internet. Today, drivers, dispatchers, shippers, carriers and anyone connected with freight management can access a nationwide system with current data on available loads and available trucks. As with any industry, not every participant is Internet-savvy, so DAT also handles over 3,000 calls a day to a call center that has access to the same information. The majority of DAT's revenue is earned through charging a subscription fee to all users. Additional fees are charged for more specific searches and matching of load to truck.

Over time, DAT has realized that their customers need more than the ability to find a load or a truck. Originally, once a deal was struck, the shipper and the trucker were left to complete the payment for the services off-line in a traditional method of invoice and check-processing. To address this need, DAT introduced a new service that allowed for the settlement of the transaction on-line. As soon as truckers and shippers fully embrace this service, DAT will institute a settlement fee (similar to a back checking fee), but for the time being, the company offers the service at no charge.

Today DAT serves over 17,000 customers and handles over 100,000 transactions a day.

DAT is a remarkable success story. Was the reason for their success their choice of business model, or was it luck?

That DAT had been a successful bricks-and-mortar company for nearly twenty years was no guarantee that the company would succeed when they went on-line in 1997. Their history did, however, give their management team a head start when it came to building liquidity and to identifying a need in the market where customers were demanding a service.

Unlike such emerging dotcoms as Transportation.com and NTE.com, who are pursuing DAT's market, DAT did not have to start from scratch when it came to soliciting carriers and shippers. DAT had already staked out its place in the demand chain and had a proven track record of delivering the services, albeit in a rather non-technical manner.

The dotcom competitors in this segment are not failing because of technology problems. They are failing on the demand dimension. They are perilously close to the underside of the Rule of Two. These companies find it difficult to build liquidity because they are having a hard time convincing enough carriers (P) to sign up and use (T) their technology.

From a technology standpoint, DAT has been able to take a successful business model that worked for two decades off-line and transform it to a successful model on-line, which at time of writing has been thriving for four years. DAT provides an easy-to-use, always-available and flexible technology that allows the industry to retain its institutions and business model without requiring the constituent users of the service to change the way they do business. DAT understood that even though the Internet allows for "any time, anywhere" access, not all truckers would be willing to carry a wireless device that put them in contact with more than one Net Market on-line exchange. This is exactly what NTE and Transportation.com hope will change quickly.

Having engaged in the activities of the trucking industry since 1978, DAT have learned the mechanics of the trucking business. DAT management knows, especially, how helping make deals for fulfilling shipments has evolved over the past quarter century. From its humble origins as a process of posting notices on bulletin boards or using sticky notes and then calling a call center, the solution to the time-worn problem of eliminating or reducing the deadhead now has truckers logging on to the Internet. DAT's technology has proved to be robust and allows for near real-time price setting and demand/supply peak fluctuations.

The Internet-based DAT service complements traditional activities and influences the growth of the demand and supply of empty truck capacity. Increased demand due to real-time bulletin boards meant that DAT needed to have a stronger back-end that was capable of fulfilling and organizing the order.

Having been immersed in the dynamics of the match/load business model, DAT has altered the way deals were set by moving the practices from PA systems and sticky notes to electronic bulletin boards. They kept the well-established institution and really did not change it after incorporating the Internet into their business. They made no attempt to force institutional changes or business process changes on the industry and, therefore, engendered strong use by both buyers and sellers. The result was liquidity in their marketplace as the Rule of Two applies in the positive direction—sizeable participation (P), strong propensity among truckers and shippers to use (T) the DAT service.

Because DAT captures the trucking and shipping information in digital form in nearly real-time, DAT adds value by providing customers with the right products at the right place at the right time.

GOFISH.COM INC./SEAFAX

Another example of an organization that attempted to capitalize on its current customer base and move to a B2B business model is Gofish.com. Gofish did not achieve its original objectives for its Net Market, the Seafood Exchange; but it has expanded its business partly because of its experiment with the Seafood Exchange. Gofish was established in 1998 as a new venture by the owner of Seafax, a company that provided credit-rating information to the seafood industry. Seafax has been around since 1985 and is well established in the seafood industry. Seafax sells credit reports and insurance to fishermen and their fleets to manage against payment risk, which is common in the industry.

In combining its existing business of credit management with the new exchange which allows for the buying and selling of fresh fish, Gofish.com saw the B2B initiative as an extension of the current business, not as a totally new strategy. On the Gofish.com Web site, buyers and sellers could enter the Seafood Exchange to see current prices for a wide variety of seafood products. Prices changed in real time as new transactions were consummated. In much the same way as stock markets operate by providing real-time trade information, Gofish.com could provide information to buyers and sellers to guide their transactions. Additionally, based on its extensive database of credit information, Gofish.com could ensure that new members to its trading community pass stringent credit checks.

Gofish.com has also taken the approach that trading is not the only, or at least not the most important, component of its service offering. Traditions in the industry are strong, where small-business seafood stores, fishermen and distributors have built relationships off-line that have, in some cases, spanned generations of family operations. Trust in this business is critical and tends to be cultivated by long-standing personal relationships. Participants are especially sensitive to the risks of non-payment, as fresh fish cannot retain market value if a supplier must repossess inventories from a buyer who defaults on a promise to pay.

Gofish.com offers participants in the fresh seafood market system a creative value proposition, and the value proposition is based on promises of cost and risk reduction rather than on price discounts. Gofish.com has combined trading with credit validation and added the option for the seller to receive an electronic transfer of the payment in the seller's bank account within 48 hours. In a business where payment typically takes 30 days, sellers find great value in the accelerated cash flow.

Although Gofish.com ceased to offer active product listings on its Seafood Exchange in June 2001, it has opted to sell the software platform to other players in the industry who are interested in organizing trade with their seafood suppliers.

Gofish.com faced its own set of challenges to achieve liquidity. Commercial fishermen and seafood stores do not evoke images of leadership in information technology. The basic infrastructure of computers and Internet connections is not likely to be in place for the tens of thousands of potential buyers and sellers. Moreover, the seafood trading business has been in existence for thousands of years, and in some countries, the one-to-one relationship between a typical buyer and a typical seller has spanned many generations. The ability of Gofish.com to intervene in such relationships, potentially even severing some, would need the justification of a significant value proposition that is much stronger than the low-price value proposition touted by many Net Markets. In addition, while electronic payment may be a strong value proposition for larger players, the typical institution for payment in the industry is likely to be cash. Changing this institution may ultimately prove to be much more of a challenge in a specific segment of the industry than Gofish.com could manage.

At least initially, the opportunity for Gofish.com may have been most compelling in working with very large buyers (major supermarket chains, major restaurant chains) and very large suppliers (very large seafood processors) where the volume of transactions, the drive for lower prices and profitability, and the cost efficiencies that might be achieved through streamlined payment processes could yield decidedly positive returns. Gofish.com did create some excitement in the industry with such large and diverse players as Wal-Mart and High Liner Foods Inc., a very large supplier and seafood processor, showing interest in testing the Seafood Exchange software.

In November 2001, three members of management, George Babeu, Jim Bonnvie, and David Weatherbie, succeeded in buying the enterprise. Signalling a return to the company's core business information and credit services, they changed the company name back to Seafax. Seafax will continue to offer its web-based credit reports and risk monitoring products. Seafax will also continue to operate One Source Risk Management, which includes credit insurance, factoring, and receivables outsourcing services. Information services will be offered via the Seafax website exclusively.

"The market has spoken," said Bonnvie in the press release of November 5, 2001. "What it's told us is that the Internet is a terrific way of distributing information, but not transacting business. We are looking forward to continuing to push the capabilities of the Internet to deliver the Seafax product—the best information in the business." One might take issue with this claim, but there is no question that the complementary information and risk management services address a key need in the fresh seafood industry. The challenge of managing a virtual market place in a commodity with fluctuating, perishable supply just proved to be too complicated for the Gofish.com management team and investors, given the geographic distribution of the customers who would seek fulfillment of their orders.

EBAY

One famous and, by Internet standards, enduring example of a successful Net Market is eBay. eBay typically gets thrown into the dotcom mix and is often misclassified as being in the same category as Priceline.com and Amazon.com. In fact, eBay is an example of a C2C exchange that is extremely successful. It is now applying its skills to the B2C and B2B markets.

In its simplest form, eBay offers a person-to-person Internet-based trading community. Sellers list their items for sale at auction or at fixed prices, and buyers may bid for items on auction or order items offered at fixed prices. In addition, eBay has focused on providing and creating communities of interest around thousands of categories of items. With over 22 million registered users, eBay has been extremely successful in giving its users a place to share their experiences and their passion for collecting things. They have essentially responded to the remarkably broad interest of people to attend the world's largest virtual flea market.

By such traditional success measures as revenues, growth, profitability or branding, eBay has become a leading example of a dotcom done right. The company expects growth to continue at 50 percent or better until 2005. In 2000 the site managed 80 million sales with transaction value in excess of $5 billion. Its gross margins are exceptionally high for any business, over 80 percent. Below the surface, the company can boast, much like the Jerry Seinfeld show, to be about nothing:

- since all goods are shipped by the selling party, eBay has no distribution costs to speak of
- it has no risk of financial loss due to non-payment; the majority of the transactions (including the eBay fee) are paid via credit card
- it has insignificant costs associated with incrementally growing the business—the eBay infrastructure is scalable to progressively higher volumes of business
- the company has no inventory and therefore no carrying costs
- it has zero merchandising and product marketing costs because it has no inventory

Like other successful Net Markets, eBay realized that providing a simple means of buying and selling goods was not sufficient to drive exponential growth. They continue to provide a means of simplifying the customer's experience and to add value through new services. eBay now can provide service for financing, inspection, escrow, shipping, insurance and other needs, which collectively contribute to easing the pain of transacting on-line. Building trust is a strong component of the business, as eBay clearly identified and understood the concern of dealing anonymously over the Web. Customer feedback forums and rating systems allow participants to have some level of independent evaluation of the potential trading partner. This means of building trust is fundamental to driving ongoing use of the site.

eBay also understood that the infrastructure required to operate the business (primarily the hardware and software that power their site) was a significant investment and strategic advantage. It had to be leveraged across a broad set of markets and geographies. eBay is now used in over 150 countries worldwide, and has specific sites to service countries such as the United Kingdom, Canada, France, Germany, Japan, Australia and the United States.

When we look at the success of eBay, it is clear that it succeeds in several dimensions.

In terms of technology, eBay has created a unique set of software to automate and facilitate the auction process. Automatic notification of bids and acceptances makes it easy for buyers and sellers to keep track of their potential deals. The site has been designed to be easy to use and has had relatively few issues with availability and performance.

eBay has also been very successful in identifying and satisfying potential demand to trade second-hand goods. Actually, they have created a huge supply of goods that some people do not want but that others might want. Demand has been magnified through a network effect, as announcing a good for sale to an Internet audience dwarfs the social networks touched by a local newspaper. Moreover, the seller enjoys the network effect at a fraction of the cost of buying a classified advertisement in the newspaper. More precisely, there is no cost to list; the vendor only incurs a cost when the item is sold. eBay has tapped the latent demand in the market for the buying and selling of used goods. They unlocked that demand through a much more valuable way of transacting business.

eBay delivers value by creating real efficiencies in the market. Their organization of auctions is key to the creation of efficiencies that were unattainable before the Internet. Considering the large numbers of sellers and buyers with heterogeneous goods and requirements, at any point in time eBay matches supply and demand more precisely than markets with fewer participants. Especially for those goods that have narrow or highly specialized appeal (used goods, collectibles, antiques) eBay opens up new possibilities for market clearing. Additionally, eBay provides efficiencies to the seller and buyer by providing simple means of listing, transacting and paying for goods. In short, it allows people to easily turn marginal assets into cash.

It would be impossible to have an auction through traditional means for the number of items and the general value that these items usually represent (under $100). By conventional face-to-face means, negotiating every transaction would be impractical and expensive. The costs of making the deal could easily exceed the value of the product. By bringing efficiency and scale to the participants, eBay provides a unique value proposition that is only possible through the Internet.

eBay has also preserved the essence of the interactions of the garage sale, the flea market and the market organized through classified advertising. It has not attempted to change the cultural aspects of these types of transaction. eBay retains the nature and historical aspects of the deal, while augmenting it with an English auction-based (highest bidder wins) value proposition. With the creation of mechanisms to preserve trust and ensure that buyers and sellers receive value, eBay injects trading elements that are analogous to the face-to-face aspects of the traditional yard sale.

Other success stories in later chapters will highlight how various successful Net Markets operate and thrive. eBay clearly shows that Net Markets can work, and that their value and power in bringing buyers and sellers together can be spectacular. If Net Markets can work for obscure fifty-dollar trinkets, it can work for well-specified $10,000 medical equipment. The key is to know what it takes to drive success and how to create that value.

Summary

1. Just like most other areas of business, the B2B space is strewn with examples of failure and buoyed by examples of success. A pessimist's view of this might be that the domain is too risky to enter. An optimist might conclude that with attention to the fundamentals of business, anyone who is committed to systematic thinking can prosper in the new environment of Net Markets.

2. The refrain of the hapless loser is that the Net Market did not achieve liquidity. We have described the result of liquidity in the context of three interacting factors: P (number of potential exchange parties) x T (frequency of trade or percent of the parties actually transacting) x R (rate or intensity of the transactions). We have also presented the liquidity Rule of Two: two of the liquidity factors must be at high levels in order to achieve liquidity; when any two of the factors are at low levels, then illiquidity is assured.

3. Often liquidity does not matter. An ill-conceived business model could be the culprit. A key element of the business model is the pricing model—that is, how the enterprise will capture for itself some of the value it creates for its customers. Failing to price value-creating offerings of the enterprise makes it more difficult for the enterprise to succeed.

4. Examples of failure in Net Markets:
    - BizBuyer.com was saddled by a business model that did not tap the liquidity that it might have built.
    - Encryptix.com oversold its prospective customers and investors on a technology that had not been proved in the applications fundamental to the business. Additionally, Encryptix management assumed customers would change deep-seated behaviors and attitudes once the Encryptix product technology arrived on the market, a far from certain proposition.
    - Chemdex.com successfully built transactional activity on its site, but it sacrificed potential earnings to do so. Eager to gain the participation of large, marquee participants, it succeeded in securing the active participation of Dupont and Genentech who required deep discounts. Other parties joined, but trades

in their product areas were not so robust. Their experience introduces the concept of assortment bias for an exchange—if some items on the exchange are traded more efficiently than others, then the exchange suffers from some degree of assortment inefficiency.

CEO's Playbook for the Boardroom

Consider the context: one of your most prominent investors has read an article about a Net Market in your industry, and she wants to know why your company is not mentioned as a participant. One of the board members, trying to be helpful, speculates that the Net Market in question doesn't have liquidity. You observe the furrowed brows of the other board members, as some utter knowing "Hmmmm"s. You would like to speak to the issue to demonstrate that you have solid understanding of the trade-offs facing your company in deciding to join, build, or abstain from participating in a Net Market.

Observation: Any Net Market could fail if it does not build sufficient liquidity.

Here is what is important to mention: What is "sufficient liquidity"? There are at least two things to consider.

1. Sufficiently high levels of two of the following (Liquidity Rule of Two):
   - the number of participating parties (P)
   - the frequency of their transacting on the Net Market (T)
   - the size of their transactions (R)
2. A carefully tuned business model that prices what is valued by the participants of the Net Market.

Since Net Market participants would value liquidity, then its determinants should be priced in some way. This means, prices must be set to relate to P and to T and to R. Failing to price these means that the Net Market would not generate revenues even if the Net Market achieves high levels of liquidity. That is, no matter what the liquidity level, it would not be sufficient for sustaining the Net Market if prices are set to zero!

Observation: there have been a lot of failures in the B2B space, but there have also been a lot of successes.
Here are six important points learned by fellow travelers on the B2B journey:

1. Basic, well-known business principles apply to running even the most novel Net Markets as businesses (remember BizBuyer.com).
2. Technology never built a business (remember Encryptix).
3. Giving away the farm (in the form of free services) to assure early adoption only raises the stakes in making the Net Market successful as a business (remember Chemdex).
4. Enhancing the value to your customers by using technology is consistent with good business practice (remember DAT services).
5. Expanding the business into a Net Market to deliver value to the broad range of complementary concerns and activities of your customers in the transactional context that they identify with you can be consistent with growing your business profitably (remember Gofish.com).
6. Using the Internet to organize a Net Market for goods that have geographically dispersed, heterogeneous, highly specialized demand and supply exploits the potential of positive network effects (remember eBay).

2

B2B Success Drivers

OVERVIEW AND GOALS OF THE CHAPTER

In this chapter we shall weave together a set of common principles into what we call The MIDST Success Driver Framework, a simple and powerful tool for evaluating the potential of a B2B initiative and for understanding the key factors influencing the initiative's success or failure. Whether your company is considering a B2B initiative, starting a Net Market, or providing ancillary services to a Net Market, the MIDST Success Driver Framework is a tool to help filter and organize information to clarify what needs to be done for the business to be successful. The success drivers for B2B initiatives are organized into five broad dimensions. As a first step, the executive should identify and ask questions about these five dimensions. As a second step, the executive should seek to understand how these dimensions interact.

The Five Dimensions of MIDST

To see what is so special about the electronic contexts of markets and business models in the B2B space, it is helpful to view developments through the lens of a framework. The MIDST framework identifies five interacting categories of influence:

- Market systems
- Institutions
- Demand
- State policy
- Technology

These five factors are the principal drivers of success for Net Markets, and any senior executive of either a firm participating in a Net Market or of a firm organizing one should know how to acknowledge and interpret these drivers. We use the mnemonic "MIDST" to help us remember the component drivers. For purposes of describing the five drivers, we shall examine them in this order: technology (T), state policy (S), market systems (M), demand (D), and institutions (I).

Figure 2.1: THE MIDST FRAMEWORK

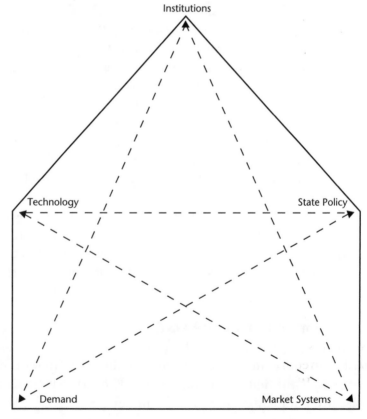

Institutions

Technology

State Policy

Demand

Market Systems

Technology

The inescapable influences of advanced communications and information technologies have presented momentous opportunities for enterprises, both new and mature, to do things they had not been able to do only a few years ago. In the simplest sense, the combination of digital representation of information and extremely rapid processing has enabled the technological revolution—the dramatically improved use of certain applied sciences—and has created the structure on which Net Markets build. Technological progress has undeniably contributed to the development of the landscape upon which Net Marketers of all kinds seek to stake their respective claims.

Technological progress rushes on. As new technological vistas are emerging from the drive to digitally represent all data, images and voice communication, and as the possibilities of digitizing information and processes become better understood, there is an evolving push to virtualize the communications and information infrastructure of contemporary business, as Tennenhouse has pointed out in *Virtual Infrastructure: Putting the Information Infrastructure on the Technology Curve.* Virtualization presents novel opportunities to separate or combine economic activities in space and in time.

As an example of such virtualization, consider the spatial separation and temporal alignment associated with the commercial fisherman and Gofish.com. Digital information and communication technologies may also enable the exploitation of the same facilities (space) asynchronously and more flexibly than can non-digital means of communications and information rendering. A good example of attempts to accomplish this is DAT's success in making a market for empty truck capacity on the deadhead.

Simply stated, digitalization of communications and information opens the possibility for virtual coordination and control of complex processes that in a non-digital age may have necessitated close personal supervision and inflexible rules of administration. One challenge for exploiting the technological possibilities, then, is to wean ourselves from a dependence on the manual administrative rules that evolved to support the exploitation of old technologies of an earlier era. We shall come to this issue later in our discussion of another element of the framework.

The arrival of the Internet is a technological event of historical proportions. There are at least five general characteristics of the Internet that are relevant for the senior management of a firm to evaluate in a decision relating to a Net Market:

1. The Internet is a network of networks designed to enable data communications, not voice communications. Voice communications are possible over the Internet (so-called "voice over IP"), but voice communications have not significantly influenced design characteristics of the Internet. *For a Net Market to successfully serve the interests of its users, either the Net Market must duplicate communications capabilities that approximate interactions that people have practiced (for example, a telephone conversation), or create and coach the user through a new, novel form of communication or social interaction.*

2. The Internet offers multiple points of access. Although "gatekeepers" can function to govern access for members of specific user groups, such as the employees of an enterprise or the members of a Net Market, the "network of networks" characteristic of the Internet presents to the most curious and persistent users creative opportunities to bypass gatekeepers. *For a Net Market to be successful, the Net Market organizer must assure members that real controls and processes are in place to manage secure, authorized participation.*

3. The Internet has grown in popularity in large measure because users all over the globe have adopted a common protocol for gaining access and transferring data. The protocol effectively defines the World Wide Web and enables a large number of users to connect to each other by means of data communications. *For a Net Market to be successful, the Net Market organizer should provide incentives for participants to exploit the low-cost reach of the Internet.*

4. The Internet is primarily an open or public communications and information infrastructure. Data are moved in packets—a software standard that encapsulates small segments of a data communication—and routes each packet in a dynamically optimal way (path of least resistance), re-assembling the packets at their intended destination in a logical and comprehensible order. *For a*

Net Market to be successful, the Net Market organizer must assure members that credible means of maintaining the integrity of the data are in place.
5. The users of the Internet maintain quasi-anonymity, as their identities are revealed only in terms of an Internet address. There are at least two potentially troubling consequences of this: first, the quasi-anonymous user could assume or steal an identity, and second, an interloper could use another user's computer and identity. To manage network capacity and to enhance security, administrators of networks local to their enterprises may dynamically and randomly re-assign an Internet address to a user each time the user logs on to the network. *For a Net Market to be successful, the Net Market organizer must assure members that the means to authenticate users are reliable and credible.*

One would expect that progress in making the Internet even more accessible, flexible and usable will continue. For purposes of understanding the way that Internet-related technologies influence the working of a Net Market, consider a rather stereotypical transaction flow that one might observe in a Net Market (See Figure 2.2). The building blocks of any computing or processing environment must be in place for the transaction flow to achieve its purpose. These building blocks are hardware (for example, computers), operating systems (for example, Unix or Windows), and applications (steps in the transaction flow).

Additionally, to assure that users of the Net Market may interact—either in real time or with some lag (asynchronously)—the building blocks of the communications network must be in place. There are numerous components in a communications network, but those of prime importance are:

- bandwidth
- access
- authorization and authentication
- search/query process
- post/bid or offer/match and clear process
- processing and confirmation
- archiving

Figure 2.2: THE STEREOTYPICAL ONLINE TRANSACTION
PROCESS

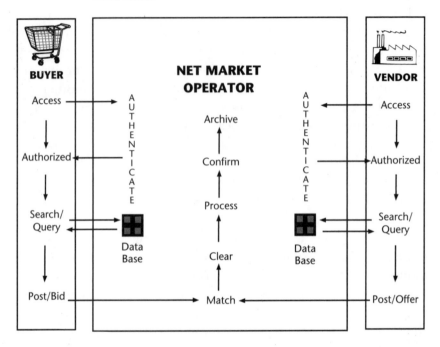

Bandwidth

Roughly defined, bandwidth is a capacity measure accounting for
the number of simultaneous signals; the speed of delivery of the data
and the richness of the information that can be carried; transmission;
switching; and addressing (finding users who originate or receive
communications).

Access

Both prospective buyers and prospective vendors must gain access to
the Net Market. The ease and speed of access is determined by a
combination of hardware characteristics and Web site design characteristics of the Net Market. The hardware characteristics depend
on the appropriateness of the end users' and the Net Market's hardware infrastructure, both fundamental to creating acceptable performance and transaction-processing and communications speed.

Bandwidth varies over local networks and even within the public network infrastructure. The Net Market's performance in providing convenient access is partly a function of characteristics of the end users' network and public networks (the Internet service providers) that its users must use.

Web site design characteristics will also influence the speed of presentation of a Web page on the Net Market site and the speed and ease at which a user may enter and use the site. The coding of the business processes of a site, as well as the layout of information on the site, will influence response times.

The key issue for the user in entering the Net Market is whether one is obliged to install special software on local computers (conceivably introducing complexity at the user's premises).

Authorization and Authentication

In recent years, there have been significant advances in preserving secure access to Internet sites. Popular means of security including the use of login names, passwords and PINs are giving way to newer means of identifying users and managing their access to only those areas they are authorized to enter. Public key infrastructure (PKI), a suite of solutions based upon applied number theory and abstract algebras, and biometric procedures, such as confirming identity by measuring heart rhythms, fingerprints and aspects of the human eye, are slowly moving into the mainstream. These innovations typically entail installing a file on a user's device and comparing it with a file installed on a third party's device. Security, however, is only as great as the weakest link in the procedures that individuals at points of control follow.

Search/Query Process

Users of a Net Market will engage in some form of search to inform themselves of relevant market events or to find potential buyers or sellers. One of the most remarkable developments in the use of the Internet has been the development of high-performing search engines. These are intelligent agents, or software programs, that penetrate in mere seconds the mind-boggling complexity of information on the Internet and render guides or links to information a user seeks. Search engines supporting a Net Market could be configured to search the entire Internet, just the conditional domain of the Net Market itself, or both.

If the Net Market user seeks to query information, then some level of analysis must be performed. The analysis may be simple (for example, reviewing the assessments that a third party may have conducted of Web transactions in some setting) or complex (for example, correlating the characteristics of visitors to a site with their choices of options at the site). The greater the number of visitors to a Net Market, the more opportunity there is to capture data about their visits. To demonstrate the volume of data that could be captured, consider the case of BizBuyer.com, which attracted 1.3 million unique visitors to its site each month. If the average visitor visited the site once a week, provided two elements of identifying information and engaged in a string of eight actions ("clicks") during each visit, then BizBuyer.com would have had the opportunity to capture 26 million fields of information on users each month. If BizBuyer.com responded to just one of the eight clicks of the average visitor, then that would add yet another 5.2 million elements of data to keep track of. Assuming that BizBuyer.com were to have operated at this level for, say, a period of 12 months, then the database would accumulate to nearly 400 million elements of distinct information pertaining to the use of the site. The technologies of data warehousing, data mining and customer analytics apply to storing and organizing data in anticipation of the analysis that might be applied to it, organizing means for reviewing it, and interpreting it, respectively.

Post/Bid or Offer/Match and Clear Process

Participants of a Net Market will likely need to provide information regarding inventory status, availability or delivery of goods to their customers and seek the same information from their suppliers. The simplest approach to accomplishing this is for the Net Market organizer to create catalogs of fixed positions (bid prices, offer prices, product specifications, and so on). The utility of the catalog depends on the frequency with which the Net Market organizer can update the catalog with real-time data. This is analogous to the utility of a telephone directory that must be updated depending on the flow of subscribers connecting to and disconnecting from the telephone network.

A more advanced approach is to organize a real-time exchange, listing current positions and current transactions. The major complication this introduces is matching and clearing offers and bids. In such organized capital markets as the New York Stock Exchange, the matching and clearing originally took place on the trading floor as brokers and dealers who were members of the exchange would shout their positions to each other. The Net Market organizer may emulate this to some extent by using algorithms that create queues of positions on both sides of the market, enable adjustments in counter positions through some form of negotiation or automation, and determine when agreements have been struck. These algorithms are analogous to programmed trading models used by institutional investors on the organized capital markets. The issue for the CEO of a participant firm in such a Net Market is to know whether the technology assures that unbiased trades will occur. For example, prices should not tend to favor one side of the market or the other because of the way the algorithm sets the rules of the trade—which positions are considered first, how price adjustments are executed and so on.

Processing and Confirmation

These steps are sometimes referred to as the "messy middle." They entail communication and coordination with all of the parties and enterprise-based systems that will handle aspects of fulfilling the consequences of the transaction. Third parties, such as credit agencies, insurers and banks, as well as shipping departments, warehousing units and third-party transportation firms, may be involved in these steps. Not all Net Markets offer to conduct all of these process communications and coordination functions, but many do. It is not unusual for the various applications that drive these processes to have incompatible architectures or operating systems that cannot pass information between them. In the latter instance, the Net Market organizer or the trading parties themselves must resolve the application integration issues. The confirmation step is critical, as the Net Market must be able to formally confirm the terms of the agreement that each transaction constitutes. This means that the information captured and reported for each transaction must identify the terms of the agreement and the identities and commitments of each party to the transaction.

To be successful, the Net Market must demonstrate a capacity to perform both the integration of the communications and coordination processes and the confirmation step. As Net Markets will vary in their performance on these functions, especially as scales of transactional activity vary, CEOs should ask for assurances from the organizer of the Net Market in which their firms wish to participate that these critical functions are conducted at desired levels.

Archiving

Upon completion of a transaction, the *Net Market maker* must record and retain the terms of the agreement between the transacting parties, as well as their identities. In all cases, as trade among parties becomes more anonymous or impersonal, in order for the market to function it must have inviolable means of measuring transactions and enforcing transactional terms whenever conflicts arise. This requirement expands the requirement to build specialized data warehouses that can be mined, if needed, to respond unequivocally to contractual and legal queries. Thus, data storage requirements of a Net Market extend beyond the BizBuyer.com illustration discussed earlier.

How is technology a success driver for Net Markets? The digital technologies of the modern era have provided the necessary conditions for Net Markets to be established. As innovation naturally accompanies any technology—as humans struggle to learn new ways to do things better—it is safe to assume that the potential pitfalls of organizing and operating a Net Market today will be scrutinized by technologists hell-bent on overcoming them.

The best way for the CEO to stay abreast of the influence of the digital technologies is by using them to the extent practicable and to avoid the sure trap of relegating management of the technology to the CIO within the organization. Technological progress will continue, and the progress is driven in good measure by the learning of users in all functional areas of the business, at all levels, including senior management.

Of course, the story of the emergence and viability of Net Markets is not only a story of the technology associated with the Internet. It is not only technology that has produced the economic opportunity in a Net Market-driven business world. The other four drivers influence the conduct and performance of economic activities of Net Markets: state decisions and policies, market systems, demand and institutions.

State Policy

States have considerable discretion in wielding influence. They may impose constraints, threaten market participants with the imposition of constraints, directly encourage private investment in specific sectors in specific ways or invest in or operate economic activities in specific sectors. The Internet, for example, began in 1969 as ARPAnet, an American state-owned and controlled activity to serve the Advanced Research Projects Agency of the U.S. Department of Defense during the Cold War.

There are examples of state influence even farther reaching than the development of the original ARPAnet. The development of the global computing industry took a remarkable turn in June 1969 when IBM announced that it would unbundle its hardware, software and services. Strictly speaking this was not a state decision, but it was provoked by the U.S. Justice Department's threat of anti-trust litigation in December 1968. One consequence of IBM's decision was that competitors and new entrants for the first time had access to IBM operating systems. Another consequence of the decision was that IBM satisfied a requirement to supply the ARPAnet, a network based on open standards so as to provide flexibility and robustness to assure communications even under catastrophic circumstances.

In the communications sector, state decisions have had similarly far-reaching influences. Recognizing that communications and data processing technologies were beginning to disrupt market structures and undermine the terms of a 1956 consent decree, the U.S. Federal Communications Commission opened the First Computer Inquiry to review state policy of the unregulated computing industry and the regulated telecommunications industry. The introduction of smart communications terminals rendered meaningless the simple distinctions concluded by Computer I and the FCC was prompted to initiate Computer II. The conclusion of Computer II was to deregulate the U.S. customer premises telephone equipment market, which effectively opened a Pandora's box of new competitors for AT&T from consumer electronics (principally Japanese firms) and computing firms (for example, IBM and Siemens).

The United States does not have a monopoly on momentous state decisions that have influenced the evolution of computing and communications markets. In France, the Office of the President launched an ambitious plan in the late 1970s to digitize the nation's communications infrastructure. By the mid-1980s at the behest of the Télétel project, France transformed itself from one of the most backward telecommunications markets to one of the most advanced in the world. The U.K. had already taken dramatic steps, as Parliament passed the Privatization Act of 1981 that paved the way both for competition in domestic communications and for privatization of the state-owned British Telecommunications.

Europe, generally, has pursued a path, often rocky, of progressively liberalizing the communications and computing sectors, beginning with the 1957 Treaty of Rome and arriving at the Single European Act of 1987 and the 1987 Greenpaper on the Development of a Common Market for Telecommunications Services and Equipment. The consequences have been momentous, as procurement practices have induced a competitive, albeit rationalized, European computing industry and an intensely competitive communications sector.

It is a challenge to unequivocally establish the causal direction of changes. Certainly, the drive to globalize business has pressured states of a variety of political persuasions to liberalize their communications and information infrastructures, as very few would shun the benefits of expansive market exchange that robust digital communications and information infrastructures make possible. In this respect, state policy and decisions across the globe have provided for the enabling of the development of Net Markets.

How is state policy a B2B success driver? It is essential that CEOs of any firm that would participate in or build a Net Market would inform themselves of decisions in the state environment. Generally, the state decisions fall into three categories: constraints (taxes, regulations, anti-trust), incentives (such as subsidies and social policies) and investments/disinvestments (for example, privatization versus state ownership). In modern liberal democracies, state decisions are often motivated by an attempt to satisfy special interests but typically are subject to support from the general public. The states of some liberal democracies, though, are more capable of leading the people with initiatives that are undertaken even if there is no broad public support.

Market Systems

A classical question that has occupied the minds of top executives of all enterprises and of the economics profession is "What are the bounds of the firm?" Recent trends to downsize firms, to rely on contractors and temporary workers and to create strategic alliances and partnerships reveal that the question still inspires a multitude of interpretations—both in practice and in theory.

Ronald H. Coase, winner of the 1991 Nobel Prize in Economics, has argued eloquently that the bounds of the firm are determined by its willingness to incur certain transaction costs associated with procuring on markets the inputs for its relevant economic activities. In a very narrow sense, this reduces all business to a set of "make-or-buy" decisions. Since no firm chooses to "make" everything, the decision to "buy" obligates the firm to participate in open markets to procure these needed inputs.

A simple concatenation of make-or-buy decisions of a set of firms depicts what is known as either a supply chain (from the perspective of a downstream agent) or a demand chain (from the perspective of an upstream agent). Typically, firms are complex. Any given firm may depend upon more than one supply chain and contribute to more than one demand chain. (The full set of make-or-buy decisions can be described as a set of flows; see Chapter 4.) The mix of supply and demand chains associated with any firm or collection of firms, as well as the firms that assist or enable exchange by providing such ancillary services as credit, advertising and consulting, is called a *market system*.

There are a few ways that digital communications and information technologies influence the line between a firm and the market boundaries within a market system. These technologies present the prospect of *efficiency* or *productivity gains.*

Efficiency Gain at the Firm

Digitizing processes and information within the firm may allow it to save certain costs, such as purchase of paper, archival costs of physical documents, postage and courier expenses, and personnel costs associated with managing information. If the firm chooses merely to replace, where possible, analog or physical forms with digital forms and employ the same quantities of supporting resources for the same basic activities, then its costs should reduce. The firm may do this in the interest of increasing its margins or of gaining some flexibility to reduce its prices in its most competitive product markets. Vendors such as PeopleSoft, Niku and SAP provide services to help their clients to realize efficiency gains on various dimensions, including human resource management, project management and corporate finance.

Efficiency Gain in the Market

Digitizing information and communications may also produce efficiencies in markets. If markets become more efficient, then prices for procuring a given set of inputs tend to stabilize, in which case, the firm may substitute "making" for "buying." Indeed, several firms may choose to organize in some way so as to exploit these potential efficiency gains. Such organizing schemes range from the creation of B2B exchanges to portals that accelerate the reliable exchange of information. The process of "e-enabling" procurement is a means to capture the efficiency gains from the electronic marketplace (for example, Ariba, CommerceOne, Intellsys, and RightWorks).

Productivity Gains

If the firm can incur lower costs in producing a given level of output, then it might decide to produce more and simply maintain costs at historical levels. The *customer relationship management (CRM)* systems of vendors such as E.Piphany and Siebel effectively position themselves to enable their clients to realize productivity gains.

Re-Orientation of the Firm or of an Activity

By reducing costs through automation a firm may free up resources to engage in other activities it previously deemed too costly or to abandon some activities that cannot be easily digitized. In addition, a firm may decide to procure inputs from the market at a lower cost. Firms may have historically conducted an activity because of a constraint of a conventional technology that in a digital age may no longer have a clear purpose. When a firm redirects its activities, possibly redefining its business mission, it often creates the opportunity for some downstream player to reap an efficiency gain or a productivity gain. The evolution of Reuters, from its origins in providing a carrier-pigeon messaging service bridging the gap in European telegraphy, to a diversified business information services firm (without pigeons) is an extreme illustration of the point. The original consumer of the Reuters messaging services was the London-based investment broker, and as Reuters redirected its activities these brokers and other players such as business journalists found it progressively easier to accomplish their activities.

Firms tend to be complex combinations of disparate, but interdependent, economic activities. It is very difficult for any firm to expect that the process of digitizing some of its activities would not ultimately lead to a re-orientation of the firm.

Moreover, digital technologies touch almost all firms that interact with each other in a market system. Two firms that have interacted over some period of time may choose to exploit potential efficiency and productivity gains in ways that fundamentally change their relationship. This means that if a change takes place in any firm, as a component member in a market system, the system is likely to foster additional changes in the interactions between participants.

This point is key and significant. A firm that is interested in creating a Net Market and redefining its role in a market system seeks to have an impact on the system and to change the value proposition and the economic activities of upstream or downstream participants. A CEO must understand what that impact may be to all parties in order to clearly assess the role of the firm in the affected market system.

Why is the market system dimension considered a success factor for Net Markets? The CEO of a participating firm in a Net Market must recognize that all firms throughout the market system are facing make-or-buy trade-offs. It is essential for any CEO to acknowledge the choices that other firms could make when participating in Net Markets and consider whether any other given firm would become a competitor, a trading partner, or both. Adam Brandenburger and Barry Nalebuff, professors of business at Harvard and Yale, respectively, have recently developed a simple framework to help executives think through the possibilities. In their book *Co-opetition*, their concept of a "value net" refines the description of the possible market dynamics that Michael Porter earlier articulated in his "Five Forces" diagram found in his book on competitive strategy. The value net incorporates the interactions between any firm and its competitors, customers, suppliers and collaborators. And all of them could be present in a Net Market, and that could help build the transaction volume and liquidity to sustain the Net Market.

Demand

A market system can be sustained only if it adequately serves some demand. To understand demand deeply, one must understand the fundamental driver of demand, "consumption activity." The end consumer demands products (that is, goods and services) offered on a market exchange because the end consumer has chosen to "buy" rather than to "make" something. So, the relevant demand is the demand for inputs into some productive activity, and the relevant productive activity for the consumer is a consumption activity. This is true even for an industrial or business consumer, which could be a large complex organization. Industrial and other business consumers populate the downstream of B2B Net Markets.

Rarely do buyers find turnkey solutions to their needs on markets. Typically, consumers or their representative buyers find solutions that can be *adapted* to serve the purposes of their consumption aims. This means that such consumers can realize benefits from products available on markets only if they apply themselves to the tasks of extracting those benefits. Sometimes the extraction of benefits entails considerable work and cost. For any consumer, there is likely to be a continuum between one extreme, in which the consumer only "makes," and another, in which the consumer only "buys."

Buyers and sellers view consumption activities with specific degrees of precision. Products available on markets are suited to consumption aims with varying degrees of precision. Net markets that are organized for routine, repetitive transactions are likely to attract buyers and sellers who view the consumption activities at relatively aggregated levels, that is, with little precision. The typical buyer would be likely to procure items in such a Net Market for a consumption activity that applies to many users and across many situations. For example, paperclips are used to bind documents in the marketing department, the legal department, at the reception desk and so forth. It is unlikely that many buyers would disaggregate the consumption activities of their legal department, their marketing department and their reception desk to consider procuring specific paperclips for each department separately. One might expect that buyers who participate in Net Markets would be interested in buying at low prices, possibly at frequent intervals, given the repetitive occurrence of the consumption activity (binding a document). Sellers who participate in such markets would seek to produce or supply in quantities that permit maximizing volume so that unit costs could be low enough to assure reasonable margins at low prices.

We would therefore expect that to attract a supplier, the organizer of a Net Market offering goods and services that meet the needs of aggregated consumption activities (paperclips) would have to ensure high transaction volumes to the supplier so that they could profitably satisfy buyers.

A Net Market that presents an assortment of goods and services that serves highly *disaggregated* consumption activities exposes itself to the risk of inefficiency. Consider once again the case of Chemdex. The transaction volume of this Net Market was dominated by activities of only two participants, Dupont and Genentech. Though each firm is a diversified enterprise, both conceivably have specialized requirements for chemicals to support their activities. As Chemdex adopted a business model that took possession and title of all of the products sold on the Net Market, it became increasingly difficult for

Chemdex to supply the increasingly specialized requirements of the buyers from other firms.

One of the key inputs that industrial or business consumers must always use in the pursuit of a consumption activity is time. As the consumer pursues an increasing number of consumption activities, and participates in an increasing number of activities in the market economy, the opportunity cost of time devoted to these pursuits rises. In an industrial setting, as consumers take on the characteristics of complex organizations, the opportunity cost of time spikes with the pressures to manage the complexity. The dynamics of demand respond, in part, to the marginal value of time.

One clear influence on demand from the electronic environment is that consumption activities may be defined now more precisely than before. A CEO who suffers a poverty of time and storage capacity may use a caterer with on-line services to accomplish "just-in-time" production of a meal at a specific time to accompany a specific meeting.

How is demand a B2B success driver? Demand is, in some real sense, the critical dimension of success. Every demand that can be served by a Net Market is derived from some consumption activity or set of consumption activities. The value proposition that the organizer of the Net Market delivers to buyers participating in the Net Market must not simply attract them to the Net Market; the buyers must use the Net Market to buy. Only by identifying and quantifying the demand will the Net Market organizer attract sellers to assure that the Net Market generates the transaction volume and liquidity to sustain it.

Institutions

How exchange takes place is determined by institutions, the constraints we either choose to observe or are obliged to observe—both formal and informal. Examples of formal institutions are laws and rules, which delimit behavior that we consider acceptable to society in general (stopping at a red light, reporting one's income to the state) or to a segment of society (driving on the right-hand side of the street, paying excise taxes). Examples of informal institutions abound and determine to a great extent the character of a culture (shaking hands as a greeting, informing a business associate of a decision that one might have made). In fact, a business model is an institution, at least for those who adhere to it. If the business model becomes enshrined as a convention (the credit-card industry applies a business model that charges merchants a percentage of the transaction amount and cardholders an annual fee plus interest on outstanding balances), then the business model becomes an institution for a segment of society or an industry. Whatever helps us govern our behavior, the choices and trade-offs we make, qualifies as an institution.

The growth of the Internet over the past ten years has been driven in large measure by the adoption of certain important standards. The definition of the open standards protocol suite TCP/IP and the adoption of HTML to create "Web pages" that enable easy access to information on the Internet qualify as important institutions governing human interaction on the Web. New protocols that further simplify information access (for example, XML) or provide enhanced flexibility (WAP) are being adopted to encourage even greater growth.

Other institutions influence the evolution of the Internet and the use of the Internet in other ways. For example, the debate about universal access to the Internet as a utility—should no one be denied the right to access the Internet?—or universal service—are there certain Internet-based services that should be made available to everyone irrespective of the cost to produce those services?—is yet unresolved in most countries. Moreover, the issue of whether sales taxes or value-added taxes should be assessed on Internet-based transactions has not been resolved, partly because of the difficulties in measurement and enforcement and in the payment and collection of such taxes. These examples are formal, state-related institutional questions.

Not all relevant institutions that influence the conduct of social and commercial interchange on the Internet are formal. Two important informal institutions that should be acknowledged and that are still in the process of evolving are:

1. pricing conventions and
2. information handling.

Pricing as an Institution

For the better part of the 20th century, fixed prices have been a convention in most market systems, especially those involving end consumers. We owe this to the successful emergence of the department store in the 1880s, first in Amsterdam, then in Paris, and later in the U.S. The fixed pricing convention of the department store was emulated by other succeeding retailing innovations, such as the supermarket, the chain store and the warehouse store. Negotiated pricing conventions are more common in industrial markets, but fixed prices tend to be the norm in most conventional market systems characterized by impersonal exchange.

Especially with the introduction of auctions, the Internet has created a remarkable shift away from fixed prices as the dominant form of pricing. Portals, in particular vertical portals that qualify the credit-worthiness of members, may also re-institutionalize negotiated prices as a norm.

Information-Handling as an Institution

In organizational settings, it is common for power to correlate with the information that an individual can control. Hierarchical organizational forms convey power and prestige with the control of information. The Internet defies conventional hierarchies, as the utility of information is enhanced by propagation and sharing—not in its archiving in the brain of an individual. Organizations, especially those committed to delivering high levels of professional services, must adapt quickly to the vagaries of a changing, ill-structured marketplace. Information capture and control is not the key to power in such organizations. The consequence of the changing modes of information-handling is the changing of rules for running and managing organizations. This change is confusing for those who have adapted to the performance measures of organizations that have emphasized and rewarded control. New organizational forms must encourage coordination and rapid adaptation, and new institutions will most likely arise to help people adjust their information-handling behavior in manners that are consistent with the interests of the organizations that employ them.

How is the institutional dimension a success driver for B2B? Institutions are the pervasive mediating force in the environment. Technology cannot be exploited profitably without institutions (for example, Morse and his code; the Internet and TCP/IP). Market systems do not function without institutions: rules and procedures for managing the interactions and exchanges of goods and services in a market. States specialize in establishing certain formal institutions: regulations and laws that exist on the books to resolve trade disputes as they might arise. Even demand is predicated on institutions: conventions for doing business.

MIDST: Toward a Methodology

What makes Net Markets distinctive is that the five drivers *interact* in distinctive ways. The methodology for conducting analysis of a Net Market context requires that we first catalog the factors that constitute each of the drivers. In a second step, we consider the first-order interactions among technology, market systems, demand and state policy. The third step is to consider how the interactions of the drivers induce change and are mediated by institutions and institutional adaptation. This is fundamentally an exercise in mixing objective and subjective data, but the important point to recognize is that the step-by-step approach creates a systematic approach to the assessment of the five dimensions and the business model of the Net Market.

Applying MIDST—a Three-Step Approach

Step 1: Base Measurement of MIDST

Gauging the Market System Driver

The market system will present the potential for organizing a successful Net Market whenever it offers the opportunities for efficiency and productivity gains for at least some players. There are two factors that would contribute to making the opportunity significant. We gauge each contributing factor on a five-point scale:

1	3	5
low drive for success		high drive for success

M1: Conjecture 1: The less vertically integrated an industry, the greater the tendency for firms to seek benefits of efficiency in the market. The rationale: When firms are vertically integrated, they have chosen secure access to reliable supply, to favorable down-stream markets, or to both over market mechanisms that may provide stable or lower prices but at a risk of "failure." Failure would mean that either suppliers or buyers might cease to conduct business.

M2: Conjecture 2: The more concentrated an industry at any point in the market system, the more difficult it is for the smaller firms to organize a market of sustainable transaction volume. Rationale: This is a corollary to the disadvantages of monopolistic and anti-competitive structures in the market and in the activities of players throughout the system. Indications of concentration can be measured by a concentration ratio, such as the sum of market shares of the largest two firms in an industry.

In summary, the gauge of the strength of the market system as a driver for B2B Net Market success is the sum of the scale values for each of the three conjectures divided by two. This produces a number on a scale from one to five, interpreted consistently with the scale above, and we designate this as the base measure for the strength of the Market System Success Driver.

Gauging the Demand Driver

Only by identifying and quantifying the demand will the Net Market organizer attract sellers to assure that the Net Market generates the transaction volume to sustain it. Gauging the strength of this driver is tantamount to assessing the size of the markets served by the Net Market. This is a monumental task, and one that is typically fraught with error. However, a base measure must be established if only to serve to be revised as market information is discovered. We suggest using a simple relative measure for the demand driver to follow the strength of the driver on the simple, standard five-point scale as before:

1	3	5
low drive		high drive
for success		for success

A straightforward way to create an index that is consistent with this scale is, first, to establish a demand benchmark. The benchmark should be a sizeable Net Market, such as Motorplace.com, a B2B site for automotive dealers and auto industry professionals. Its primary goal is to provide a dynamic dealer-to-dealer marketplace with vehicles and parts for more than 12,000 dealer clients. Hence, the base measure for the demand driver index for Net Market X would be

$$\mathbf{D} = 5 \times \text{(potential transactional value of Net Market X)} / \text{(transactional value of Motorplace.com)}$$

Gauging the State Driver

The state driver is the net effect of restrictions and incentives that relate to the creation and operation of a Net Market. We suggest applying the standard five-point scale above to assess the strength of restrictions and incentives, separately. So, factor S1 would indicate the strength of regulations, restrictions and other constraints imposed by the state, and factor S2 would indicate the strength of incentives, subsidies and other inducements provided by the state. Recognizing that these factors interact, to establish the base measure for the strength of the state driver we suggest multiplying the two factors to create a composite base score as follows.

(S1)(S2)= **S** score
1 to 5 = 1
6 to 10 = 2
11 to 15 = 3
16 to 20 = 4
21 to 25 = 5

Gauging the Technology Driver

In some sense technology has become a generic driver in the Information Age. However, aspects of technology that may vary across Net Markets relate to the ability of the Net Market to manage the specific transaction process flows that will characterize the Net Market. (See Figure 2.2). Complex transaction flows may be handled easily if the technology can be installed and operated reliably, and simple transactions may be disrupted if the technology cannot be easily installed and operated reliably. This is fundamentally a judgment call on the part of knowledgeable observers. We represent the base measure for the technology driver on the five-point scale:

1	3	5
low drive		high drive
for success		for success

Step 2: Acknowledging Interactions Among the MIDST Drivers

The four drivers may interact in ways to accentuate or diminish the influences of each other. To assure that we capture this systematically, we create a simple table relating the base measures, established in Step 1, to each other. For each interaction, we document our judgment of whether the drivers will enhance (+), diminish (-), or have negligible effect on (0) the drivers' influences on the success of the Net Market in question.

	M1	M2	
D	+/0/–	+/0/–	Revised D
S1	+/0/–	+/0/–	Revised S1
S2	+/0/–	+/0/–	Revised S2
T	+/0/–	+/0/-	Revised T
	Revised M1	Revised M2	

Let's consider the interactions in the table briefly. The first row addresses to what extent the strength of demand influences the strength of vertical integration or concentration to inhibit or enable productivity and efficiency gains, if at all. Conversely, the two market systems factors may or may not cause us to consider revising the strength of the demand driver if we think that concentration or vertical integration in the industry makes it easier or more difficult to tap the potential demand in the market.

The second and third rows address the influences of concentration and integration on the effectiveness of constraints (S1) and incentives (S2) in influencing the success of the Net Market, and vice versa. The fourth row addresses the interaction of technology and the market system factors. For example, an industry that is highly integrated would probably be one in which a large share of transactional processes would be internal to an enterprise, thus possibly reducing the requirements of a technology to support a Net Market. In this vein, consider the differences in complexity of a transaction involving an investment property (escrow, credit, title, insurer, buyer, broker, seller) and a simple procurement transaction (buyer and seller). Similarly, concentration should indicate how many different parties on one side of the market could engage in a transaction. The fewer the parties on one side of the market, the less onerous might the requirements of the technology be to enable the transaction processing.

Step 3: Acknowledging the Influence of Institutions

Gauging the Institutional Driver

The key aspect of institutions is the degree of impersonal exchange. In general, the simpler the value chain (the fewer the levels), the lower the incentive for firms to organize a Net Market. The fewer the levels of a value chain, the easier it should be to conduct transactions by personal exchange. The reasons for the significance of impersonal exchange revolve around the magnitude of two kinds of costs: measurement costs and enforcement costs. Both of the costs tend to be low in environments characterized by personal exchange, that is, in environments where the transacting parties know each other or can otherwise personally interact.

Measurement costs are the costs the parties incur in recognizing what the other party has agreed to exchange in the transaction. Enforcement costs are those costs that each party would incur in the event that the other party does not live up to the terms of the trade. There are various sub-dimensions of each of the cost categories. We establish a base measure of each on a scale from 1 (high cost) to 5 (low cost).

Measurement Categories

I1 Degree of identity (1: anonymous exchange vs. 5: blood relative)

I2 Degree of prior inspection (1: no prior inspection vs. 5: extensive prior inspection)

Enforcement Categories

I3 Degree of authentication of vendor (1: no guarantee for compliance to specification or fulfillment vs. 5: comprehensive guarantee)

I4 Degree of authentication of buyer (1: No guarantee of payment vs. 5: comprehensive guarantee)

I5 Recourse for non-performance (1: No recourse for non-performance vs. 5: comprehensive recourse)

To judge the influences of institutions on the other four drivers, we create a table similar to that of Step 2:

	I1 base	I2 base	I3 base	I4 base	I5 base	
Revised M	+/0/–	+/0/–	+/0/	+/0/–	+/0/–	Net M
Revised D	+/0/–	+/0/–	+/0/–	+/0/–	+/0/–	Net D
Revised S	+/0/–	+/0/–	+/0/–	+/0/–	+/0/–	Net S
Revised T	+/0/–	+/0/–	+/0/–	+/0/–	+/0/–	Net T
	Revised I1	Revised I2	Revised I3	Revised I4	Revised I5	Net I

We capture the adjustments from the interactions systematically and produce a net measure for each of the five drivers in the far right-hand column.

Applying MIDST: Illustrations

The following three examples—Figures 2.3, 2.4 and 2.5—illustrate results of the MIDST methodology for presenting graphically the assessments of the success drivers for specific Net Markets. In each case, these are our own judgments based on information available to us at a moment in time. We would modify these as we accumulate more information.

Figure 2.3: MOTORPLACE.COM

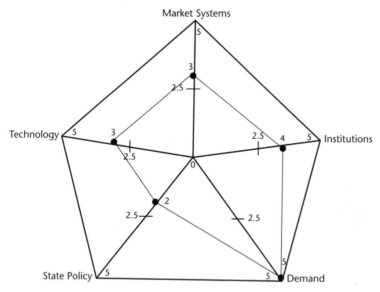

Figure 2.4: DAT SERVICES

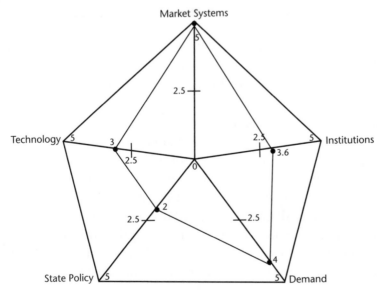

Figure 2.5: BIZBUYER

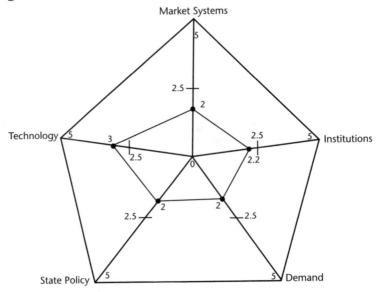

Summary

In the environment of Net Markets there are five categories of drivers that will necessarily determine how successful any B2B Net Market could be. The drivers are:

1. **Market System:** this is the engine of the Net Market. Market systems describe who the players are and how they relate to each other. The players are related through an extensive series of make-or-buy decisions.
2. **Institutions:** the most complex and the most pervasive driver. Institutions are constraints on human interaction. One of the most important classes of institutions for Net Markets is the set of formal and informal rules and conventions that would encourage the impersonal exchange characteristic of a Net Market.
3. **Demand:** to understand whether buyers will flock to a Net Market, it is helpful to understand what consumption aims buyers have or represent. The level of participation of buyers in a Net Market will directly influence the level of supplier participation.

4. **State Policy**: generally classified into incentives, constraints and investments of the state. State policies can deliberately or inadvertently create the basic conditions for certain Net Markets to exist; they can also undermine the economic rationale for selected Net Markets.

5. **Technology**: a complex suite of uses of various applied sciences. The key macro driver is the transformation that digitalization of information, communications and computing has enabled. In the narrow context of a Net Market, there are specific technological considerations surrounding the transaction flow within the Net Market.

The MIDST Success Driver Framework can be used to provide a guideline for rating the individual importance of the five dimensions on a B2B initiative. As each of the five dimensions also interact and influence each other, the scoring requires an assessment of this cause and effect. By using the assessment framework, CEOs can begin to understand the importance of the various dimensions and ensure that appropriate information is gathered to make an informed business decision.

CEO's Playbook for the Boardroom

Remember the context: one of your most prominent investors has read an article about a Net Market in your industry, and she wants to know why your company is not mentioned as a participant. One of the board members, in trying to be helpful to you, speculates that the Net Market in question doesn't have liquidity. You observe the furrowed brows of the other board members, as some utter knowing "Hmmmm"s. You would like to speak to the issue to demonstrate that you have solid understanding of the trade-offs facing your company in deciding to join, build or abstain from participating in a Net Market.

Observation: The environment may or may not be conducive to organizing a Net Market.

Here are the important issues to raise:

- How have the relationships between the participants of the Net Market and those who depend on them changed? Has any player altered a make-or-buy decision as a result of the creation of the Net Market? If so, should that be expected to support or undermine the building of transaction volume on the Net Market? (**M**arket system)
- How would the standard business conventions be altered as a result of the creation of the Net Market? Can we expect that players would adopt new business conventions, especially to support broader incidence of transactions among parties that do not know each other? (**I**nstitutions)
- Is there a sufficient number of buyers with sufficiently strong incentives to transact on the Net Market? (**D**emand)
- Are there any changes in public policy, such as tax policies and subsidies, that would support the establishment and growth of the Net Market? (**S**tate)
- Is the technology of the Net Market adequately supportive of the transaction flow to which we would be committing? Are there more reliable technologies available or announced for other Net Markets? (**T**echnology)

3

Sources of Value in the B2B Spectrum

OVERVIEW AND GOALS OF THE CHAPTER

The B2B domain suffers from one important aspect of its youth: it lacks a *taxonomy*. A classification system helps to both simplify communications and build confidence in and understanding of the domain. Without such a system, identifying and critically evaluating different B2B models in the environment becomes that much more complicated for the CEO. The absence of a taxonomy also complicates the task of determining whether any "new" B2B model is truly new. However, it is safe to say that even the most unique models have historical roots of one kind or another, and in this chapter we shall introduce a simple tool, the MaRCoT Value Framework, with which to compare models, both old and new.

Unifying Examples

We are not certain who coined the term B2B, but clearly its history would include such well-established concepts as industrial purchasing, marketing, logistics and materials management. What is truly new about B2B is that the Internet is now inextricably linked to the activities of commercial enterprises. Let's consider a simple B2B case study.

SNATCHING DEFEAT FROM THE JAWS OF SUCCESS: THE CASE OF MERCATA.COM

Mercata, a B2C group-buying site backed by the venture capital firm of Microsoft co-founder Paul Allen, launched in May 1999. By the end of January 2001, it had ceased operations.

Andrew Bartles, a senior e-commerce analyst with Giga Information Group, explained Mercata's demise: "The difficulty that Mercata faced was that it wasn't able to capture great discounts and, in fact, the search bots such as Ask Jeeves turned up better prices than Mercata...So for all the effort to be part of the pool, the reality was you didn't get as good... prices as [available through] other sites." He added that Mercata was hurt by its small selection in various categories and by the threat that sites such as Yahoo and America Online could start up similar businesses but with many more participants. Mercata chief executive Tom Van Horn argued in *The Industry Standard* (4 January 2001) that the company simply fell victim to the general disinterest among investors toward e-commerce. Let us take a closer look.

Mercata's business model was applicable only to the Web. Originally, it ran on-line *reverse auctions* on a broad range of products such as electronics, jewelry, luggage, sporting goods and watches. In a reverse auction the vendor begins with a reference price and then ratchets it lower until a buyer steps forward, so Mercata's lure to customers was its promise to drive prices down as the number of customers on the site increased. The reverse auctions were limited to a time interval. If at the end of the time interval there was no buyer, the item on the block was then offered to the highest bidder. Mercata made money by charging manufacturers to list their items in its auctions and took a small percentage on the sales.

To survive, Mercata needed to attract enough buyers to its site to drive the kind of volume needed to turn a profit. Although Mercata said it had hundreds of thousands of customers and half were repeat buyers, it was not making money. During its last year, Mercata expanded its e-commerce offerings beyond reverse auctions, launching an on-line marketplace where small businesses could set up their own limited-time sales. Mercata did succeed in engaging some big corporate clients, such as General Motors, Microsoft and Sun Microsystems, which used Mercata technology to run reverse auctions for their own products.

B2C auctions like Mercata have been regarded as potentially superior substitutes for C2C sites, as they reduce the risk of fraud by acting as middlemen for reputable merchants. The challenge for Mercata was twofold, though. First, Mercata had to attract reputable merchants or manufacturers to list their wares on its Net Market. Second, Mercata had to attract a sufficiently large number of customers to the site not only to make the market but to make a profit.

The mental hurdle for the first challenge was to convince vendors that there were potential cost savings to be enjoyed by listing products on the Mercata site rather than sending products through conventional channels. With an emphasis on declining retail prices, Mercata would have to make an argument based on explicit proof that the costs the vendor would incur in engaging customers on the Mercata site were so low as to more than make up for the reduced margins the vendor would earn. As we've seen in the case studies of Chapter 1, institutions are difficult to change quickly, and the conventions the vendors followed in going to market through known channels were deep-rooted barriers to the uncertain prospects of Mercata's value proposition.

The prospects of meeting the second challenge dimmed when Mercata realized that it was competing with numerous similar Net Markets. The conundrum that Mercata faced is the chicken-and-egg problem that new magazines face. A magazine earns most of its revenues from advertisers, but advertisers will advertise in the magazine only if they can be assured that the readership profiles are consistent with the market that the advertisers seek to reach. Similarly, if Mercata could not attract a long list of reputable vendors, then the customers would not visit the site. Perhaps Mercata could have found a way out of this by attracting the "right" kinds of customers for the vendors, but those customers would not likely have been ones openly seeking price discounts. And, if customers would not come to the site, then Mercata would have attracted vendors offering items that could not find purchasers through conventional channels. It is unlikely that such vendors or their wares would have conjured images of high quality in the minds of the smaller and smaller numbers of customers attracted to transact on the Mercata site.

MaRCoT: The B2B Value Framework

In Chapter 2 we introduced the MIDST Success Driver Framework to provide a broad diagnosis for why certain B2B models failed or succeeded. The MIDST framework can be applied to successes and to failures to give the CEO a disciplined and systematic overview of all the pieces that must fit together to assure success. In this chapter we use the MaRCoT Value Framework to drill down on the value that any given B2B model might produce. The MaRCoT framework is linked to the relation between the *Demand* and *Market Systems* components in the MIDST framework. It is in this relation where value is created. Each of the other drivers of MIDST influences the value created by each of the other factors.

Highlighting the Distinctions Among the Efficiencies

The Case of Organized Capital Markets

The basic market condition that economics seeks to address is scarcity. Capital is a scarce resource. In the case of the formation of the corporation as an economic institution, the innovation was the pooling of financial interests to provide the capital for the creation and growth of an enterprise in such a way as to protect the owners (that is, the capitalists) from claims or liabilities separately from the enterprise. Standard corporate finance and investments textbooks, such as Bodie and Merton (2000), have documented the significance of the corporate form of enterprise in fostering the growth and distribution of wealth in the United States.

The popularity of the corporate enterprise form also supported the demand for pooling capital—an activity that was difficult to organize in post-colonial America. The Buttonwood Agreement of 1798 was a singular event that established the economic ground rules for organizing a relatively large-scale capital market. There are two significant intermediaries that made the NYSE work. The first was the *broker*. The role of the broker was to reduce overall search costs in the market and to provide the facilities to execute orders. In this role the broker acted as an agent on behalf of a principal (investor). The broker was the focal point for incoming orders, kept records of unfulfilled bids and asks, and transacted. However, this fledgling organized capital market could not perform sufficiently well without the emergence of another institution: the *dealer*, a player who acted as a principal, taking positions for his own account. Together the broker and the dealer made the market. Importantly, when the flow of buy orders and the flow of sell orders are unbalanced, the dealer enters that side of the market that is deficient and takes a position to buy or to sell. When bid and ask prices are spread too much, the dealer enters one side of the market to solicit buy or sell orders and to negotiate. Together, these intermediaries reduce uncertainty on the part of investors, and the dealer in particular functions to dampen imbalances, thereby promoting the liquidity of the market. For the original investors to try to organize their own trades would most likely have resulted in higher overall search costs, higher costs of negotiation and closing, higher levels of risk and, ultimately, lower levels of liquidity (hence more widely varying short-run clearing prices).

The momentous agreement over 200 years ago to organize a capital exchange to help pool investments of many individual savers for the purpose of supporting budding economic enterprises was a B2B solution that enhanced market efficiency in the market for capital, enhanced cost efficiency in the complex activities of finding and securing investors, enhanced risk efficiency through aggregation to diffuse the claims and obligations of individual players, and enhanced time efficiencies of players, many of whom would have missed the opportunities to earn the returns they sought without the organized capital market.

The Case of Electronic Data Interchange (EDI)

The interest and activity surrounding B2B are not restricted to exchanges or organized markets. Firms of all kinds have had a long-standing interest in trying to engineer efficiencies from their activities. The reasons for this are relatively straightforward. Efficient operations mean greater margins, faster response to market events and, conceivably, competitive advantage. For example, there are five stereotypical stages of operations that firms producing manufactured goods must manage:

1. Customer response: The firm must detect and act on indications of demand.
2. Procurement and production: The firm must order raw materials, hire labor and manage the manufacture of the goods it will sell into the market.
3. Inventory management: The firm may need to stock elements that it will use in manufacture in the event that it has to respond to demand before it can be assured of receiving timely delivery of the resources required.
4. Transportation: Having produced goods, the firm must transport the goods to or near the ultimate markets.
5. Warehousing: When goods produced arrive at or near destination markets before customers can consume them, the goods must be stored and maintained so that they do not lose value.

Over the past fifty years, manufacturing firms have learned to exploit computer technology to automate such activities as ordering, invoicing, bill payment and even inventory management. Each of these activities is an element of the five stereotypical stages; the stages together constitute what is called "supply chain management." The technologies that have revolutionized supply chain management since the early 1980s have been flexible manufacturing and electronic data interchange (EDI). The results of exploiting these two technologies have been measured in terms of rapid order processing, reduced inventories and just-in-time manufacturing.

In short, the exploitation of computer technology in integrating manufacturing and procurement processes has produced significant improvements in operational efficiencies and reduced process costs. The operational efficiencies are achieved by coordinating players' activities that serve a central manufacturing demand. The coordination does not resort to market mechanisms as much as it integrates activities across the boundaries of firms. The principal result is the achievement of cost efficiencies in the supply chain, as redundant work is eliminated.

Additionally, by virtue of the integration and coordination provided by EDI, uncertainty in the system is significantly reduced.

Downstream demands emanating from the manufacturing activity are known and disseminated quickly to all relevant suppliers. This means that all players, recognizing that they will be informed quickly and accurately of manufacturing demands, product availability and progress of shipments and payments, will be able to produce goods with greater assurance that the resources to produce the activity will not be wasted. The timely dissemination of rich information afforded by EDI enhances both cost and time efficiencies in the system.

The Distinctiveness of B2B in the Domain of Net Markets

The Internet really is a big deal, and one can see what it has made possible in the realm of supply chain management. Flexible manufacturing and EDI were clever combinations of computing, information and communications technologies and the Internet have taken the combinations one step further. EDI connected a producer with various suppliers, usually through a private or proprietary network or dedicated connection, allowing suppliers to be integrated into various aspects of the production process of the manufacturer; the resultant operational efficiencies have often been impressive.

Typically, an EDI architecture would be designed to automate processes of a small number of suppliers for a single producer. Boeing, for example, might have dedicated electronic connections with several key suppliers, coordinating the order and delivery of key components at different stages of the production of a 737.

The Internet is a *public infrastructure*. Not only is the backbone network accessible to almost anyone, a common protocol supporting the World Wide Web, hypertext transfer protocol or http, has been adopted worldwide. By using specific security and authentication systems on the Web, a producer could create an EDI-like architecture to accomplish supply chain management. Although there are various examples of Internet EDI solutions, perhaps the most prominent example is GE Interchange Solutions. GE offers Desktop EDI, a software service that enables small- and medium- sized enterprises to take advantage of electronic data interchange and electronic commerce. In general such examples are curious extensions of an institution of procurement, a protocol for coordinated activities sponsored by a downstream producer. They are curious because they are applying a protocol to an infrastructure that would be capable of delivering more.

Because it is a public infrastructure, the Internet makes it relatively easy to organize markets with many producers (buyers) and many suppliers (sellers). This significantly changes the economics for all participants, at least potentially. One organizes a market to achieve *market* efficiency, which is distinct from the *operational cost* efficiency of EDI and flexible manufacturing combinations. Whereas operational efficiency addresses process cost reduction, market efficiency should enhance liquidity.

One of the several features of liquidity is a tendency toward creating *price uniformity*. Well-organized markets are efficient if there tend to be no wild variations in prices.

In the B2B space, if producers band together in an on-line exchange to satisfy their procurement needs, each may be giving up some market power that could be wielded over suppliers in an EDI environment. However, producers would gladly do this to reduce uncertainty by stabilizing prices.

The Internet, as a public infrastructure, is pulling many well-known, distinctive activities together. The goals of supply chain management and organized markets haven't changed. What is new in the B2B Net Markets space is that the Internet presents the opportunity for firms to economize in their pursuit of these two goals. The following diagram is an attempt to map out the conceptual distinction. On the one hand, logistics has been revolutionized by the progressive exploitation of computing and information technologies, bringing dramatic reductions in process costs. On the other hand, market systems are emerging that capture both the liquidity enhancement provided by organized markets and the reduced transaction costs offered by new **intermediaries** such as the **infomediary**.

B2B Net Markets seek to exploit the Internet, which permits the simultaneous pursuit of both market and risk efficiencies of traditional organized markets and market intermediaries, on the one hand, and cost and time efficiencies of EDI, on the other hand.

Figure 3.1: B2B NET MARKETS AND THE INTERNET

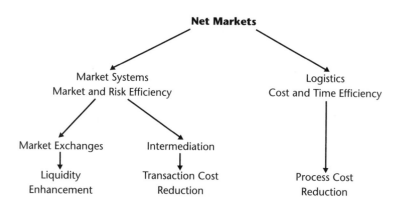

The Efficiency Dimensions of Net Markets

We now address each of the specific elements of the MaRCoT framework in turn. For each efficiency dimension, we discuss both the concept and approaches to measurement.

Market Efficiency (Ma)

The value or benefits from successfully organizing a market arise from enhanced liquidity and reduced transaction costs. An asset is liquid if the owner can find another who would be willing to exchange cash or a money instrument either for the asset or for some other instrument secured by the asset.

If markets become more efficient, then prices for procuring a given set of resources tend to stabilize. The reason prices stabilize is that the parties to an exchange in an organized market tend to be more informed than they would be were they forced to trade outside an organized market, and price-setting reflects the enhanced information. The prospect of stabilized prices has three possible effects:

1. It attracts a large number of buyers at a point in time, buying in quantities that may exceed the requirements of immediate use, or

2. It lowers costs of coordination through exchange outside of the firm (that is, in the market) rather than inside the firm (transaction cost reduction), or

3. It does both.

The tension between what is done in the market and what is done within the firm is a time-worn tussle. The more efficient the market, the greater the desire for organizations to go to the market for inputs rather than to produce what they need themselves.

Liquidity was a major stumbling block in the example of Mercata. There was no assurance that a sufficient number of potential transacting partners would appear on either one side of the market for any proposed transaction (offer to buy or offer to sell), making it hard for any player to participate in the Mercata exchange to *hedge*. One reason players participate in any organized exchange is to take positions to protect themselves against unfavorable future circumstances. One way to hedge is to buy at a known price in advance of the need to use something. Additionally, in the Mercata exchange the risk of taking a position to sell something that might deteriorate in value was heightened because the prospect of the small number of participants in the exchange would put pressure on sellers to reduce prices. So there was no potential up-side to *speculate* on. Consequently, Mercata suffered because of its inability to organize a market and distribute the benefits of relatively stable prices to market participants.

Measuring Market Efficiency

Conceptually, market efficiency would mean that a Net Market had both achieved heightened liquidity (ease of establishing prices and enabling trade) and dampened price volatility. In practice these two characteristics are difficult to observe directly, so we indicate how a Net Market would perform on five sub-dimensions. We measure performance of any given Net Market on each of the five sub-dimensions using a standard five-point scale. The degree of market efficiency correlates with each sub-dimension.

Sub-dimension M_1: Derivative Products

The extent to which the Net Market permits creation of derivatives on the underlying physicals traded should attract more participants (P) to the Net Market. Examples of derivative products would be options to buy or sell a physical product at a specific price, within a specific time frame. Adding derivative products increases the choices for buyers and sellers and, consequently, the propensity for transactions to take place (T).

Scale:

High: 5	4	3	2	Low: 1
(many derivatives)				(no derivatives)

Sub-dimension M_2: Liquidity

As we have defined liquidity, it is a component of the overall market efficiency calculation.

The liquidity index applies, with P as potential trading partners, T as percent transacting or frequency of transacting, and R as intensity or rate of transacting:

$$P \times T \times R$$

Applying the "Rule of Two," there must be high levels of two of these to achieve liquidity; having low levels of two of these assures illiquidity.

Scale:

High: 5	4	3	2	Low: 1
(many derivatives)				(no derivatives)

P,T,R—all high
At least two P,T, and/or R high
Mixed
Any two low
P,T,R all low

Sub-dimension M_3: Internal Rules

Internal rules govern the participants and their behaviors in the Net Market. Specific internal rules that influence market efficiency govern how the market is cleared and how orders are processed, both buy and sell.

Scale:

High: 5	4	3	2	Low: 1
Internal rules that organize the Net Market make things run very efficiently, leaving no surpluses on either side of the market		Internal rules have no influence on surpluses on either side of the market		Internal rules prevent exchange from occuring

Sub-dimension M_4: External Rules

Rules may also be imposed on the exchange from outside parties, such as governments and industry associations. These rules may also govern the participants and their behaviors. A simple example would be a rule requiring the reporting of terms of a transaction so that parties to the transaction could be assessed taxes. Other rules, such as information privacy-protection provisions and equal treatment requirements, may influence how the market is cleared and how orders may be processed. Some external rules promote market efficiency by reducing uncertainty (such as reporting requirements); others help to expand choice (tax relief, for example).

Scale:

| Rules may | **Expand Choice** | or | **Reduce Uncertainty** | |
5	4	3	2	1
If external rules significantly expand choice and reduce uncertainty	If external rules significantly expand choice but do not reduce uncertainty	If external rules do not expand choice but significantly reduce uncertainty	If external rules moderately expand choice and moderately reduce uncertainty	If external rules neither expand choice nor reduce uncertainty

Sub-dimension M_5: Assortment Bias

Some markets may be very efficient in enabling trade in a few goods and services, some may be very efficient in enabling trade of a broad variety of goods and services. If any given exchange is efficient in organizing trade for one item in its assortment, but inefficient in organizing trade in all other items in its assortment, it would be misleading to say that the Net Market is particularly efficient. To capture the balance of efficiency in exchanges for all items in the assortment of items offered for trade on a given Net Market, we use a Herfindahl index:

M_5 = *the sum of squared transactions of each product in the assortment divided by the square of the sum of all transactions for all products in the assortment. This is the same as the sum of market shares.*

A highly efficient market without assortment bias would have equal market shares for all N products traded in the market. This means that the Herfindahl index would be $1/N$. Conversely, a maximally inefficient market would have one of the N products in the assortment accounting for all transactions, and the Herfindahl index would equal 1. The scale to gauge the depth of assortment bias that is consistent with the degree of market efficiency can be generalized for a Net Market with N products offered for trade in the assortment as:

Scale:

		Herfindahl Index		
5	4	3	2	1
1/N most efficient/ no assort- ment bias		(N-1)/2N		Least efficient maximal assortmnet bias

In practice it may be expedient to calculate this index on only a sub-sample of the items offered on a given Net Market.

$$\text{Ma score} = (\ M1 + M2 + M3 + M4 + M5)\ /\ 5$$

For any Net Market, this score will be between 1 and 5. The closer the score is to 5, the more evidence there is that it has a high degree of market efficiency.

Risk Efficiency (R)

Risk is a special case of uncertainty, and uncertainty has many dimensions or causes. One indicator of uncertainty is variability either in expectations—not really knowing what will happen—or in past performance—observing what has already happened. The latter form of variability often fuels the former. Risk is uncertainty that has potential consequences one would otherwise wish to avoid. Not all forms of uncertainty harbor consequences, but all forms of risk do entail the potential of problems of some kind. When different parties to a transaction have different levels of information, a special class of problems arise from uncertainty. These cases are identified as *information asymmetries*, and there are two kinds of problems associated with information asymmetries:

- adverse selection
- moral hazard

When one party cannot ascertain relevant characteristics of a counterparty, then the first party faces a problem of potential *adverse selection* stemming from hidden information. Consider the hypothetical example of Bob Smith of Olympia, Washington, who seeks to purchase authentic replicas of Honus Wagner's baseball glove and Duke Snider's baseball bat listed on the Mercata exchange by Billy Don MacDonald Enterprises (BDME) of Brownsville, Texas. BDME is a small business not previously known to Bob. Under these circumstances it would probably occur to Bob that there would be certain assurances he would appreciate having from BDME. Is the glove made from real cow leather and is the bat from real ash? If Bob cannot verify these aspects of BDME's items on offer, then Bob cannot determine with certainty whether the products offered by BDME would "perform" up to his expectations. Since Bob does not know Billy Don or BDME, he does not know whether BDME has a record of bilking its customers by selling inferior goods or whether BDME has satisfied its customers with its products and customer service in this business for fifty years. In transacting with BDME, Bob exposes himself to risk that BDME might deliver products that do not perform up to Bob's expectations.

A second variant of information asymmetry is the problem of *moral hazard*, which arises when one party to a transaction cannot be assured of the performance or behavior of the counterparty after the transaction. Moral hazard is a problem stemming from hidden or unknown circumstances. For example, though Bob and BDME agree on price, grade and shipping terms, Bob would find it difficult to know if BDME might consciously substitute the items for cheaper items made from non-authentic materials before shipping them to Bob. In general, Bob cannot verify if BDME has performed in a way that supports his expectations for the products' performance.

The extent to which the transacting parties do not know each other exacerbates the unfavorable effects from information asymmetries for at least one of the transacting parties. As Net Markets can be viewed as only the latest step in progressively impersonal exchange evolving over the past 150 years, transacting parties and their intermediaries seek remedies for the potentially damaging consequences from uncertainty in knowing who they are transacting with and how the counterparty will behave after the transaction. There are four common remedies for reducing information asymmetries arising from impersonal exchange:

1. Contingent contracting
2. Certification and compliance monitoring
3. Signaling
4. Reputation.

Remedy 1: Contingent Contracting

An important special case of a direct contract between two transacting parties is a **contingent contract** that ties the seller's compensation to performance of the product in use after the transaction. A second form of contracting is for one party to contract with a third party who insures the first party against costs associated with an unfavorable outcome, typically subject to certain requirements of the first party. The challenge of both forms of contingent contracting is that parties to the contract must envisage all relevant contingencies, and they must be able to observe performance by each party under the terms of the contract. Contingent contracts are helpful, but they are not perfect remedies for information asymmetry problems.

Although there may have been a need for it, contingent contracting was difficult to execute in the impersonal exchange of the Mercata Net Market, primarily because there was no provision for an independent assessment of the performance of the product in use.

Remedy 2: Certification and Compliance Monitoring

To avoid contracting, parties to a transaction may only transact with each other so long as one or both have qualifications to perform as expected. Sellers may need to be certified whenever the production, distribution or installation of a product requires specific expertise. Buyers may need to be certified whenever the success of the product in use—hence the good name of the vendor—requires expertise on the part of the user. Certification is typically accompanied by monitoring by one party or its agent to assure that the counterparty complies with requirements. Certification is often established under a franchise arrangement. Mercata sought to certify transacting parties, at least to some extent, through the member registration process. On the Mercata Net Market, physical products were traded on a spot market where violations of promises might have been difficult to monitor and redress.

Remedy 3: Signaling

Signaling among potential transacting parties economizes on information retrieval and transmission. An effective signal would inform without necessarily revealing explicit information about the quality of the product exchanged, for example. A seller who is willing to engage in a formal contingent contract would be signaling confidence in the ability of the product to perform up to expected quality levels. In many instances, advertising is fundamentally signaling, as its sponsor conveys confidence in exposing a position (products on offer, for example) that may be appreciated by both potential transacting parties interested in the position, as well as by organizers of an exchange interested in listing the position.

Remedy 4: Reputation

To the extent that a seller is concerned about future demand for his product, his reputation serves as an implicit contract. The greater the level of demand the seller can serve, the more effective reputation is as a substitute for any explicit contingent contract. For reputation to serve as a remedy for information asymmetries, the identity of the party wishing to transact—buy or sell—must be evident to others entering a Net Market. In the case of Motorplace.com, the reputation of the Cobalt Group as the party that warrants that every vehicle on offer has been professionally inspected is key to driving the trading volumes. Reputation, as an implicit contract that trades would be consummated or that trading parties had relevant trading histories, could not be used effectively on Mercata.

One can imagine various creative combinations of these remedies to reduce risk in the environment of a B2B Net Market. Consider an example of combining the second and fourth remedies, *certification and compliance monitoring* and *reputation*. To counteract the risks that arise when trading parties do not really know each other, a third party could specialize in providing a reputation rating system. This is, in fact, a service that eBay provides on its C2C Net Market.

Some players have a greater tolerance for uncertainty in their decision-making than others. A player's tolerance for uncertainty would relate to what the player foresaw as possible costs or gains brought about under alternative future scenarios. The willingness of players to expose themselves to risk depends on certain individual characteristics such as circumstance, history, intentions and personality, as well as to environmental characteristics that influence the probabilities of outcomes and their associated costs or gains. Those who take positions to reduce their exposure to risk are hedgers; and those who take positions to profit from increasing their exposure to risk are speculators. Modern markets accommodate both hedging and speculating, which together help sustain market liquidity.

Risk efficiency is achieved when trading partners engage in exchange without subjecting themselves to greater uncertainty and higher associated costs than they would otherwise desire to trade under. Some players consciously choose to reduce their risk of uncertain but major loss in exchange for incurring a known, smaller loss. In fact, the insurance industry has emerged to guarantee compensation to players in the event of undesirable, uncertain outcomes, in exchange for the players' incurring a guaranteed loss—the premium paid to the insurer.

Market systems that are more risk-efficient tend to encourage higher volumes of exchange than those that are less risk-efficient. A great variety of information services, from journalism to market analysis, provide information to diminish the uncertainty that players in a market system might otherwise face.

Measuring Risk Efficiency

Risk efficiency varies directly with the extent to which the Net Market presents opportunities for hedging, speculating or otherwise adapting one's position in light of emerging information on market conditions or conditions of the parties with whom one might transact.

The risk efficiency criterion will be revealed in assessments of counterparty risk and in the extent to which such risks can be identified and qualified. If a first party cannot assess the prospect of a counterparty to perform according to any of the various elements of a trade, such as payment or delivery, then there would be little opportunity for any party to hedge or speculate.

Sub-dimension R_1: Credit Risk

If counterparties in the Net Market cannot marshal the resources to buy what is offered, an imbalance in the market will be created.

Suppliers may initially supply. But if buyers cannot buy, then suppliers will not keep supplying. The more pervasive the evidence that buyers do not have the means to purchase, the fewer opportunities for suppliers to hedge. The Net Market may encourage third parties to enter to provide credit at prices that make both parties and counterparties better off. A Net Market with high levels of risk efficiency will support third parties who specialize in providing credit. A Net Market with low levels of risk efficiency will require either buyers or sellers to extend credit across the market. When sellers finance the purchases of their buyers, they expose themselves to the prospect of a buyer ultimately defaulting. When buyers pay in advance of delivery, they are financing the production activities of sellers who may ultimately fail to deliver. Either way, buyers and sellers are extending credit across the market, which is less efficient than having a third party that specializes in the provision of credit services, such as a bank or credit agency, provide credit to buyers and sellers. A third party is an efficient solution because its involvement limits losses to buyers or sellers who would otherwise expose themselves to higher levels of risk.

Scale:

5	4	3	2	1
no risk to the seller		moderate		high credit risk to the seller

Sub-dimension R_2: Delivery Risk

In the event that suppliers cannot produce sufficient quantities, adhere to specifications or meet buyer's deadlines, then buyers will expose themselves to unwanted risk with little prospect for profit.

Scale:

5	4	3	2	1
(certainty that suppliers can supply) no risk		moderate risk		(no assurance that suppliers can supply) high risk

Sub-dimension R_3: Market Risk

When the time horizon of exchange over which trades can be organized does not afford suppliers the opportunity to liquidate their inventories, efficiency is jeopardized by market risk. If a Net Market affords players opportunities to adjust their positions, to buy or to sell at negotiated prices, in light of information as it is made available, then risk efficiency is enhanced. If the trading horizon is so short as not to permit parties to incorporate new information into the adjustment of their positions, then risk efficiency of the Net Market declines.

Scale:

5	4	3	2	1
maximally lengthy trading horizon to permit turnover of inventory		moderate		extremely short trading horizon

Sub-dimension R_4: Strength of Opportunity for Hedging and Speculating

Opportunities for hedging and speculating depend on two factors: first, that the market permits easy entry by qualified traders, and second, that the market operations must quickly disseminate new information accurately.

Scale:

5	4	3	2	1
extremely strong	somewhat strong	neutral	somewhat weak	extremely weak

Sub-dimension R_5: Availability of Third Party Insurance, Settlement, and Clearing Services

The presence of third parties that pool risk to indemnify principals who seek to buy and sell will limit the losses principals would incur in the event of unfavorable outcomes. The greater such pooling of risk, the more risk efficient is the Net Market. Similarly, the presence of third parties to provide clearing and settlement of trades by guaranteeing transfer of title and payment will enhance the risk efficiency of the Net Market.

Scale:

5	4	3	2	1
extremely available	somewhat available	neutral	somewhat unavailable	extremely unavailable

Cost Efficiency (Co)

Each side of a market is a boundary of a chain of activities. Work takes place on both sides of the market, and work consumes resources. For example, the exchange of corn on a spot market is linked to the work on the upstream side of the market that is associated with planting, irrigating and harvesting the fields, among other activities. The exchange of corn on a spot market is also linked to work on the downstream side of the market associated with milling, processing, packaging, storing and other activities.

Organizing a market can have consequences for the costs of conducting the linked activities on either the upstream or downstream sides of the chain. The success of Motorplace.com demonstrates that it can make a market at various stages in the motor vehicle supply chain.

Some market systems are more cost-efficient than others as they enable the upstream and downstream activities to take place with minimal waste of resources. More fundamentally, the pursuit of cost efficiency on the part of the various individual players in the market ultimately determines which activities are left to market forces (buy and sell) and which are produced within the enterprises of the respective individual players (make). The pursuit of cost efficiency determines to a great extent the structure and dynamics within the market system.

Measuring Cost Efficiency

Cost efficiencies are achieved by re-engineering various activities conducted by downstream and upstream players. We identify five primary activities that both upstream and downstream players may re-engineer to reduce costs.

Sub-dimension C_1: Market Information-Gathering and Dissemination

Firms expend considerable efforts to collect information from the market about prices, sources of supply and demand, specifications, inventories and competitive movements. Firms also seek to inform customers and suppliers as well as units within their organizations so that identified opportunities can be exploited and identified threats avoided. The scale of measure indicates the extent to which a given Net Market offers the opportunity to reduce costs associated with information-gathering and dissemination.

Scale:

5	4	3	2	1
major cost reduction				no cost reduction

Sub-dimension C_2: Production and Procurement

All firms produce something and, typically, to do so they must procure inputs. The organization and conduct of production consume resources, some of which are obtained at market prices through a procurement process. The clearest examples of production and procurement are manufacturing enterprises. But service firms also produce and procure, although outputs may be intangible and inputs may tend to be exclusively operating supplies. Some Net Markets may simplify the procurement and production processes.

Scale:

5	4	3	2	1
major cost reduction				no cost reduction

Sub-dimension C_3: Inventory and Storage

Production is often difficult to align in time with demand. Consequently, manufacturers commonly produce more than can be cleared from the market at any point in time, and inventories accumulate only to be depleted when demand subsequently outstrips the rate of production. This balancing act applies equally to service producers, as inventories accumulate in the form of idle or underutilized service professionals or service capacity. As "storage," in whatever form, takes place, firms incur costs that would be reduced if storage were not necessary. Some Net Markets may obviate the need for storage by providing information that synchronizes production with demand. For example, one could imagine a Net Market in the book trade that would signal to the publisher to produce a copy of a book only when a reader were to ask for it.

Scale:

5	4	3	2	1
major cost reduction				no cost reduction

Sub-dimension C_4: Warehousing and Materials Conditioning

After production, outputs may be moved near to the points of demand before buyers require them or can pay for them. They may be moved in unfinished form and require maintenance, assembly, and conditioning or finishing to retain or realize their market value. If demand were known in advance and if the economics of production and the economics of demand were consistent in supporting the same levels of outputs, warehousing would not be required. To the extent that warehousing is required, it causes producers to incur costs, which are embedded in the market prices of the outputs buyers purchase. Some Net Markets may reduce or even eliminate these costs.

Scale:

5	4	3	2	1
major cost reduction				no cost reduction

Sub-dimension C_5: Administration and Organization

Coordinating the production, procurement, inventory and warehousing activities in a supply chain consumes resources. To the extent that a Net Market can simplify the coordination of these activities, then cost will be reduced.

Scale:

5	4	3	2	1
major cost reduction				no cost reduction

Downstream and Upstream Weights

Some Net Markets are oriented to serving the interests of **downstream players**, some serve primarily the interests of **upstream players**, and others are balanced in serving the interests of both downstream and upstream players, presenting two measurement issues:

1. The assessment of performance on the cost sub-dimensions must be done for downstream players separately from the performance for upstream players. Consequently, there are two measures on each sub-dimension: a downstream measure (C_{iD}) and an upstream measure (C_{iU}).
2. The performance of the Net Market in terms of cost efficiency should give more weight to that side of the market whose interests the Net Market serves most. We denote the downstream weight as W_D such that W_D lies on the interval between 0 and 1 and the upstream weight, $W_U = 1 - W_D$.

    The composite score on cost efficiency may be constructed as a weighted sum of the scores on the sub-dimensions for the upstream performance and the downstream performance:

$$Co\ score = (W_D [C_{1D} + C_{2D} + C_{3D} + C_{4D} + C_{5D}] + W_U [C_{1U} + C_{2U} + C_{3U} + C_{4U} + C_{5U}])/5$$

Time Efficiency (T)

Time is a commodity we find difficult to preserve and so we value those market systems that consume little of it. In the market system, high levels of time efficiency are achieved when the collection of players incur minimal waiting costs.

Although we may recognize this goal, we also know that it is difficult to achieve. For example, as buyers and sellers do not necessarily share coincident impulses to enter into exchange, time efficiency may be achieved by permitting exchange to take place asynchronously. Various forms of impersonal exchange accomplish this, and perhaps the extreme case is that of vending machines.

Generally, the pursuit of time efficiency in the market system opens opportunities either for agents representing upstream or downstream principals to emerge or for organized markets to emerge at one or more points in the system. Some of these markets, as we have seen in the example of Mercata, are made in the physical products intended for production or consumption. Often time efficiency associated with these markets is achieved by eliminating the need for storage on one side of the market or the other, as the markets are organized to match instantaneous demand and supply. To be liquid, these markets require high values of P as transacting parties may only enter the market when needs to consume or produce arise and, then, require only low levels of R.

Other markets, such as Motorplace.com, achieve time efficiency as a consequence of tailoring offers of vehicles and parts to peculiar temporal demands. The heightened transparency of trades in the Motorplace.com market guides players to schedule their production and consumption decisions with full knowledge of their decisions to participate in the market.

Measuring Time Efficiency

One can organize conceptually the series of decisions that a market participant must make, into a simple process of three steps: search for information, list information, and execute a decision to trade. Searching (T_1) incorporates entering the market, actively looking for relevant information, and passively receiving information. Listing (T_2) involves posting information for broad undefined audiences as well as delivering tailored information to specific target audiences. Execution (T_3) entails evaluating offers or bids, arranging trades, and responding to the obligations of the terms of trades. Net markets may vary in their responsiveness to each of these steps of the decision process and so vary with respect to time efficiency.

We classify these three steps of the decision process under "responsiveness" and measure performance of the Net Market on a five-point scale, where 5 denotes a highly responsive Net Market to the time efficiency sub-dimension and 1 denotes a highly unresponsive Net Market.

Scale:

Sub-dimension T_1: Search:

5	4	3	2	1
highly responsive				highly unresponsive

Sub-dimension T_2: Listing

5	4	3	2	1
highly responsive				highly unresponsive

Sub-dimension T_3: Execution

5	4	3	2	1
highly responsive				highly unresponsive

Time efficiency also depends on the temporal sensitivity of demand and supply. There are some outputs that are highly perishable (T_4): their market value declines quickly as time elapses. A time-efficient Net Market is one that preserves the market value of the output. Gofish.com is one example of a Net Market that specializes in producing high levels of time efficiency with respect to preserving the market value of fresh seafood.

There are also cases of highly perishable demands (T_5). These are demands that spike at a moment in time. A highly time-efficient Net Market would be one that would perform well in accommodating such spikes. A good example of a Net Market that specializes in producing high levels of time efficiency with respect to satisfying perishable demand is DAT Services. That is, the DAT Net Market organizes a means to meet the demand for filling empty backhaul capacity, thus stimulating a flow of similar perishable demands among truckers and trucking firms.

We classify these aspects of time efficiency as "preservation" and measure performance on a five-point scale, where 5 means "high preservation" and 1 means "low preservation."

Scale:
Sub-dimension T_4: Supply

5	4	3	2	1
high				low
preservation				preservation

Sub-dimension T_5: Demand

5	4	3	2	1
high				low
preservation				preservation

A composite score for time efficiency is the arithmetic average of the scores on the five sub-dimensions:

$$T \; score = (T_1 + T_2 + T_3 + T_4 + T_5)/5$$

Classification Using the MaRCoT Framework

At present there is no taxonomy for B2B models, a situation which makes decision-making more complex for the CEO who is considering whether to commit to a specific B2B model as either an investor or a participant. As an aid to the CEO with this dilemma, we will apply the efficiency measures described in this chapter to several different models in the marketplace. Essentially, one could place any given B2B model on a scale, with four dimensionals to represent its performance or intended performance on each of the efficiency dimensions—market, risk, cost and time. Because the B2B Net Market space will continue to evolve, keeping track of a B2B's performance on the four efficiency dimensions may be more useful for the CEO than trying to remember an ever changing list of alternative models. Knowing how any given model might perform with respect to efficiency is more important than knowing if the model is really novel.

Steven Kaplan and Mohanbir Sawhney have proposed a classification system that is based on how business buying is conducted, and on what businesses buy. For example, catalog hubs, they argue, are suited to serving buyers who systematically source manufacturing inputs; MRO hubs serve businesses that systematically source operating supplies; B2B yield managers serve buyers who procure operating supplies on spot markets; and B2B exchanges serve businesses that source manufacturing inputs on spot markets. Their classification system is insightful and helpful, but it begs an important question: will the evolution of alternative forms of B2B models influence how businesses buy or what they buy? So, for example, as the B2B space develops, could one expect, for example, that businesses would find or seek opportunities to consolidate purchases of both operating supplies and manufacturing inputs on a common Net Market, or alter procurement policies so that an item previously negotiated in a systematic purchase might be included among those procured by spot buying? We cannot answer such questions unless we establish the economic benefits that any player potentially could enjoy by participating in one kind of B2B Net Market or another. The economic benefits or value, we argue, reduce to various forms of efficiency.

We propose three broad categories of B2B Net Markets that can be described in terms of their performance or expected performance on the four MaRCoT efficiency dimensions:

- Balanced
- Specialized
- Focused

Balanced B2B Net Markets perform at high levels on at least three of the efficiency dimensions; *Specialized* B2B Net Markets perform at high levels on any two of the dimensions; and *Focused* B2B Net Markets perform at high levels on one exclusive dimension. A "high" level of efficiency would correspond to a score of at least 4 on the five-point scale that we have employed throughout the measurement methodology. There are 15 different possible sub-classes of B2B Net Markets:

Balanced B2B Net Markets having high levels on:
1. Ma, R, Co, T
2. Ma, R, Co
3. Ma, R, T
4. Ma, Co, T
5. R, Co, T

Specialized B2B Net Markets having high levels on:
6. Ma and R
7. Ma and Co
8. Ma and T
9. R and Co
10. R and T
11. Co and T

Focused B2B Net Markets having high levels on:
12. Ma only
13. R only
14. Co only
15. T only

   Any B2B Net Market that does not perform at a high level on any efficiency dimension, we argue, is risking failure. After all, B2B Net Markets are just like any other economic enterprise: in order for a B2B Net Market to survive, it must deliver value to some collection of customers. Value in the environment of B2B Net Markets is efficiency, and efficiency has four dimensions: market, risk, cost and time. The B2B Net Market sponsor has 15 different ways to create value for stakeholders. The trick for the B2B Net Market sponsor is to organize and operate the Net Market to offer the specific efficiencies to those players consistent with the specific trade-offs those players make, so the 15 different sub-classes of B2B Net Markets must align with 15 different segments in the market. Although there is no guarantee that any given one of the 15 segments of players is sufficiently large or active to sustain a Net Market that would cater to the efficiency trade-offs its members make, we are bullish on the general domain of B2B Net Markets precisely because there are so many different ways for a sponsor to deliver value to the market.

Illustrations of Specific Cases of MaRCoT

To illustrate how efficiency considerations apply to different kinds of B2B models, we apply the MaRCoT Value Framework to six different Net Markets. The six Net Markets we have chosen span a variety of descriptors: public, private markets, *e-procurement*, e-sales, and vertical Net Markets. As the B2B Net Market space has evolved, we would expect that it will become harder and harder to find pure cases of any of the Net Market model descriptors. (This is yet another reason for the CEO to focus on the underlying four efficiency dimensions, which are not likely to change.) Indeed, commonly cited categories are often combinations of characteristics shared across categories.

The following four B2B Net Markets—one example of a balanced Net Market, two examples of specialized Net Markets, and the last an example of a focused Net Market—were scored on the efficiency dimensions. We present their assessments and rationale for the two extreme cases, and the resultant Value diagrams the efficiency dimension scores created for all four.

A Balanced Net Market

Motorplace.com is a successful private, vertical Net Market that does not easily conform to the Kaplan and Sawhney classification, but in certain product categories operates as a B2B exchange. In terms of the MaRCoT efficiency dimensions, Motorplace.com is a good example of a balanced Net Market that operates at high levels on all four efficiency dimensions.

Market
- M1: Derivative products. Futures contracts and other options are not offered for the underlying physicals. M1 = 2.
- M2: Liquidity. P, T, and R are all high. M2 = 5.
- M3: Internal rules. The system is replete with support to negotiate special terms quickly with any counterparty. M3 = 5.
- M4: External rules. Operating opportunistically in markets to expand choice. M4 = 5.

- M5: Assortment bias. Not only does Motorplace.com organize markets, it offers a full spectrum of complementary services for dealers, such as parts directories, information services, and lead tracking. M5 = 3.

$$Ma = (2+5+5+5+3)/5 = 4.0$$

Risk

- R1: Credit risk. Site registration pre-qualifies with rigorous due diligence upon transaction. R1 = 5.
- R2: Delivery risk. Same as for R1. R2 = 5.
- R3: Inventory risk. Time horizons for trade have been extended in most categories beyond industry standards. R3 = 5.
- R4: Hedging/speculating. High transaction volumes, wide and timely dissemination of information and negotiated prices combine to attract large number of participants, creating environment conducive for hedging and speculating. R4 = 5.
- R5: Facilitation services. Contracting responsiveness is excellent, clearing is internal, and settlement uses standard institutions. R5 = 3.

$$R = (5+5+5+5+3)/5 = 4.6$$

Cost

As the market is a vertical exchange, Motorplace.com seeks to serve the downstream player. However, by aggregating dealers at the site, parts manufacturers and distributors also benefit. Hence the sides of the market are weighted equally.

- C1: Information. Posted at a 4, listed items, had industry news. C1 = 4.
- C2: Production/procurement. Timely availability of product and pricing information streamlines production and procurement decisions for both upstream and downstream players. C2 = 4.
- C3: Inventory and storage. Information on bids and offers (quantities, source and price) is updated dynamically. Information relieves pressure on inventory management for both upstream and downstream players. C3 = 4.
- C4: Warehousing. Similar to C3. C4 = 4.

- C5: Administration. Motorplace.com uses a dedicated legal and contracting staff to quickly craft terms of all contracts reflecting all elements of negotiation. C5 = 5.

$$Co = (4+4+4+4+5)/5 = 4.2$$

Time

- T1: Search. Easy to find out if desired product or customer is available. T1 = 5.
- T2: Listing. Posting of bids and offers is a routine process. T2 = 4.
- T3: Execution. Well-organized process established and executed. T3 = 5.
- T4: Perishable supply. Product line can be perishable, flexibility in the types of transactions and transactional horizons are flexible. T4 = 5.
- T5: Perishable demand. Spot buying is transparent. T5 = 5.

$$T= (5+4+5+5+5)/5 = 4.8$$

Figure 3.2: MOTORPLACE.COM

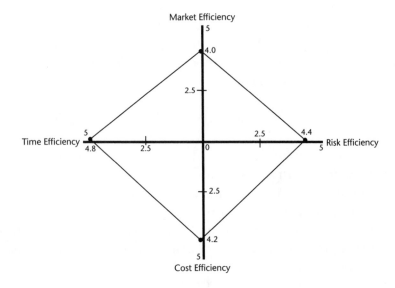

Specialized Net Markets

DAT Services is a successful public, vertical Net Market that arguably fits with the "yield manager" category of Kaplan and Sawhney. DAT Services is a specialized Net Market, offering high levels of time and cost efficiencies to trucking firms and their agents.

Figure 3.3: DAT SERVICES

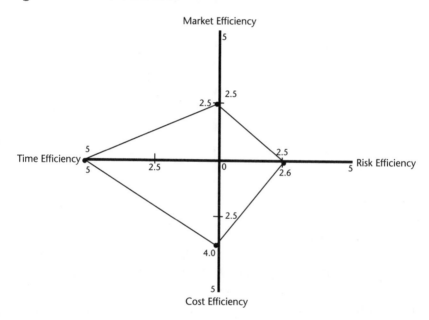

Gofish.com is another example of a specialized Net Market. It is a public, vertical Net Market that began as an on-line credit service for the fresh seafood vertical. It now has diversified into providing e-sales and e-procurement services. Gofish would also be a yield manager. Considering the highly perishable nature of the physical product, it is a challenge to produce high levels of market and risk efficiencies. At present we view Gofish as a specialized Net Market, offering high levels of time and cost efficiencies. Its long-term success would seem to require that it produce high levels of both market and risk efficiencies, though.

Figure 3.4: GOFISH

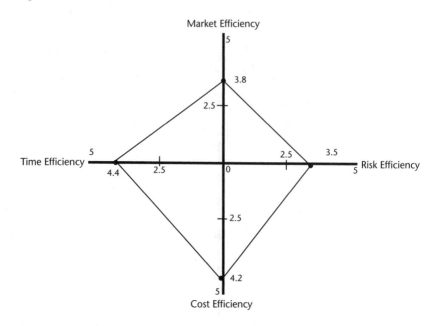

A Focused Net Market

Chemdex was a public vertical market that did not succeed in generating sufficient transactional volume to satisfy its sponsors. Chemdex was a mixture of a catalog hub and an MRO hub. In terms of its MaRCoT attributes, Chemdex was a focused Net Market with moderately high levels of cost efficiency.

Market

- M1: Derivative products. It enabled transactions for the direct procurement of goods rather than for options on the goods. M1 = 1.
- M2: Liquidity. In PTR, T and R appeared to be relatively low. M2 = 2.
- M3: Internal rules. Intention was to create an extensive assortment of goods for the chemicals vertical, offered at catalog prices. Simple rules that should have made processing efficient, aiding timely dissemination of relevant offer information, but no provision for rapid updating of bid information. M3 = 3.

- M4: External rules. No exceptionally binding constraints imposed by the state or external entities. M4 = 4.
- M5: Assortment bias. There were two primary players that probably purchased the same items on a regular basis and those did not cover the full spectrum of items listed. M5 = 1.

$$Ma = (1+2+3+4+1)/5 = 2.2$$

Risk

- R1: Credit risk. Site registration procedure provided a moderately high level of pre-qualification. R1 = 4.
- R2: Delivery risk. Site registration procedure pre-qualified sellers. R2 = 4.
- R3: Market risk. Posted items were available until depleted. R3 = 4.
- R4: Hedging/speculation opportunities. Catalog format without rapidly updated prices tied to spot or futures markets reduced opportunities for hedging and speculating. R4 = 2.
- R5: Facilitation services. Clearing provided by operator, settlement through conventional financial institutions, and insurance coverage at standard levels. R5 = 3.

$$R = (4+4+4+2+3)/5 = 3.4$$

Cost

Chemdex operated a catalog-based exchange essentially to serve as a central location for buyers and sellers to trade relatively undifferentiated scientific equipment and instruments. We have weighted the upstream and the downstream cost efficiency elements equally.

- C1: Information gathering. Fairly standard for the industry, approximating the information-processing at a master distributor. C1 = 4.
- C2: Production/procurement. The availability of the products and the pricing information made it easy and quick to decide whether to make or buy. C2 = 4.
- C3: Inventory and storage. Product information was readily accessible with available quantities, upstream and downstream participants inventory could manage storage easily. C3 = 5.

- C4: Warehousing. Product eventually would be put on shelves for some period and other than the amount stored, there is not that much impact on the warehousing efficiency. C4 = 4.
- C5: Administration. Potential to reduce paperwork and personnel responsible for procurement of the myriad of products needed by the participant. C5 = 4.

$$Co = (4+4+5+4+4)/5 = 4.2$$

Time

- T1: Search. Fairly standard process for trying to find needed product; suppliers receive updated general information on the downstream participants in the exchange, and all participants received general industry information that could accelerate intended searches. T1 = 4.
- T2: Listing. Allowed for catalog listing, but not dynamic on its updating in the event that a bid was refused. T2 = 2.
- T3: Execution. Once desired product in the quantity desired was located, execution proceeded quickly. T3 = 4.
- T4: Perishable supply. No provision to move products that had time dependent market value other than to promote them through the catalog at discounted prices. T4 = 2.
- T5: Perishable demand. No provision to attract or deal with the spot buyer with pronounced need; relied on extensiveness of assortment in catalog. T5 = 2.

$$T = (4+2+4+2+2)/5 = 2.8$$

Summary

In this chapter we have endeavored to classify the various sub dimensions of efficiency and risk that affect the success or failure of an initiative within the B2B space. Classification is important to both simplify communications and build confidence in and understanding of the domain. The MaRCoT Value Framework provides a tool that demystifies the ever changing landscape of B2B while simplifying the process of determining the value offered in different B2B models, both old and new.

Figure 3.5: CHEMDEX

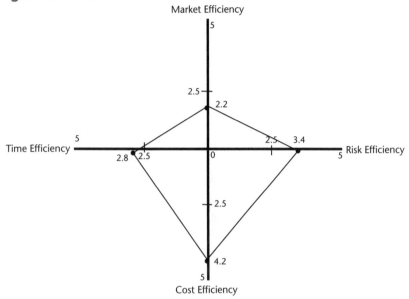

A CEO's Playbook for the Boardroom

Remember the context from Chapter 2: one of your most prominent investors has read an article about a Net Market in your product area, and she wants to know why your company is not mentioned as a participant. One of the board members, in trying to be helpful to you, speculates that the Net Market in question doesn't have liquidity. You observe the furrowed brows of the other board members, as some utter knowing "Hmmmm"s. You would like to speak to the issue to demonstrate that you have solid understanding of the trade-offs facing your company in deciding to join, build or abstain from participating in a Net Market.

Set the Tone. B2B Is Not New...

B2B has significant historical precedents, and it is helpful for the board to appreciate that the B2B models current or prospective are potential solutions to longstanding problems that face enterprise. It is just that the context has evolved (and will continue to do so) and that the means for resolving the problems have evolved as well.

Use the MaRCoT Value Framework...

All B2B models can (must) be evaluated in terms of the efficiencies that they may deliver to their participants.

1. Understand the dimensions of value:
    *   Market efficiencies
    *   Risk efficiencies
    *   Cost efficiencies
    *   Time efficiencies
2. How should the busy CEO use the MaRCoT framework to make life easier?
3. Apply the Value Framework diagram tool: encountering a B2B Net Market, ask yourself the following:
    *   Can you expect prices to be relatively stable over a period of time or in reference to general price levels in the economy? A positive answer would indicate that the Net Market is achieving or likely to achieve market efficiencies.
    *   How visible are all transactions on the Net Market? To what extent are there opportunities for you to hedge, speculate or insure yourself against market price risks? The more opportunities, the more risk efficient the Net Market is likely to be.
    *   Does the Net Market make some of your processes and activities redundant? The more there are, the greater the opportunities for cost efficiencies.
    *   Can you enter the market to transact whenever you want or is it prudent for you to enter the market only when your need to buy or sell arises? Or must you plan carefully when and how you enter the market? The more likely is the former, the more pronounced are the opportunities for achieving time efficiencies.

4

The B2B
Networked Economy

Why Net Markets Can Survive and Thrive

OVERVIEW AND GOALS OF THE CHAPTER

A key development in the recent expansion of economies around the world is the formation of markets and B2B presents new promise for further market formation. Markets, like any other business mechanism, require systems to operate. In B2B, new business models and market systems have been touted as revolutionary and fundamentally better than traditional systems. For the CEO to understand in broad terms whether market systems—new and emerging or long established—are viable alternatives, we explore in this chapter how a market system forms and functions, using the concept and application of the five primitive flows.

We will also look at the economic function and value delivered by the different players in a market system, discussing the distribution services and costs produced and incurred by each. An enterprise may seek to engage many players within a market system. Knowing how to assess the economic function of any given player as the system accommodates Net Markets will provide useful insight into the prospects for the player's survival.

We close the chapter with an illustration of the trade-offs that players in a well-established market system might make in responding to the creation of a Net Market.

The CEO must become a critical evaluator of alternative ways of organizing and operating a business within a market system. Not long ago a common promise of sponsors and supporters of various e-businesses was that the Internet would permit them to accomplish *disintermediation.* The presumption was that this would be a good thing. Many of these e-businesses are no longer in business, and there is probably more than a tenuous connection between their pursuit of disintermediation and their demise.

Our goal is to demonstrate that intermediation in a market system is generally desirable. This does not mean that market systems cannot be improved by re-engineering the way that intermediation is accomplished. Indeed, the form intermediation takes in a market system will be influenced by the pursuit of efficiencies by the individual organizations in the system. B2B Net Markets present certain challenges within market systems because they present opportunities and risks for accomplishing intermediation in new ways. The chief executive of any firm within a market system must become comfortable and skilled in assessing these opportunities and risks.

How a Market System Functions: Primitive Flows

Whether trade or exchange takes place along a rural road in Nova Scotia, in a dark alley in New York City, on the "Strip" in LA, in the pit of a commodities exchange in Chicago, at the checkout lane in a supermarket in a suburb of Windsor, or somewhere in cyberspace, there are five primitive flows that, collectively, inevitably make the trade or exchange happen. These form the foundation of any market system.

Market systems can be extremely simple—for example, a cobbler producing a pair of shoes from the hides of livestock he owns and selling the shoes directly to anyone who will pay him. Market systems can also be extremely complex, such as a consortium of producers interacting to create a microprocessor that may be sold to various intermediate and final buyers who modify, consume or resell the product or associated services in unique ways. Generally, there is only weak correlation between the complexity of the product and the complexity of the market systems through which the product may be conveyed from original producer to ultimate consumer.

It is important to remember that it is the number of players who contribute to enabling the five primitive flows that determines the complexity of the market system.

The five primitive flows are:

1. Product flow
2. Information flow
3. Payment flow
4. Property rights flow and
5. Risk flow

A B2B Net Market exists within a market system, and the market system is defined by its primitive flows. Whether the Net Market is economically viable or not, it will influence and alter the flows. In most cases, a Net Market can alter the function of at least one player or a class of players that enable at least one primitive flow in a market system. In any case, players within the system will adapt in ways to either impede or enhance the flows, and this is what the CEO must anticipate.

In addition, Net Market makers and ancillary service providers must strive to understand the primitive flows in their industry or target market so that they can identify their impact on the market system in which they participate. Understanding the flows' potential impact on value will allow the participants to determine their role in the system and the consequences of different strategies of participation.

Product Flow

A product is anything valued by some downstream player (a buyer of some kind) and provided by some upstream player (a supplier of some thing). Both upstream and downstream players derive value from something produced by the other. The value the downstream player attributes to the product is derived from its use. The value the upstream player attributes to the product is derived from a conjecture that some downstream player will use or resell the product to another player, in exchange for some economic recompense. Products vary in terms of their completeness in enabling the intended or conjectured use or consumption. In all cases, downstream players may choose to produce for themselves the product in question.

The value realized by the user of a product is fundamentally grounded in a stream of services that the user can extract from the product. The costs that the player would otherwise incur in some form of self-production or in the exploitation of substitutes define a product's real value to the user.

Commercial products can be neither purely goods nor purely services. Services typically require some goods to enable consumption, and goods typically require some service to enable consumption. For example, a telephone has almost no utility without an accompanying network, and a network service has no utility without some kind of telephone.

The product flow results from a multitude of players in the system who process, assemble, modify, package and configure something they procure from an upstream player. What generates the product flow is the intention of the players to refine the solution for consumption or use by downstream players. The product flow is the progression of steps that ultimately completes the production of value for the end user. One key part of the value creation is the step of physically moving the product from point of original production to point of ultimate consumption.

Consider two extreme examples of products that have two very different flows in two very different market systems.

EXAMPLE 1

Nokia designs, manufactures and markets, among other things, cell phones. The consumption activities into which Nokia's cell phones are used vary widely over time and place. Downstream players, such as wireless carriers, evaluate carefully the specifications of Nokia cell phones, attempting to match their utility to different kinds of users and use situations. Ultimately, the choice of cell phones that will be sold in the market will rest upon the assessments of end users, who are downstream from the wireless carriers. The value of Nokia cell phones depends, in large part, on the services that the wireless carriers associate with them. A carrier such as ATT Wireless may influence the specification of Nokia cell phones, to assure that they are designed to deliver the network services ATT Wireless intends to deliver to end users. ATT Wireless may also make some minor modification to the Nokia cell phone, such as placing its logo prominently on the dialing pad.

The product flow is rather complex in this case. The cell phone product begins its definition once Nokia designs it, assembles the parts, assigns the Nokia trademark to it and distributes it to downstream players at various levels of the market system. The product takes on an added dimension once a carrier such as ATT Wireless associates a service with it. End users attribute value to the Nokia phone, and Nokia and its downstream partners speculate what that value is and how much of the value they might capture through some pricing arrangement.

EXAMPLE 2

Imagine a Net Market for cell phones that permits players to conduct business at various levels of the market system. One of the reasons for creating such a Net Market might be to accumulate key market information for all participants to ensure that specifications of the cell phones are quickly adapted to meet genuine demands of end users.

To encourage players throughout the market system to innovate continuously, one might create financial instruments that let parties in the system take conditional delivery of the goods. One kind of instrument could be a *promise to purchase,* at a specified price, a cell phone with specific features that may not yet exist on the market. Another kind of instrument could be a *promise to produce,* at a specified price, a cell phone model with features not yet on the market. These instruments would be products just as the cell phones are products. That is, players within the system could value the instruments, betting with varying degrees of confidence that the conditions specified would arise. In short, a market could be made in the instruments separately from the tangible or "physical" cell phones. If the derived markets for these instruments were to be made, then there could be some incentive for resources to flow into the design, manufacture and marketing of these new and, as yet, uncreated cell phones.

The point of these two examples is to suggest that a market system supporting production and consumption of a product (in this case, cell phones and their complementary network services) can be transformed by altering the product flow. In Example 1, the product flow is rather linear or sequential: manufacturer to network operator to user. Example 2 suggests a way to refine the creation of value to match the desired value that downstream players might seek. In doing so the example suggests a product flow that is not so linear, as promises to produce and to consume are bought and sold to improve the flow of the complementary physical product.

Information Flow

All players in a market system contribute to information flow. At a simple level, the information sets of upstream players differ from those of downstream players in terms of what the former know about production and what the latter know about consumption or re-sale. The relevance of information for players throughout the market system is determined by knowledge of prices—offer prices and asking prices. Among the factors that influence these prices is information that maps out supply and demand schedules, that is, quantities available or desired, respectively, at points within the system. Prices for a good or service will vary widely with the quality of the information about quantities available in the system and quantities demanded from the system. Improved availability and quality of information will generally improve pricing data and therefore assist in stabilizing prices.

But there is other information that influences prices. The product flow embodies information about product specifications, supply sources and demand destinations. The higher the quality and availability of information about what is demanded and what can be supplied in terms of product specifications, the more variable prices will tend to be.

In addition, the payment flow contains information relating to the willingness and ability of downstream players to pay. Upstream players who struggle to pay their suppliers are not reliable counter parties. Information relating to the ability and willingness of both downstream and upstream players to pay will influence price stability.

Knowledge of the rights flow reveals claims that players throughout the system make on property. Typically, the rights any player may claim are incomplete. If information about the claims that players make is restricted, prices tend to vary more widely.

Risk-taking exists in any market system partly because all parties do not equally share relevant information about prices. The more distorted the distribution of information among players within the system, the more variable prices will tend to be.

In the late forties, Claude Shannon and Warren Weaver developed the foundation of modern communications theory. Applying our context to their terms, communication occurs when information flows between parties. The transfer originates with the sending party, who encodes a signal or element of information and transmits it via a medium until it is ultimately decoded by the receiver. Specialist players may evolve to facilitate specific steps of the process thereby enabling the flow. For example, advertising agencies provide expertise in encoding, network operators and carriers provide expertise in transmission, and analysts of various kinds provide assistance in decoding or interpreting information. Communications networks can be formal, such as a modern public switched telecommunications network, and they can be informal, such as a social network of friends and acquaintances. The distinctions between the two are subtle. The Internet, for example, is a combination of both formal electronic networks and a collection of ill-defined, though resilient, social networks. Information can flow on either kind of network.

Finally, a player may hold information that varies from any other player's with respect to completeness, accuracy, precision, reliability and durability. This variability in the quality of information has a direct impact on prices and on the value of the information throughout the whole market system.

Information flow is essential to a market system and fundamental to its success. In the last five years, there has been strong growth in the number of new Net Market makers and other intermediaries trading on the value of information in an attempt to improve upon its quality and reliability as a key source of value creation for their organizations.

Payment Flow

Payment is a promise, taking a wide variety of forms, to settle a claim. Money is only one form of payment and a variable form itself. Table 4.1 compares five common forms of money using 17 criteria. *Legal tender* is money that the state accepts in payment of its claims against its citizens and residents. *Notional money* is a weaker kind of money that requires an accounting of cumulative positions that parties claim against each other. Credit or methods of deferred payment abound in modern economies, and their provision provides great impetus to trade. The availability of credit depends on the existence of institutions, especially those sponsored and enforced by the state that protect both creditors and debtors (such as bankruptcy protections).

Variability of payment methods depends in one respect on whether the claimants are members of a closed or open system of claims. Because of the highly impersonal nature of the Internet, new challenges exist to ensure settlement of claims. Closed systems create "private money" that has reduced purchasing power outside of the system. Players engaged in any transaction, whether in a closed or an open system, have different preferences for payment methods, because the methods impose different benefits and costs on the players in different ways. The speed and certainty with which payment flows from buyers to sellers are also influenced by the costs and risks associated with the payment type. As an example, credit-card payment has a specific cost associated with it for the vendor accepting this type of payment.

Table 4.1 COMPARISONS OF CONVENTIONAL FORMS OF PAYMENT INSTRUMENTS

Characteristics	Explanation of Characteristic	Cash	Check	Credit Card	Debit Card	Money Order
Easily Exchangeable	Easy to exchange as payment; fungible	yes	some-what	no	no	yes
Locally Scalable	Adding users does not create slower transactions	yes	yes	yes	yes	yes
Low Transaction Delay	Time required to complete transaction	yes	yes	some-what	some-what	no
Low Transaction Cost	Cost associated with each transaction					
– For Micro		yes	no	no	no	no
– For Large		no	yes	yes	no	yes
Non-refutable	Transactions can be verified	no	yes	yes	yes	yes?
Transferable	Payment instrument is not bonded to one party	yes	no	no	no	yes?
Low Financial Risk	Parties involved in the transactions are not subject to risk; mostly a function of the security of the payment mechanism	no	no	some-what	some-what	sellers face no risk; buyer might
Unobtrusive	Few steps are required to carry out transactions; increased transparency	yes	yes	yes	yes	no
Anonymous	Identity of one or more parties is hidden					
– For Buyer		yes	no	no	no	yes
– For Seller		yes	no	no	no	possible
Immediately Respendable	Payee does not have to take an intermediate step after receiving payment to respend	yes	no	no	no	possible
Two-way	Possibility of peer-peer payments	yes	yes	no (unless tied in with something like PayPal)	no	yes
Security	Not easily stolen, secure against eavesdropping during transactions	no	some-what	some-what	some-what	no
Atomic Transactions	All-or-nothing nature of transactions	no	no	no	no	no
Portable	Security and use of payment mechanism are not dependent on physical location	yes	yes	yes	some-what	some-what
Float	Does buyer keep the float generated before and after transactions?	NA	yes	yes	yes before; no after	no
Low Fixed Costs	Cost of adopting the payment protocol is low; function of hardware, software and account start-up costs	yes	yes	yes	yes	yes
Account Required	Mechanism requires that users set up an account	no	yes	yes	yes	no

Net Market models of various kinds present a host of new issues relating to the payment flow. The prospect of digital payments is one issue that parties throughout any market system must be able to evaluate. Table 4.2 presents interaction between parties to enable a digital payment flow.

Table 4.2: ILLUSTRATIVE DIGITAL PAYMENT LANDSCAPE

Device	Transaction Channel	Application Server	Transaction Processor	Destination Payment Mechanism	
Cellular Phone, PDA, Browser and Mini-Browser	Blue Tooth Terminal	Vending Machine	Application Provider *Web site owner or Merchant owner*	On-line Secure Payment	
	Wireless Network	PC		Account	
	Internet	Toll Booth	Telco Operator *Vodafone Deutsche Telekom*	On-line Secure Payment	
	British Telecom Cellnet	Kiosk		Phone Bill	
Nokia Ericsson Motorola Palm Pilot Handspring	Deutsche Telekom	Internet Merchant (Amazon)	Financial Institutions *Amex, Visa, MC*	On-line Secure Payment	
	Vodafone			Account	
	Telstra				
	IMode	SET SSL			
Smart Card (SIM, stand-alone)					

Public Key Infrastructure (PKI)

There at least six reasons why digital payments receive serious attention in Net Market environments:

1. **Digital payments may encourage trust.** Exchange in on-line environments tends to be impersonal. Trust among transacting parties who do not know each other may be supported by some form of a digital payment that quickly settles the coincidence of claims.
2. **Digital payments may encourage liquidity in Net Markets.** To the extent that a Net Market succeeds in building high levels of liquidity, the digital payments could support markets with numerous and dispersed transactions.

3. **Digital payments may diminish the need for parties of electronic trades to have identifiable places of business.** Transactions in on-line environments may bring together parties that are spread far and wide over the globe. Moreover, a Net Market may permit parties to transact without acknowledging or declaring a place of business. If two parties were to meet on the street and the payer were to pay in cash, then the claim would be settled without either party having to disclose to the other his or her place of business. In much the same way, digital payments could function as cash for transacting parties in the virtual space of an electronic environment.

4. **Digital payments may ensure privacy.** To the extent that digital payments function like cash, then transacting parties need to know very little about each other.

5. **Digital payments are suited to micro-payments.** Certain pricing models in Net Market environments assess charges on transactions that are smaller than standard currency units. Digital money can be divided into arbitrarily small units, thus enabling transactions even when the monetary value is small. One way to organize a digital payment scheme would be to have a specialized third party sell to potential transacting parties, in conventional monetary denominations, blocks of arbitrarily divisible digital money. The third party redeems cumulative positions of transacting parties in conventional denominations. The cumulative positions result from receipt of a series of micro-payments. See Table 4.3 for illustrations of two such third parties, NetBill and Millicent.

6. **Digital payments may accommodate non-traditional players in the payment flow.** Certain third parties are in positions within on-line market systems that permit them to lead the establishment of digital payment as an institution in Net Market environments. In particular, telephone carriers, given the extensiveness of their coverage, have begun to exploit their positions as bill collectors. For example, NTT DoCoMo have more than 40 million subscribers, who can use the i-mode technology to make on-line payments. NTT charges by volume of data transferred and not by the traditional telephone rule of pricing by length of connection time.

Table 4.3: MICRO-PAYMENTS

@ Millicent

- Customers buy scrip from brokers
- Scrip is vendor-specific
- Scrip contains name of vendor, some customer properties, value, expiry and some ID material
- No centralized server to verify scrip
- Inexpensive encryption (cost of breaking encryption <value from breaking)

@ NetBill

- Suitable for information goods
- NetBill software verifies that the goods were received intact (arrives encrypted) and sends verification of this to the merchant's server
- Merchant sends verification message, account information and the decryption key to the NetBill server
- NetBill server verifies that there is enough money in the account. If so, it transfers the funds, stores the decryption key and sends a report back to the merchant's server
- The merchant then sends the decryption key

A final development that will influence the payment flow in B2B Net Market environments is *electronic bill presentment* (EBP). The objectives of EBP are to:

1 Improve customer review
2. Develop structured ways to handle payments
3. Create more efficient payment processing by:
    - streamlining accounts receivable and accounts payable functions
    - reducing billing costs
    - accelerating cash flow

The innovations presented by both digital payments and electronic bill presentment combine either to reduce or eliminate the risks and lead times associated with current payment methods. Although these innovations will most likely accelerate and simplify payment flows in many market systems, they will also impose pressures on players within the system to manage their customer relationships in new ways to maintain loyalty.

Property Rights Flow

Property rights are established in both legal and economic terms. Legal rights may enhance economic rights, but legal rights do not completely establish or preclude economic rights. This is important because for legal rights to render effective claims, two activities must be assured:

1. Measurement of the rights is competent and clear and
2. Enforcement of the legal claims is credible and swift.

Market systems struggle to conduct these activities to support all legitimate claims. Even with the use of such institutions as written contracts, contracting parties often discover that they interpret terms of an agreement in inconsistent ways. And, even when measurement may be accomplished, if a claimant can rely neither upon the force of the law nor upon his own powers of coercion to assure sufficient enforcement of a legitimate claim, then the legal right has no effective value. In short, it is costly to measure and enforce claims, and parties realizing this often choose not to assert their rights.

We identify five distinct rights that one might exercise over an asset or property. These rights are a blend of economic and legal rights:

1. *The right to possess and restrict access.* Example: The owner of a house possesses a deed to the house and the land on which it sits. However, a neighbor may effectively restrict access in many creative ways, such as by playing very loud music in the evening hours.
2. *The right to use or deplete.* Example: The owner of a house may choose to sleep, eat meals and listen to music in the house. However, a passerby may help himself to the delicious mushrooms growing in the front yard or an apple from the tree by the sidewalk.
3. *The right to transform.* Example: The owner of a house may choose to build a garage on the land and create a master suite with a view of the ocean out of two bedrooms on the second floor of the house. However, the municipal government could construct a high-rise office building that obstructs the view.
4. *The right to use as a source of income.* Example: The owner of the home may choose to rent the house to a temporary occupant.

However, an enterprising individual may take up a station on the sidewalk outside the house, selling historical accounts of the house because it represents a significant architectural style.

5. *The right to alienate (to dispose of or sell to a third party).* Example: The owner of the house may choose to sell the house. However, the bank holding the mortgage may decide to offer the house for auction because the owner has been in arrears on the mortgage payments.

In any exchange, one or more of these rights are conveyed from the upstream player to the downstream player. This means that an exchange may deliberately attempt to convey only one or two of these rights while leaving the remaining rights intact. However, it is typically difficult for any player to exercise all of these rights with equal force. The reason for this, again, is that the exercise of rights to property requires measurement and enforcement of claims, which we argue are costly to perform. *Capture*—the use of property without a valid claim to it—occurs because it is costly to measure and enforce rights. The flow of property rights in a market system will depend on the quality and quantity of the efforts that players in the system exert to measure and enforce rights.

It often surprises us to account for the extensiveness of capture. Consider the following two instances of capture.

CAPTURE EXAMPLE 1

When a traveler purchases an airline ticket, he may notice that although he possesses the ticket it may be no more than an incomplete claim to a seat on a flight. He certainly does not own the seat or the storage space anywhere near the seat. The claim he has purchased in the form of the ticket conveys a limited use right and is likely to carry severe restrictions with respect to all of the other four rights listed above. What are the limits of the traveler's use right? The airline does not specify rights as completely as the passenger might think, and sometimes that may not matter. But when the passenger finds himself sitting in a middle seat in economy class on a crowded, trans-oceanic flight, and the large fellow stuffing enough carry-on luggage for three people into several overhead bins and under other passengers' seats announces, "I am sitting in the window seat next to you," the passenger might consider his own rights to be violated.

CAPTURE EXAMPLE 2

Many people have found it convenient to malign telephone companies. They are an easy target, but consider the kind of capture behavior they subject themselves to. For some years, the tariffs of the European phone companies were much higher than those for North American phone companies. Recognizing this, certain North American-based enterprises seeking to deliver low-cost international calling to European-based clients offered what became known as "call back services." For a small fee, a client in Paris, say, could call a toll-free number on the French telephone network requesting to place an international call to someone outside of France. The service would then call back the client, having originated the call on the North American network, and charge the client at North American rates as though she were in North America. This is capture because the client is still using the French network, at least partially, to complete the call, but the client is not paying the market price for use of the French network.

Some instances of capture reveal egregious behavior and some simply speak to the opportunism that is characteristic of dynamic market systems. In any case, one should expect capture to occur—it is the norm—because property rights are never completely delineated even under the best of circumstances. Players emerge in market systems to manage the conveyance of different property rights. Certain institutional approaches, such as licenses, attempt to delineate use rights, rights to transform, and rights to earn income from such assets as software or network services. Nevertheless, these attempts cannot possibly fully delineate these rights because it is impossible to anticipate every possible use. Besides, to measure and enforce every subsequent claim would probably prove too costly for the conveyor or for the conveyor's agents. So capture cannot be stamped out of any market system.

There is a significant institutional influence on the rights flow. The more reliable and consistent are the law courts and enforcement agencies within a society, the lower are the measurement and enforcement costs associated with the assertion of property rights. Douglass C. North, co-winner of the Nobel Prize for Economics in 1993, has noted that market exchange, especially impersonal exchange, is typically easier to accomplish in developed economies because formal institutions tend to be more reliable in these settings.

Risk Flow

Risk arises in exchange—hence in market systems—because of the variability in the preceding flows:

1. *Variability in the product flow.* Because producers throughout the system are not necessarily certain what specifications customers might demand, players throughout the system produce different product specifications. Additionally, because producers are not certain of the depth of the demand throughout the system, players will speculate in holding different levels of inventories at different points of the system.
2. *Variability in the payment flow.* Because players on the downstream side of markets throughout the system differ in terms of their willingness and abilities to pay for products, the timing of the flow of funds between transacting parties will vary.
3. *Variability in the information flow.* Because players are rarely completely informed with respect to all relevant and desired aspects associated with a transaction, the flow of information throughout the system will vary.
4. *Variability in the rights flow.* The difficulty in completely delineating rights encourages variability in the exercise of rights among players throughout the system.

Variability produces uncertainty. Just as different players in the system have different tolerance levels for uncertainty, some players will specialize in accepting risk whereas others will seek or pay to avoid it. Thus, exchange throughout a system may see various strategies among transacting players to shift risk across the market. The shifting of risk throughout the system is tantamount to producing risk flows.

In any given market system, these five primitive flows are likely to flow in different ways and among different players. A catalog retailer may not take possession of a product listed in the catalog, as a conventional store-based retailer might, much less title to it. The catalog retailer may act only as an agent, or take inventory on consignment. A conventional store-based retailer may permit the payment flow to be accomplished by a financial network administered by a credit-card issuer. In this instance, risk is borne primarily by the credit-card issuer.

Market systems tend to evolve to become progressively more complex, because the two players in the simplest possible exchange do not want to manage all of these flows. The reason that intermediaries exist is to enable one or more of these flows more efficiently or more effectively than the transacting players can themselves. A great variety of market systems arise and co-exist because companies discover that they are more competent than others in enabling some of these flows. Because inevitably there are multiple flows, the net economic result for any given player in the system can usually be produced in more than one way—that is, by other players who may manage the other flows in unique ways.

Illustrations of the Primitive Flows

Below are two illustrations of the primitive flows in two well-established industries, hotels and mortgages. In each case, we provide a schematic diagram of the stereotypical conventional system. We then suggest at least one way that a B2B Net Market model could be introduced and illustrate how introducing the B2B model might alter the primitive flows.

CASE EXAMPLE: HOTELS

A traditional structure of the hotel market system is diagrammed in Figure 4.1, isolating the context of the product and information flows in the procurement and distribution systems.

Figure 4.1: TRADITIONAL HOTEL MARKET SYSTEM

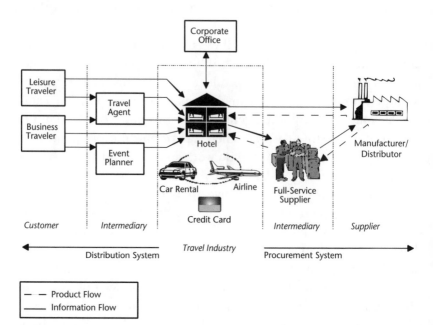

The payment flows of traditional hotel systems is diagrammed in Figure 4.2 and reveals the relatively complex combination of ordering, billing and payment in conjunction with the flow of information.

Figure 4.2: **PAYMENT FLOWS IN THE TRADITIONAL PURCHASE PROCESSES OF HOTELS**

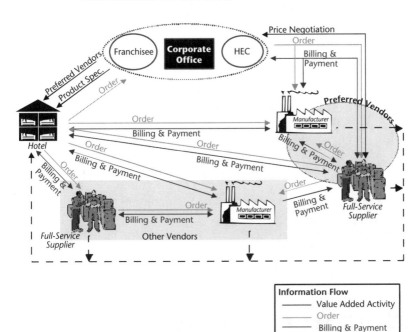

A B2B Net Marketplace could alter the structure and flows of the hotel market system. One possibility for streamlining the system, as depicted in Figure 4.3, would be to create a downstream-oriented auction and an upstream-oriented on-line procurement mechanism.

Figure 4.3: AN AUCTION AND E-PROCUREMENT SYSTEM
ALTERS PRODUCT AND INFORMATION FLOWS

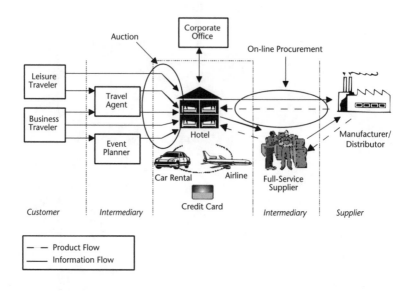

CASE EXAMPLE: MORTGAGES

The structure and dynamics of the conventional market system supporting mortgages may be depicted schematically according to the various primitive flows.

Figure 4.4 depicts the information flows at a macro level.

Figure 4.5 depicts the product and payment flows.

Figure 4.6 depicts the property rights flows.

Figure 4.4: **INFORMATION FLOWS:**
              MACRO LEVEL

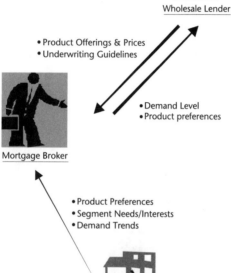

Wholesale Lender

• Product Offerings & Prices
• Underwriting Guidelines

• Demand Level
• Product preferences

Mortgage Broker

• Product Preferences
• Segment Needs/Interests
• Demand Trends

Borrower

Figure 4.5: **PRODUCT AND**
              PAYMENT FLOWS

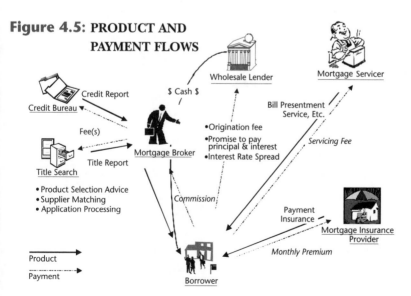

Wholesale Lender

Mortgage Servicer

Credit Report

Credit Bureau

$ Cash $

Bill Presentment
Service, Etc.

Fee(s)

•Origination fee
•Promise to pay
 principal & interest
•Interest Rate Spread

Servicing Fee

Title Report

Mortgage Broker

Title Search

• Product Selection Advice
• Supplier Matching
• Application Processing

Commission

Payment
Insurance

Mortgage Insurance
Provider

Product

Monthly Premium

Payment

Borrower

Figure 4.6: PROPERTY RIGHTS FLOWS

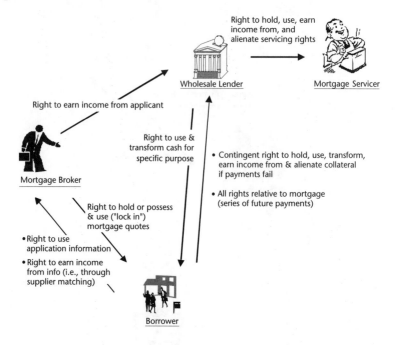

The information flows may also be observed at the transactional level, as in Figure 4.7.

Finally, the risk flows of a conventional market system for mortgages are depicted in Figure 4.8.

Figure 4.7: INFORMATION FLOWS:
TRANSACTION LEVEL

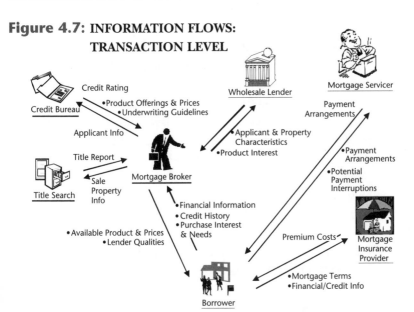

Figure 4.8: RISK FLOWS

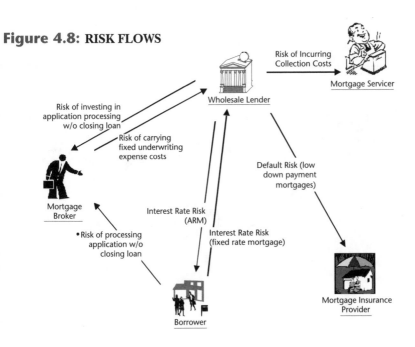

Clearly, as the various primitive flows reveal, the conventional market system for mortgages is an intricate collection of relationships and interactions on various levels among numerous parties. The introduction of a B2B Net Market could take the form of a wholesale lender/mortgage broker exchange. Such Net Markets have emerged, and IMX Exchange, FINet.com, and OpenClose.com are examples. IMX Exchange retains suppliers (that is, lenders and underwriters) to bid or supply quotes for applications submitted for customers by brokers. IMX supplies such "niche loan" products as stated income, NINA, high LT, and EZ DOC loans. Figure 4.9 depicts one possible reformulation of the market system for mortgages.

Figure 4.9: **A B2B NET MARKET CONCEPT FOR THE MARKET SYSTEM FOR MORTGAGES**

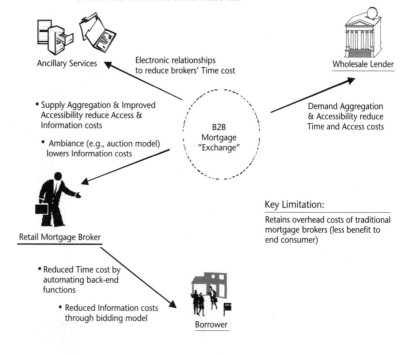

Ancillary Services

Electronic relationships to reduce brokers' Time cost

Wholesale Lender

• Supply Aggregation & Improved Accessibility reduce Access & Information costs

• Ambiance (e.g., auction model) lowers Information costs

B2B Mortgage "Exchange"

Demand Aggregation & Accessibility reduce Time and Access costs

Retail Mortgage Broker

Key Limitation:

Retains overhead costs of traditional mortgage brokers (less benefit to end consumer)

• Reduced Time cost by automating back-end functions

• Reduced Information costs through bidding model

Borrower

Interactions of the Primitive Flows in On-line Environments

Perhaps the flow most significantly influenced directly by the Internet, specifically, and by the digitization of communications and computing, generally, is the information flow. The Internet has "democratized" access to information, permitted manipulation of information and encouraged, simultaneously, both broad and targeted dissemination of information.

In any market system, the change in an information flow resulting from the application of the electronic medium—the digitization of information—invariably induces change in at least some of the other four primitive flows.

Information Flow Influence on Product Flows

In some instances, the product (that which is valued by a down-stream player) may be rendered purely in logical form. Newspapers, magazines and books presently exist in purely logical form (for example, as binary files) for several intermediate stages in their production. Printing may be shifted to the end user, so long as the end user has the requisite mechanisms to capture the logical form and convert it to paper form. Music can be recorded, edited, mixed and re-mixed, and stored in logical form. Playing the music may be shifted to the user through such mechanisms as streaming and MP3, requiring only that the user have a computer connected to sufficiently fast communications media and enabling translation software. In both of these cases (books and music), changing the information to digital form has presented opportunities for new, complementary products to enter the product flow (computers, printers, software, communications services and so on).

Information Flow Influence on Payment Flows

The key to the payment flow is the nature of settlement—how it is accomplished and how quickly. In this respect, the payment flow is inextricably linked to the liquidity of the exchange. An on-line vertical portal that succeeds in establishing a critical mass of participants also accumulates extremely valuable information, in the form of bid and ask prices, inventories, specifications, and buyer and seller qualifications, which enhances liquidity. Similarly, Web-based procurement exchanges consolidate information about the timing and nature of demand and supply.

Information Flow Influence on Property Rights Flows

Technology has inspired the organization of a variety of markets—for example, capital (NASDAQ), steel (e-Steel), electricity (houston-street.com), events (eventsource.com), bandwidth (universalaccess.com) and so forth. In fact, many of these markets, such as events and bandwidth, had not previously been organized at all under off-line conditions. A remarkable aspect of these on-line markets is that trade may now be organized not only in the physical products, but also in claims to products in these markets. The claims may adhere to standard conditions as specified in a futures contract or in specialized conditions as specified in forward contracts. In any case, because of the depth of information on bid and ask prices and because of the speed at which digital information may be transmitted to market participants, complex exchange of both restricted and unrestricted rights or claims may be accomplished.

Information Flow Influence on Risk Flows

Information is the antithesis of uncertainty. A distinctive feature of the Net Market environment is that access to information may not be easily restricted. Instances of asymmetries in the information levels of market participants are harder to sustain in the Internet environment. Variability of risk preferences among market participants following from different levels of information should be lower in on-line market environments than in conventional market environments.

Justifying the Economic Purpose of a Player in the Market System: Intermediary Functions and the Distribution Costs/Services Framework

Intermediaries are the Rodney Dangerfields of market systems: over the centuries, few kind words have been wasted on middlemen. "Disintermediation" has been both overblown and misguided.

Intermediaries exist because they do things that players, including consumers, value.

In some sense every firm performs at least some intermediary function: if a firm exists in a market system anywhere between the point of original production and ultimate consumption, then it is intermediating, and this is as true of firms that sell directly to their customers as it is of firms that sell through wholesalers and retailers. Each of these firms likely procures unfinished products in the form of raw materials, transforms them—if only to prolong their marketable life by storing them—and sells them for another downstream player's use.

What is the product of market intermediation? What is produced in market intermediation that is valued by other players in a market system?

We define the product of market intermediation as a composite of six services that all firms produce at some level. Some firms in the market system specialize in producing some of these services at high levels, and these firms are called *market intermediaries*. We call the six services of market intermediation *distribution services* and they are:

1. Aggregation of supply
2. Aggregation of demand
3. Accessibility
4. Assurance of product delivery
5. Availability of information
6. Ambiance

Aggregation of Supply

Aggregation of supply is an intermediation service provided for the benefit of downstream players, covering breadth and depth of the assortment of products available in the market system. Breadth relates to the diversity of demands that the assortment may fulfill, and depth relates to the various means in which the assortment may satisfy a given demand. A convenient example to illustrate the differences between depth and breadth would be one of a *value added reseller* (VAR) that offers deep expertise in a narrow category of chemicals, versus a master distributor that offers an extremely wide variety of chemicals. Traditionally, these two players are located at different levels of the market system, as the VAR is typically downstream close to customers and the master distributor is upstream. These two dimensions of assortment are both sensitive to the time, place and precision of demand. Aggregation of supply enables both product and information flows.

Aggregation of Demand

Aggregation of demand is an intermediation service provided for the benefit of upstream players and in some circumstances is provided jointly with the service to aggregate supply. In determining what to supply the market at an aggregation point, an intermediary may want to service a specific mix of downstream customers. This mix of downstream customers may be characterized in terms of the homogeneity of their demands and represent a specific target market. Common examples of demand aggregation are the subscriber base that magazines sell to their advertisers, the niche clientele to which a retailer supplies a desired designer label, and the potential buyers that a Net Market exchange tells suppliers will be attracted to the site. The strength of demand varies in terms of its durability, its location and its precision. Aggregation of demand enables both product and information flows.

Accessibility

Accessibility is an intermediation service that is provided for the benefit of both upstream and downstream players. The accessibility service renders it easier for upstream and downstream players to find it easier to transact business in the market. Accessibility may be defined in physical space (store location) or virtual space (toll-free number, Web site and so on). The level of accessibility that may be achieved at any point in a market system will depend in large measure on the infrastructure in place, including the number of players connected to the network and the characteristics (quality) of the connections. Accessibility enables both product and information flows.

Assurance of Product Delivery

Assurance of product *delivery* is an intermediation service that provides assurance to either the downstream or the upstream player or both that a product desired by the downstream player is delivered within the time desired or in the form desired by the upstream or downstream player. Commonly, the service forces players to make trade-offs. For example, one may seek to purchase a book on-line at Amazon.com, thereby assuring the form of the product but trading off on the availability of the book for immediate consumption (the purchaser will have to wait at least one day). The other trade-off arises when a consumer goes to the local Barnes and Noble store looking for a specific CD by an artist, but finds a different one by the artist in stock. If the consumer opts to buy the CD in stock, then he or she has made a trade-off to take delivery of a substitution now, rather than wait a day or two for the specific selection that motivated the trip to the store in the first place. Assurance of product delivery enables property rights, payment and risk flows.

Availability of Information

Every business performs some market intermediation, consolidating products from upstream players and demands from downstream players, so it is in a position to provide information to upstream players about demand and to downstream players about supply. *Availability of information* enables its flow.

Ambiance

Because buyers and sellers are likely to have preferences as to how they conduct business, a firm may provide a market intermediation service providing comforts to encourage exchange. The ***ambiance*** of the transacting points in the system may vary widely since preferences regarding the way business is conducted vary. For example, some consumers may purchase jeans from a large department store such as Wal-Mart while others purchase theirs at a boutique such as the Gap. Ambiance may influence all of the primitive flows: product, information, property rights, payment and risk.

Any vendor in a market system is obliged to intermediate at some level. Intermediaries, however, *specialize* in producing these services and differentiate themselves from each other by focusing to a high degree on a particular type of intermediation. For example, a buying agent specializes in producing high levels of accessibility for a downstream player, whereas a selling agent specializes in producing high levels of accessibility for an upstream player. A credit agency produces high levels of assurance of product delivery for both downstream and upstream players.

Therefore, the intermediary applies a business model to *commoditize* one or more of the distribution services, charging upstream or downstream players a fee representative of the value these players associate with the services the intermediary provides.

The prices that the intermediary can charge depend fundamentally on the costs the services help other players avoid. At any point in the system, downstream players, for example, will incur six kinds of *distribution costs* in addition to the market prices they expect to pay. These distribution costs include:

1. *Direct time costs*: the opportunity costs associated with the time the player expends finding supply on the market.
2. *Direct transport or access costs*: the out-of-pocket and opportunity costs the downstream player incurs in transporting goods from a supplier.
3. *Storage costs*: the out-of-pocket and opportunity costs the downstream agent incurs to secure rights to a product and retain these rights before the time of intended use.
4. *Adjustment or waiting costs*: the out-of-pocket and opportunity costs the downstream player incurs waiting for the desired product to be supplied, including substitution for a second-best alternative when the desired product is not available, the search for another supplier when the desired product is not available, or simply doing without when the desired product is not immediately available.
5. *Information acquisition costs*: the costs the downstream player incurs in searching the market for product specifications, prices, points of supply and so on.

6. *Psychic costs*: the implicit but real, costs the downstream agent incurs relating to disagreeable or unpleasant elements of the transaction.

The distribution services that the intermediary produces reduce the distribution costs for the downstream player. As downstream players are not consistent with respect to their willingness to incur these distribution costs, the intermediary seeks to reduce those distribution costs the target downstream player is most interested in avoiding—a critical point, because it dictates the range of business models that the intermediary might consider adopting.

As intermediaries themselves incur costs in producing the distribution services, the business model that they select must allow them to do two important things:

1. Produce those distribution services at a justifiable price to achieve a high return and
2. Minimize those services not demanded to assure efficient (low-cost) operations.

Primitive Flows and Distribution Costs/Services

Consider the situation of a publishing company that has signed a contract to publish an author's first book. The publishers, recognizing that the author is not known to the market, are interested in printing and distributing the book based on prior knowledge of what the ultimate market demand could be. Predicting the number of copies that a new author's first book will sell is really impossible to do with much confidence. The publishers would consider a range of alternatives to mitigate the business risk and to enhance the possible return from publishing the book. In what follows, we describe two alternative possibilities to bring the book to market, each illustrating different mixes of primitive flows and trade-offs of the distribution costs that players in the system would have to make.

THE CASE OF THE PUBLISHING INDUSTRY

A typical breakdown of the costs of publishing and distributing a book would be:

Book list price	100%
Wholesaler/retailer discount	48%
Production cost	10%
Overhead	15%
Returns and allowances	15%
Royalties	10%
Publishers' profit margin	2%

Recognizing that the manuscript can be edited and retained in an electronic form, the publishers might realize that they do not have to commit to a large initial print run of, say, 10,000 copies. In fact, if they decide to experiment with a new B2B model that exploits Net Market features, they may stand to realize some significant savings. The publishers build a Web site to organize a Net Market that permits the secure transmission of electronic copies of manuscripts to qualified recipients. They decide to print 500 hardbound copies and send single copies of the book to 500 booksellers with a promotional offer. They also produce 500 additional copies of just the front and back covers of the book. The promotional offer requires each participating bookseller to prominently display a single copy of the book. This single copy at the bookseller's premises functions as an exemplar that any prospective reader may examine at the bookshop. If the prospective reader decides he wants a copy of the book, he may then ask the bookseller to provide him with a formal copy of the book in one of two modes.

Mode 1: Hardcover copy. The bookseller would inform the publishers either by e-mail or via a link on the publishers' Web site that the bookseller's customer wants a copy of the book at the standard retail price. The publishers would then inform a printer, who would use digital copying technology combined with a preset hardcover assembly for the book, to assemble one copy of the book and courier it to the address of the retail customer. Delivery under this mode of operation would take five business days (two days for printing and assembly, one day for order processing, and two days for physical distribution).

Mode 2: Softcover book. The bookseller would inform the publishers of the order, secure approval from the publishers to produce a printed copy remotely, and arrange printing and assembly at a local source (such as PIP printing, IKON, Kinko's, and so on). In fact, the technology requirements for production under this mode would include the ability to exploit a high-speed Internet connection between the bookseller and the publishers for transmission of permissions and the electronic manuscript file. Additionally, the printing and assembly could be accomplished by high-speed digital printing. Under this mode, the book could conceivably be delivered to the bookseller's customer on the same day the customer orders it.

Although this is a hypothetical example, it is not really too far-fetched. Notice though that what either method presents to the parties involved are unique trade-offs that could make them all better off. Notice, as well, by postponing the printing of the book until demand in the end market is manifest, that the publishers would avoid significant costs in production and distribution. That is, the publishers could pocket all of the 15 percent traditionally set aside for returns and allowances, and could probably reduce production costs, wholesale discounts and overhead as well. In total, the publishers, using either of the modes of the promotion, could save somewhere between 15 and 30 percent of the traditional cost of delivering a new book to market, if they could convince booksellers and their customers to make an institutional change and accept these two new modes of book delivery.

These two modes present a reconfiguration of the primitive flows in the book trade. The reconfiguration of primitive flows would alter the relationships that the publishers have with wholesalers and printers in the conventional system, because publishers would no longer be reliant on their services in order to earn an economic return on the commitment to the author. The reconfiguration of the primitive flows would also alter significantly the publishers' relationship with independent booksellers, because booksellers would also be able to reduce or avoid making commitments to purchasing the book before demand is known. If publishers and booksellers were to take steps to alter their modes of doing business in a manner consistent with the reconfiguration of the primitive flows as described in this example, then it would be likely that those players whose economic purpose would be diminished—printers and wholesalers—would react with their own interests in mind. Nevertheless, if the business case for the reconfiguration of the primitive flows is compelling enough for the players who can sustain the system, then a *systemic evolution* could take place.

Table 4.4 compares the primitive flows under the conventional market system for publishing and the system illustrated by the example presented above.

Table 4.4: A RECONFIGURATION OF PRIMITIVE FLOWS IN THE BOOK PUBLISHING MARKETING SYSTEM

Flows	Conventional System	New System
Information	Publishers advertise, send catalogs to booksellers, arrange book reviews, organize author marketing tours	Publishers advertise, inform booksellers of book, send an exemplar to bookseller; Bookseller informs publishers when buyer commits and quantity of commitment
Product	Created by author, edited and modified by publishers, copies produced by printer, inventories stocked by wholesalers and booksellers; if bookseller has excess inventory, sells at heavily discounted prices or returns to publishers.	Created by author, edited and modified by publishers, copies produced near to or at bookseller's premises. No returns.
Payment	Publishers make fractional advance payment to author; bookseller makes full payment to publishers at wholesale prices; publishers make lagged royalty payment to author net of advance for confirmed sales at retail. In the event of returns, publishers reimburse bookseller.	Publishers make fractional advance payment to author, bookseller pays only upon commitment of retail customer. No reimbursements because there are no returns.

Rights	Author transfers to publishers the rights to earn income from sale of author's book, to modify (edit and package) the book, to sell secondary rights to other publishers (especially for international distribution). Publishers transfer to printer the right to reproduce the book (transform), and to bookseller the right to possess (hold without title) and to earn income from sale of the book.	Same transfers of rights between author and publishers, but publishers (a) do not transfer any rights to the printer (b) transfer to the bookseller the rights to reproduce the book and earn income from the sale of the book
Risk	In paying a fractional advance to the author the publishers are buying insurance for the right to earn a higher return from the sale of the book; the publishers assume most of the risk of selling the book in the destination markets, as the bookseller may return or destroy unsold copies and be reimbursed.	Publishers continue to buy insurance through the fractional advance to the author, but limit own risk and the risk of the booksellers by making commitments to supply the book to the market only when demand is certain.

In what ways would the publishers, the bookseller and the bookseller's customer gain from the application of the proposed market system? The trade-offs that the different players—bookseller, bookseller's customer, publishing company and author—would make in adjusting their behaviors to take advantage of the proposed market system can be articulated in terms of distribution costs and services.

The Bookseller

Accepting the terms of the publishers' promotion immediately reduces the storage costs that the bookseller would otherwise incur in featuring a new book for sale. All the bookseller would need to maintain in inventory is an exemplar of each new book. In some sense, direct time costs and direct access costs (in the form of logistics) are almost completely eliminated, compared to the conventional mode of doing business. Another aspect of access costs is also reduced for the bookseller. Because the shelf-space constraint for selling any given number of books is relaxed considerably, the bookseller could choose to offer more titles to gain access to more customers than before. Additionally, the bookseller avoids some potentially significant aspects of adjustment costs, as delivery of the electronic manuscript file could be accomplished almost instantaneously after the bookseller submits a request for the book from publishers. The bookseller conceivably would incur somewhat higher information and psychic costs under the proposed market system. Information costs could rise as the bookseller would need to learn how to navigate a new market system to find not only the books, but the terms and conditions the publishers assert for selling the book. Moreover, this adjustment could introduce new psychic costs, as running a traditional independent bookstore would seem to require more formal relationships with publishers and others in the trade.

The Bookseller's Customer

The levels of distribution costs the customer would incur depend on the customer's frame of reference. If the customer is a loyal patron of an independent bookshop, then the customer probably enjoys browsing and, generally, expects copies of books to be available on the shelves. However, if the bookseller responds by offering more books for sale (featuring single exemplars of different titles), then the customer benefits from expanded choice. The specific costs that a customer could incur at higher than conventional levels are direct time costs (cannot simply pick the book off the shelf), certain adjustment costs that require the customer to take delivery of a book in a less than ideal form, and, possibly, psychic costs due to the reduced possibilities for browsing in a traditional way.

However, the costs that the customer would incur at lower levels could strengthen the customer's loyalty to the bookshop. Lower direct access costs to a greater variety of books available on the market and the lower adjustment costs relating to a reduced likelihood of encountering stock-outs might combine to bind the customer to the bookseller. Additionally, the proposed market system would permit the customer to continue to have reasonably sustained experiences with traditional-looking booksellers that on-line (for example, Amazon.com) and super-store booksellers (for example, Barnes and Noble) do not offer; hence, the psychic costs the bookseller's customer would incur would be much less than what would be incurred in patronizing either Amazon or Barnes and Noble.

Because the publishers provide the bookseller access to the market for the book (though in an unconventional way), high assurance of product delivery at the desired time, and traditionally high levels of information in marketing a new book, the bookseller could sell the book with a negligible allocation of shelf space and no pre-sales commitment to purchase copies at wholesale. Paying the publishers only when an order is in hand would mean a significant cash flow benefit for the bookseller.

The Publishers

The publishers' challenge would be to try to earn a profit margin greater than the current two percent of list price. The proposed reconfiguration of primitive flows would not only reduce certain out-of-pocket costs that the publishers traditionally incur, but it would reduce almost all of the distribution costs. Direct time costs would decline through eliminating the need to schedule printing and to ship units of the printed copies through a lengthy physical distribution system. Direct access costs would be reduced because the publishers could communicate and transact conveniently with booksellers through a Web site or by e-mail. Storage costs would be almost completely eliminated because there would be negligible inventories to handle. Adjustment costs for the publishers would also decrease because the publishers would no longer need to plan printing in anticipation of uncertain demand. Information costs would plummet because booksellers would inform the publishers directly and instantly of market conditions that would warrant shipping copies of the book through the system electronically. And psychic costs would be significantly reduced because the publishers would no longer face the anxiety of committing to printing thousands of copies of an unknown author's first book wondering if readers would ever buy it. The distribution costs would combine to reduce or eliminate for the publishers printing costs, warehousing and logistics costs, and allowances for returns, giving the publishers room to reallocate effort and energies to the marketing of the book.

The Author

It is almost ironic that the publishing industry has evolved to such a complex state simply to support the role of the author, whose role is fundamental to the industry and yet overshadowed by the scale of the activities of a variety of other players in the system. The first-time author may have little market power, but the author could benefit from a reduction in several of the distribution costs. First of all, in the traditional market the probability is minuscule that an author will succeed in getting a publisher to accept a manuscript for publication. However, if the proposed market system were to take hold, then publishers would have less exposure to market risk and might be more inclined to speculate on more manuscripts and authors would enjoy a reduced cost of direct access to the market. Similarly, as writers commonly produce many manuscripts—many of which they might choose not to submit to a publisher's review—they effectively withhold from the market or store manuscripts for indefinite periods of time. If the proposed market system induced publishers to be more speculative, then more manuscripts might be demanded, and storage costs of the author would fall.

Table 4.5 summarizes possible changes in the distribution costs for these four players. In order to determine whether this proposed B2B solution could evolve to become the institution that governs the publishing, marketing and distribution of books, one would have to evaluate the likely reactions of those players within the current system who only stand to lose as a result of the reconfiguration of the primitive flows. These players are principally the large printing and bookbinding enterprises and wholesalers. Of course, given their special knowledge of the industry, these players could also adapt to the reconfigured market system by changing the nature of their activities. A wholesaler, for example, could integrate into the distribution of equipment and services that enable remote printing; similarly, a printer and bookbinding enterprise could market downstream its production expertise and technology.

Table 4.5: POTENTIAL CHANGES IN DISTRIBUTION COSTS INCURRED BY KEY PLAYERS

Distribution Costs	Bookseller	Bookseller's customer	Publishers	Author
Direct time	Decline	Decline	Decline	Decline
Direct access	Decline	Decline	Decline	Decline
Storage	Decline	Decline	Decline	Decline
Adjustment	Decline	Decline	Decline	Decline
Information	Increase	Decline	Decline	Increase
Psychic	Decline or Increase	Decline or Increase	Decline	No change

Summary

In this chapter we have explained how a market system forms and functions. It is important for the CEO to understand in broad terms whether alternative *market systems*—those that are already established and those that are proposed—can be viable. To accomplish this we discussed the concept and application of *primitive flows*. The second point of the chapter was to identify the economic function of different players in a market system. This is key to understanding which *players* in a market system are viable. As the CEO of any enterprise may seek to engage certain players within a market system, knowing how to assess the economic function of any given player as the system accommodates such new activities, as net markets provides useful insight into the prospects for the player's survival. To accomplish this we discussed the concepts of distribution services that are produced by and distribution costs that are incurred by players in any market system. We closed the chapter with an illustration of the trade-offs that incumbent players in the well-established market system of book publishing might make in responding to the creation of a net market.

A CEO's Playbook for the Boardroom

Context: your CFO informs you that a consortium of producers in your industry has announced that they are building a B2B Net Market. The CFO explains that the consortium claims that the Net Market should deliver significant efficiency gains to the whole industry, but he does not have details. You ask your executive team to meet with you in the morning to discuss this development. You would like to understand how the consortium's plans for the Net Market could directly affect your firm. You would also like to understand the potential indirect effects on your firm, as players up and down the value chain adapt to the establishment of the Net Market.

You prepare to ask your executive team in the morning how the consortium's proposed B2B Net Market could alter the way production and distribution are conducted. Specifically, you press to get answers to the following questions:

1. Will the Net Market change the way the products in our industry are created or delivered to the market? Will any player upstream or downstream be pressured to change the value proposition of the products they bring to market? (Product Flow)
2. Will the Net Market change the speed and accuracy of the dissemination of pricing information throughout the industry? Will certain players be at a greater advantage in receiving information faster or more accurately than other players? If so, who? (Information Flow)
3. How will bill presentment and payment be accomplished in the industry after the Net Market is established? Will the methods of invoicing and payment change? Will standard practices change? (Payment Flow)
4. Will any players have a reduced ability to generate revenues because of the Net Market? Will any players have a greater ability to generate revenues? Will licensing replace sales? Will title transfer in the way that industry participants are accustomed? (Property Rights Flow)
5. Does the Net Market reduce or change the nature of uncertainty in the industry—market risk, credit risk, liquidity risk? If so, will third-party services become more or less important? (Risk Flow)

Who could benefit and who could suffer as a consequence of the establishment of the Net Market? Specifically, you press your executive team to get answers to the following questions:

1. Which players will incur lower costs?
   - direct time costs in interacting with partners, suppliers and customers
   - direct costs in gaining access to the market
   - storage or inventory holding costs
   - adjustment costs that relate to waiting and delay, stock-outs, deviation from specifications
   - information acquisition costs relating to prices, suppliers, customers, specifications and product availability
   - psychic costs relating to the alien or unpleasant nature of transacting with other players in the industry or value chain
2. What opportunities do players have for enhancing the value they could deliver, hence the returns they could enjoy?
   - enhanced aggregation of goods and services provided
   - enhanced access to downstream markets
   - expanded variety of goods and services provided
   - increased assurance of more precisely delivered demand goods and services at more precisely defined desired times
   - expanded information services
   - more desirable, comfortable and pleasant transaction environments

5

The Seven Key Trends Shaping B2B

OVERVIEW AND GOALS OF THE CHAPTER

To this point, we have taken an historical perspective on B2B, using case studies of companies that operated in the early days of B2B. We have applied three simple but powerful analytical tools—the MIDST Success Drivers, the MaRCoT Value Framework, and the concept of the five primitive flows—to B2B success stories and failures, and provided some discussion to illuminate what has really happened in the B2B marketplace in recent history. By offering a more objective assessment of B2B we have begun to refute the generally unsupported claims that B2B is another bad idea awash in the sea of Internet euphoria. Our case studies have been used to build a foundation for the key premise of this book: B2B will survive and thrive in the years to come.

In this chapter, we take a forward-looking view on B2B and introduce the seven key trends shaping the evolution. As with the progression of any technology, trends appear, based on the focus of the technology vendors, within an area of product development that is driven by customer demand for new features and *functionality*.

Trends are also driven, in many cases, by a popularity created through hype from industry analysts and marketing machines that grasp onto an idea and elevate it from an interesting observation to the next revolution to grip an industry. In later chapters we will look at these trends in relation to the three frameworks and assess the potential influence and staying power of each in the realm of B2B.

The Seven Key Trends Shaping B2B

After extensive review of research reports, industry publications, software vendors' white papers, and interviews with B2B consultants and executives, these trends emerge as the most talked about and influential in the thinking of the leaders in the B2B industry:

1. The rise of private Net Markets
2. The formation of exchange-to-exchange Net Markets
3. The re-optimization of internal business processes for a 24 x 7 business: a first step in collaborative commerce
4. The creation of optimized value chain processes: collaborative commerce arrives
5. The development of industry-wide standards for transaction processing
6. The creation of value added risk management services
7. The maturing of Net Markets to become market-efficient

Trend No. 1: The Rise of Private Net Markets

With the failure of vertical and horizontal Net Markets to gain liquidity, many businesses are struggling to derive value from their B2B initiatives.

The challenges anticipated by most potential participants in *public, consortia*, or *vertical marketplaces*, in addition to liquidity, are:

- the simplistic nature of the exchange (simple buying and selling) does not meet their needs

- their inability to influence the direction or development of the current horizontal, public exchanges
- security and trust concerns
- limited functionality of the buying and selling processes and a one-size-fits-all approach to various "industry institutions" that are not relevant for many sub-industries existing in a larger industry
- high costs of creating transactional and process integration
- different underlying technology standards and infrastructure
- insufficient or unidentifiable benefits from participation
- lack of industry-wide standards for transaction and process integration limit the potential benefits and imposing significant costs for organizations to create the links necessary to process transactions over the Web

What Is a Private Exchange?

With these challenges being front and center, many businesses have embarked upon the creation of their own exchange, commonly referred to as a private exchange. Private exchanges are created by a single company, typically a large organization in a specific industry, to facilitate interaction exclusively with its trading partners. It is private in that participation is by invitation only and the specific operation of the exchange is done by the founding company. Although this exchange operates on a one-to-many basis and can potentially drive significant benefits for the participants, it is typically most beneficial for market-dominant organizations with a leadership position in their industry. In much the same way that *enterprise resource planning* systems (ERP) were designed to drive efficiencies in processing and data sharing within the four walls of the organizations, private exchanges are designed to drive out the inefficiencies in data sharing and processes that exist between the walls of an organization and with its suppliers and customers in a very narrow band of the industry or market. It retains the traditions of the business by retaining the relationships of companies to their known and current trading partners, and generally retains the institution of "negotiated prices" with set terms and conditions. Private exchanges typically focus on the integration of a participant's back-office ERP system to ensure that the transaction efficiencies are maximized.

Successful private exchanges exist today, including Dell, Wal-Mart and Cisco. These industry leaders were early adopters of Net Market technology, as they believed that improving the overall yield of the value chain and strengthening relationships with key buyers and suppliers in the chain comprised a strategic competitive advantage.

With private exchanges, an organization is also able to effectively place themselves in a position of importance and value in the primitive flows of the industry. Because of their industry-dominant position and their ability to ensure they are at the center of the economic value chain, private exchanges can create a dependence on their exchanges and drive compliance to the standards of operation that are set, typically, to maximize the exchange owner's unique business process requirements. This dependence, coupled with the uniqueness of the technology and processes, ensures that the costs of switching out of the private exchange for both buyer and sellers is set sufficiently high that the exchange owner can have much more certainty and control of the value chain. In industries where the ongoing supply of raw materials (such as electronic parts) is critical to success, the economic influence and control through high switching costs can be of significant strategic advantage.

For the participants the benefits can be significant as well. The ability to *leverage* the investment made in the private exchange reduces the overall time and cost to participate. More importantly, the private exchange model no longer requires companies to co-invest with competitors (as is the case with vertical public exchanges, or industry consortia exchanges). The investment is made with existing trading partners and can provide a competitive advantage over suppliers that have not been invited to participate.

The rise of private exchanges is a trend that appears to be one with economic and competitive advantages. What is not clear is whether these advantages can be realized when the issues of liquidity, industry-wide standards for transaction integration, and security and risk management have not been adequately resolved.

The drivers and value of private exchanges will be explored more fully in Chapter 6.

Trend No. 2: The Formation of Exchange-to-Exchange Net Markets

Throughout 1999 to 2001 the B2B mantra was "If you build it, they will come." The stark reality is that of the 1,700-plus Net Markets that existed, a significant number of those are no longer active (Figure 5.1 and Figure 5.2). They built it, and few, if any, came. The Internet may have rendered obsolete some precepts of competition, but all companies, including Net Market makers, still need a differentiating strategy to succeed. Factors such as reduced transaction costs will soon become "good housekeeping" features rather than long-term competitive advantages. The issue of liquidity continues to plague the Net Markets of the world—not enough buyers and not enough sellers.

Figure 5.1: NUMBER OF NET MARKETS

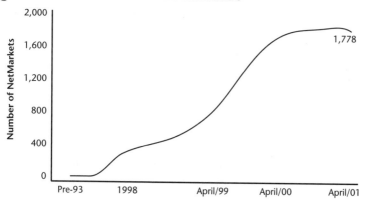

Source: Deloitte Research: Collaborative Commerce, 2001

   Liquidity is defined by the ease with which trades or exchanges occur in a marketplace. As discussed extensively in Chapter 1, a market is more liquid the greater the number of potential transactors (that is, the higher is P), the greater the percentage of potential transactors (T), and the more intensive the typical transaction (R). So, for example, reasonably high levels of market liquidity can be attained with a low number of potential transacting parties so long as they transact often (T) and/or transact intensively whenever they do transact (R).

Figure 5.2: THE U.S. RATE OF FORMATION/CONSOLIDATION

	Mid 1998*	Early 2000*	Mid 2000*
U.S.			
# of New e-Marketplaces	116	178	15
# of Failed/Merged e-Marketplaces	0	2	15
Non U.S.			
# of New e-Marketplaces	4	32	39
# of Failed/Merged e-Marketplaces	0	0	0

Source: Deloitte Research   *Two-month period

With this definition in hand, we can look at the trend in the formation of exchange-to-exchange relationships as one that meets both market need and market demand.

Essentially, the formation of exchange-to-exchange Net Markets is a direct drive to increase the value of P and T, to increase the potential number of transactors and transactions. By connecting a Net Market to another, or many other Net Markets, the operator's goal is to:

- provide potential buyers with access to more sellers and a wider variety of products
- provide sellers with access to a greater number of buyers
- leverage their investment in technologies, marketing, or industry expertise to a wider audience

As competition intensifies and investors increase the pressure to produce results, the importance of earnings is supreme and giant market capitalizations evaporate just as quickly as they were achieved. Net Market makers will seek new means that allow them to leverage their core competencies.

Therefore, Net Markets need to build a critical mass of users by forming alliances to share content, at the same time as they continue to retain their identity. They need to find ways to offer higher value without incurring higher operating costs. They need to leverage each other's capabilities. With the abundance of Net Markets, some serving vertical market needs (chemicals, food, airlines) and others serving more horizontal needs (office supplies, courier services), and the proliferation of many Net Markets in each of the horizontal and vertical markets, single Net Markets must find ways to both expand their reach and to expand their offering. One of the fastest ways to do this is by integrating and teaming up with other vertical and horizontal Net Markets.

Overall, the economic needs of a Net Market for liquidity will drive the trend for these exchange-to-exchange integrations and the long-term formation of exchange-to-exchange networks and marketplaces.

In Chapter 7 we will explore the implications of this trend on the MIDST Success Framework. We will also explore how this trend may impact the MaRCoT's Value Framework if it continues.

Trend No. 3: The Re-Optimization of Internal Business Processes for a 24 x 7 Business: A First Step in Collaborative Commerce

With the introduction of the book *Re-engineering the Corporation,* Michael Hammer started a five-year dash by most major corporations to take a critical look at their internal business processes in order to optimize for efficiency, effectiveness and contribution to the bottom line. This trend, along with others surrounding customer service excellence, integrated enterprise resource planning systems and quality management, drove senior executives to take an internal view of their business in an attempt to bring some level of order to the increasingly complex web of data and processes necessary to deliver a strategic advantage.

According to U.S. Department of Labor statistics, over half of all labor activities within an organization are related to trade partner interaction. Transforming trading partner relationships will lead to a major shift in how a company operates, and will enable the redeployment of resources for competitive advantage.

In the latter part of the 1990s, with the widespread introduction of technologies for Internet-based selling, a new channel to market was created, along with a new challenge for business. The challenge of servicing a market through a new medium was not only a challenge of technology but of people and process. The drive was to provide the capability to sell product, 24 hours a day, seven days a week, in many time zones, languages and countries.

As most organizations had been through the process re-engineering phase and believed that they had created effective systems for handling the major internal processes, they did not feel that they needed to look at processes again. Web selling was a technological challenge, not a people-and-process challenge.

The experiences and stories of failure in B2C and in many B2B cases have come to show that failures or challenges in meeting the customers' demands and delivering on the commitments and expectation could not be attributed solely to technology issues. Companies such as Amazon.com proved quite clearly that the technology could indeed handle millions of customers and millions of transactions. In fact, research and polls in the area of customer satisfaction and barriers to purchasing on the Web show that a high degree of dissatisfaction is provided by poor customer service, goods not being delivered when promised, and the inability to return goods purchased on the Web in a convenient manner. While these issues would tend to be more important to B2C, they are, in fact, generic issues that any business would need to consider when implementing a Web-based B2B sales channel.

The real issue of operating in a B2B environment is providing the capability for the customer or supplier to interact on a 24-hour-a-day, seven-day-a-week basis. This requirement is intrinsically a people issue first and a process issue second. Most organizations are not built to run 24 hours a day. Most service operations do not run 24 hours a day. The processes to manage staffing, scheduling, payroll and all of the other aspects of operational management are not obvious to a business that must move from a 12-hour day to a 24-hour day. Organizations that optimized to move from a 9:00 a.m. to 5:00 p.m. customer support hotline to a 7:00 a.m. to 7:00 p.m. customer support hotline without adding significant costs would cite this initiative as a *huge* success. Increasing the availability of support by 50 percent with a net cost reduction would be an incredible re-engineering success.

Enter the Internet. Moving from 12-hour support to 24-hour support takes much more than an incremental change. Staff may change work hours from eight hours a day, five days a week to twelve hours a day, three days a week. But nobody will do 24-hour shifts. In order to go 24 x 7, a new team would need to be hired. Night shifts would need to be supported by administrative staff. Human resources and technology support teams would need to be able to meet the needs of night-shift workers in the same way they did for day workers. New maintenance agreements would need to be in place with new suppliers able to handle night-shift issues. Areas such as shipping and receiving also entail changes that are not trivial. Starting to evaluate all of the issues related to supporting this new channel in the internal areas of people, process and technology, it becomes clear why previous efforts at re-engineering will need to be reviewed, and perhaps redone, to support any B2B initiative. While these efforts may not be quite so large (provided that the organization did an acceptable job on the initial redesign), they cannot be overlooked.

In the early days of B2C and B2B, most executives ignored the internal business-process challenges presented by this new channel. As the benefits derived from these initiatives became more difficult to find and customers began to complain about the less than stellar performances of most organizations in the Web sales arena, management began to understand and identify the large holes in their operations, particularly in the processes necessary to support B2B.

The issues of B2B are not limited to sales. They apply equally to all suppliers, customers, employees or stakeholders who have been given the expectation that they can interface with the organization for the full 525,600 minutes of every year.

Collaborative Commerce

In order to service customers and deliver value across the value chain of a business, companies must move to a collaborative business process model.

We define *collaborative commerce* as:

> A means of leveraging new technologies to enable a set of complex, cross-enterprise business processes to share decision-making, workflow, capabilities, and other information with each other to create a unique value proposition in the marketplace through the value chain.

The first step in this journey is to ensure that internal processes are effectively optimized in order to then extend outside the four walls of the enterprise to trading partners.

We therefore see the trend requiring organizations to take a step back and critically evaluate their internal processes again as potentially significant in the next five years. We will explore in Chapter 8 the value and success drivers that will legitimize this trend as B2B initiatives take hold more broadly.

Trend No. 4: The Creation of Optimized Value Chain Processes: Collaborative Commerce Arrives

With the successful adoption of B2B capabilities, companies must now turn their attention to processes that occur between trading partners. As can be seen in Figure 5.3, the touch points between an organization and its trading partners in a B2B world are more extensive and complex. In addition, while traditional electronic data interchange (EDI) provided the ability to pass raw transaction data between trading partners, it did not address a key value opportunity, the sharing and optimization of processes related to that data. The goal is to seamlessly interact and utilize all trading partner capabilities to reduce costs, increase market share and drive overall profitability up throughout the whole value chain. And this is, by its very essence, a data-sharing exercise that has *standard* processes shared by all parties in order to build and deliver component pieces to the end customer's demands and specifications.

B2B, by definition, is about inter-enterprise communications and collaboration.

Some examples of the types of efforts requiring optimized value chain processes include:

- buying and selling direct and indirect materials through a variety of e-procurement, public, vertical and horizontal exchanges
- tuning the organization and processes to deliver savings via these exchanges
- re-optimizing value chains and logistics networks
- safeguarding the continuity and stability of the core business operations and processes

- addressing security and legal issues that arise with these new types of interactions

Figure 5.3: **HEAVY LIFTING**

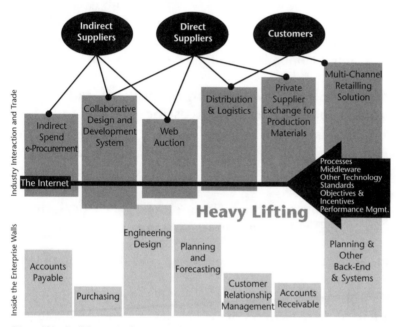

"Heavy lifting" will be required as companies optimize their enterprises around B2B capabilities

In order to achieve this value, companies will need to modify portions of their internal and external processes touch points; embrace infrastructure and process standards, middleware, XML and translation hubs, ensuring integration with exchange participants; and ensure that the supporting management controls and performance incentives are built into the system to obtain the potential value that is inherent in B2B.

The concepts of process optimization and integration are intertwined and inseparable. In this regard, the trends surrounding internal business-process re-optimizations, industry-wide standards for data sharing, and collaborative commerce process-optimization are interrelated.

In the long term, the ability of the *industry* to meet the demands of a customer, dynamically and in real-time through effective collaboration of all suppliers and customers in the value chain, can be seen as the end state of B2B. This is the pinnacle of the promise and potential value of B2B.

This promise requires many of the seven trends to become icons, particularly the need for industry-wide standards, the re-optimization of internal processes, the creation of value added risk management services, and the optimization of value chain processes.

Trend No. 5: The Development of Industry-Wide Standards for Transaction Processing

Historically, improvements in the business process have occurred largely within the four walls of an organization. The advent of B2B creates opportunities for far-reaching process transformation across the entire value chain.

The capability to achieve "inter-enterprise" process, to truly interact collaboratively, involves several fundamental abilities, to:

- seamlessly pass complex transactions and data among multiple trading partners
- pass this data among disparate systems of the trading partners (each will have its own unique business systems, technology and software standards)
- manage risks surrounding security, fraud and misrepresentation of a transaction from a trading partner
- create a transaction audit trail across the chain of trading partners

Fundamental to the ability to integrate transactional data and processes is the need for mature standards in three areas:

1. The definition and format for basic transaction data. How is an invoice, purchase order, payment or any other type of transaction structured? (In what order are the data elements such as invoice number, date and amount stored, and how long is each of these pieces of data?)
2. The definition and format of process instructions accompanying the data, to allow the business systems of the trading partners to

know what to do with the data once it arrives (for example, "when an invoice is received, post it to the accounts payable system")
3. The definition and compatibility of the technical infrastructure allowing the actual transactions to be passed between trading partners (for example, Unix or Windows).

The trend toward the development of industry-wide standards for transaction processing is one that will ease the bottleneck in bringing new B2B projects on-line, as competent technical resources tie disparate systems together, one by one.

A number of standards are beginning to emerge, through the broad support and acceptance of the major B2B technology vendors. In addition, the adoption of these technology standards by the major Net Market makers and marketplace participants is allowing for other trends such as exchange-to-exchange integration and creation of optimized inter-enterprise business-process integration to take hold.

Figure 5.4: BUILDING THE INFRASTRUCTURE: MIDDLEWARE, TRANSLATION HUBS AND XML

Building the Infrastructure:
Middleware, Translation Hubs, and XML

Middleware and translation hubs facilitate the linking of multiple e-Marketplaces and the formation of new networks and other models, accelerating the value proposition for both them and their members.

- **Middleware** is electronic integration software that helps link different B2B software platforms and facilitates the exchange of catalog content and transaction information between companies. It translates messages and transactions into specific formats, forcing integration and data compatibility for purchasing, ERP, accounts payable/receivable and financial reporting.

- **Translation hubs** enable companies to rapidly deploy transactional or process interactions to a variety of e-Marketplaces. They use standard technology and adapters to enable interface to a new exchange in a matter days.

- **XML (extensible markup language)**, the newest standard for electronic data transmission, can be transacted across the Internet and is much less rigid than its EDI predecessor. XML not only contains data pertaining to transactions, but also "tags" describing data structure, identifying what the data is and what it's for.

Source: Deloitte Research

We believe that this specific trend could be the most significant barrier or enabler of success in B2B in the next five years. It is clearly driven by the MIDST framework, particularly on the dimensions of Market and Technology.

If we believe that the inherent and maximum value of B2B initiatives is in increasing the yield of the value chain through squeezing out more effective use of the limited resources in the full chain, then the ability to share data and collapse time and processes will be fundamentally enabled by industry-wide standards for transaction- and process-sharing.

There are three components to the standard as defined in Figure 5.4. They are *middleware, translation hubs* and *XML*. We will explore in much more detail these concepts and the economic value of industry-wide transaction-processing standards in Chapter 9.

Trend No. 6: The Creation of Value Added Risk Management Services

With the rise of Net Markets and B2B exchanges, never before has so much confidential information been created, stored, shared and accessed outside of a company's internal systems and controls. Net Markets take the lifeblood of a company (that is, inventory databases, supply chain processes, financial information) and make them accessible over public and inherently insecure networks.

The greater the sensitivity of the information that organizations make available to more of the outside world, the more important it is to know with whom exactly they are sharing the information. The ideologies and concepts of trust have never been so important as they are in such scenarios, as it is quite possible and becoming more common that transactions and flows of crucial information are taking place with little or no human interaction.

There are essentially six key risk issues associated with B2B commerce. These issues drive the need for and extension of trust and risk management-related services associated with the exchange of goods and services in a Net Market:

1. Who am I dealing with?
2. Is the commitment they are making reasonable? (Can they perform/deliver?)
3. Will the goods/services meet the specifications agreed upon?
4. Can and will they pay?
5. How much risk exists that the transaction will not be completed?
6. Can they be trusted to keep the business arrangement secure and confidential?

There are also three overarching tenets to observe to ensure that the transactions are recorded properly for management purposes: the transactions must be complete, authorized and accurate.

It is important to note that these six risk areas and three tenets exist as fundamental principles of business. B2B initiatives demand a fresh look at risk management policies and procedures because the means of managing risk change in an electronic world.

These risks are created by three specific characteristics of B2B:

1. The number of trading partners could be exponentially greater than was previously managed.
2. Buyers and seller may not know each other or have ever dealt with each other before.
3. Control over corporate information is now scattered across the value chain.

These three characteristics account for the majority of the concerns regarding trading partner risk in public and vertical Net Markets. Private exchanges manage these risks simply by virtue of being closed, secure exchanges.

Other B2B exchange characteristics, such as transactions being processed without human intervention or transactions being processed in real time, are not really germane to the issue of risk. These characteristics are already part of the landscape in today's financial world and are managed through a complex set of security controls and protocols that, in essence, form a private trading exchange, for example, in the banking industry. Most banks still require businesses to provide proof of incorporation and legal details of the corporate officers before they will open a new account. This process of validation of the organization is designed to ensure that the business making the commitment on a financial transaction can be identified *and* held accountable. Even in that industry, some participants will not trade electronically with each other because of risk concerns. In the public stock markets and brokerage industry, the level of data sharing is minimal compared to that normally contemplated by a private exchange or an integrated value chain.

The level of risk in B2B has spawned a new and potentially large opportunity to manage these risks. New services and service providers are being created to ensure that B2B commerce does not expose a corporation to excess risk. We will explore each of the six key risk issues with a view to identifying how they are likely to be managed in the future.

We will explore the first five of the six key risk issues with a view to providing an introduction to the concepts of risk management and mitigation. The sixth issue, security and confidentiality, is discussed more fully in Chapter 10.

Who Am I Dealing With?

In the traditional business world, a CEO could answer this question quickly with a visit to the potential trading partner and meet the management team, talk to their suppliers and see their employees.

In a B2B environment, a company may buy from or sell to someone halfway around the world in an instant, without ever setting eyes on the transacting party or validating their existence. The real issue is that since the exchange is transacted through a computer, it is difficult to validate that the party identified as Joe is in fact Joe. His network e-mail address may be JOE@BLOW.COM, but who really knows if it is Joe, Fred, Alice or their dog sitting at the desk firing off e-mails. What is needed is a means to validate that Joe is really Joe, that he has the authority to execute transactions and that he has no way of weaseling out of his end of the deal (known as non-repudiation). If a business can ensure that every time JOE@BLOW.COM sends an order or a cancellation it is really coming from Joe, it can lower the risks associated with dealing with an unknown trading partner.

The trend in B2B will be for services that can reduce this risk to grow dramatically as electronic trading grows.

Is the Commitment They Are Making Reasonable and Can They Perform/Deliver?

Traditionally, when companies attempt to determine whether their suppliers can meet commitments, they review supplier past performance or look to static information providers such as Dun and Bradstreet (a provider of credit reporting services and business and financial information on more than 62 million public and private businesses worldwide) or others to provide information. However, static information is a potential source of significant risk since today's business operation environment is subject to quick change. Real-time data that takes into consideration a trading partner's performance on the Web and across many Net Marketplaces and geographies is what is needed. Unbiased information and the ability to rate and rank suppliers are absolute requirements.

Companies such as eccelerate.com (provider of company information and business credentials, including a database and links to other sites) and Equifax (provider of consumer credit reports) are beginning to tailor their offerings to meet the needs of a changing market, specifically around the ability of Net Market participants to meet their commitments. This service will become essential as the number of marketplaces and participants grows exponentially and the transactions' associated risks grow at the same rate.

Will the Goods/Services Meet the Specifications Agreed Upon?

Historically, underwriters used escrow accounts to manage the issues of performance guarantees and the delivery of goods as promised. The traditional methods of managing escrow and underwriting transactions is inefficient for Net Markets because of the potential volume of transactions.

The need of the buyer to ensure that the goods will be delivered at the right time and the right specifications is paramount. The invisibility of the trading partner heightens the need for a new form of underwriting and quality-assurance provider.

Companies such as Worldwidetesting.com and Insuretrust.com are among the new risk management service providers who are attempting to fill the void. Worldwidetesting.com enables both buyers and sellers to make confident and informed purchasing and selling decisions by providing sampling, surveying and testing of industrial commodities. Insuretrust.com offers a Lifecycle Risk Management solution, and was the first in the world to offer a suite of hacker insurance policies.

Can and Will They Pay?

Organizations will not participate in a Net Market if they have any concerns about how or whether they will be paid. Payment integrity is a cornerstone of liquidity in any market. The limited face-to-face involvement among participants in the Net Market context makes it even more vital that the Net Market not only meet all participants' financial service requirements, but that the process is seamless. Brand has only so much weight on the Internet—one bad experience on a Net Market can severely undermine a participant's trust.

Many e-tailers do not have an integrated payment process in place and restrict payment to credit cards. However, most B2B sales are too large to be processed on credit cards, and require wire transfers, lines of credit, instant financing and escrow services to be utilized. Accordingly, an integrated network among Net Markets, payment networks and buyers' and sellers' business processes is necessary to facilitate transactions over the Internet.

The need to process transactions in a timely way is of course an age-old problem, newly exacerbated by the Net Markets phenomenon. In the old world, letters of credit and performance bonds would suffice. The process for putting these items in place, however, is generally too slow to meet the needs of most organizations. When procuring over the Web, a buyer may be faced with a situation of having to decide on purchasing a specific item at an unbelievably good price, without time to put the financing in place. Instant payment, or at least instant guarantees of payment, are needed. The need for real-time credit brokers and financing facilitators is increasing. Companies such as eCredit.com (provider of on-line credit/financial services) are beginning to offer services that will allow for the real-time placing of short-term financing to meet the demands of the Net Markets world.

How Much Risk Exists That the Transaction Will Not Be Completed?

Even though the previous four areas of risk may be manageable, there is still risk that one party will not execute on the agreed-upon transaction. The need to manage the risks associated with non-completion exists in both Net Markets and the traditional market. Insurance against this risk is available. In a B2B world, the needs of providers and purchasers of insurance are different and unique and brokers can provide customized means to companies to purchase and claim against their policies.

Trust, security and control are critical to successful e-transformation. A new breed of ancillary service provider is addressing these five key issues. The role of the trust brokers and risk managers of the 21st century is to minimize the risks of dealing in a Net Market and increase the market efficiency of the B2B space.

We will explore further the value and drivers for these new service providers in Chapter 10.

Trend No. 7: The Maturing of Net Markets to Become Market-Efficient

As we discussed in Chapters 1 and 3, markets, whether they be on-line or off-line, are continually driven to become efficient. The foundation principles of business—profit optimization, access to information, and the matching of supply with demand—underlie the constant and continual drive for markets to become efficient.

When we look at the successful case studies of B2B businesses that have garnered liquidity, such as DAT and eBay, we see these businesses have moved closer to being market-efficient. They provide a good or service to meet a demand, and at the same time provide a marketplace for those that have excess supply of goods or services to sell them—at a price determined on a spot basis, at the time they are available *and* needed.

The development of the public stock markets is the best example of the foundational principles of business driving market efficiency.

Fundamentally, market efficiency has as its underpinning *price stability*. A market is efficient when buyers and seller are matched, in real time, to allow for the exchange of goods or services at a mutually agreed-upon price. When this match occurs, prices are stable at any point in time. Fluctuation is minimized as buyers and sellers are fully aware of all supply and demand information and so can manage their purchasing or production to match the market, at a price they believe is fair for the goods. Availability and sharing of information is the key to this market efficiency.

Figure 5.5: MATURING OF MARKETS TO BECOME MARKET-EFFICIENT

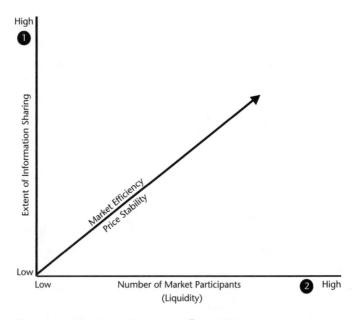

Extent of Information Sharing

High ①

Market Efficiency
Price Stability

Low

Low   Number of Market Participants   ② High
(Liquidity)

① Trends Supported by the Extent of Information Sharing:

- Development of industry-wide transaction-processing technologies
- Re-optimization of internal business processes for a 24 x 7 business
- Creation of optimized value chain processes
- Creation of value added risk management services

② Trends Supported by Market Liquidity:

- Rise of private Net Markets
- Formation of exchange-to-exchange Net Markets

When all relevant information is fully available and shared among all value chain participants, a market will be efficient, resulting in price stability.

Net Markets are likely to be driven to provide this information by participants through the financial "voting" rights they have to participate or not participate. Voting with their participation can drive liquidity. Liquidity, it bears repeating, is the lifeblood of a Net Market. Therefore, Net Market makers should be driven to provide the information because of the economic realities of any market.

The trends surrounding the creation of industry-wide transaction processing standards and optimized value chain processes have influence on the maturing of Net Markets to become market-efficient and can be facilitated by these two other trends. Both of these trends increase the availability and accessibility of relevant data. The optimizations of the value chain processes improve on the timeliness of this data. Both access and timeliness are also fundamental to any market becoming efficient.

While price stability is an ideal, even the public stock markets are not always efficient, as we have seen at various times in history, most recently through 1999 to 2001. However, the public stock markets, in the long run, have shown a clearly banded range of stable prices. We would expect that Net Markets would also experience this phenomenon in the long run.

Due to the need for almost "perfect" information, market efficiency remains a goal that will take many years to achieve. It will require all key participants in an industry, including all of the ancillary service providers (insurance, banking, credit and so on), to be fully engaged and to have achieved the highest level of inter-organization process- and data-sharing.

We do, however, see that with the creation of consortia in many industries, market efficiency could be achieved to an acceptable degree for the participants over a shortened period of, say, five years. Consortia, due to the almost forced participation by key suppliers and customers, ensure that the bulk of supply and demand information is available and shared through the value chain.

We will explore further this key trend and the drivers and value that it will create in Chapter 11.

Summary

There are seven key trends shaping B2B. Each of these trends has been influenced by the MIDST success dimensions and can be evaluated against the MaRCoT value dimensions. The seven trends are:

1. *The Rise of Private Net Markets.* Private exchanges are being created in response to the low value proposition of current horizontal and vertical public Net Markets that cannot cater to the specific needs of a major industry entity. Private Net Markets attempt to provide value to a closed group of suppliers and customers through a secure and controlled marketplace.

2. *The Formation of Exchange-to-Exchange Net Markets.* As the concept of liquidity eludes most of the existing public Net Markets, Net Market makers are being driven to increase their reach and spread their substantial investments in industry expertise and technology foundations to a wider audience. By working with other Net Markets, the formation of exchange-to-exchange Net Markets provides value to participants, Net Market makers and ancillary service providers.

3. *The Re-Optimization of Internal Business Processes for a 24 x 7 Business.* In order to meet the competitive needs of the global marketplace and to service customers 24 hours a day, 7 days a week, organizations must revisit their process, re-engineering projects with a view to improving and delivering round-the-clock business operations. This is the first step in creating a collaborative commerce environment.

4. *The Creation of Optimized Value Chain Processes.* Collaboration requires the sharing of data and processes between trading partners, requiring a reassessment and reconfiguring of people, processes and technologies to deliver value.

5. *The Development of Industry-Wide Transaction Processing Technologies.* These technologies are being developed to allow for the seamless integration of data and processes among trading partners. These technologies are driven by the need to reduce the substantial costs associated with creating customized integration points for the hundreds or thousands of participants in an industry.

6. *The Creation of Value Added Risk Management Services.* The key issues of business do not change in the B2B domain. However, B2B demands a fresh approach to risk management. A new cadre of ancillary service providers who will insure the credibility of the trading partners and provide performance guarantees for all aspects of the transaction will flourish in the Net Markets world.

7. *The Maturing of Net Markets to become Market-Efficient.* With the previous six trends converging with the overarching drive of all business and markets to become more efficient, we expect that Net Markets that survive the consolidation and fallout of the next ten years will grow to deliver value by becoming closer to markets that resemble the public stock markets. Key requirements will be open access to information and improvements in the liquidity of existing Net Markets.

We defined collaborative commerce as:

> A means of leveraging new technologies to enable a set
> of complex, cross-enterprise business processes to share
> decision-making, workflow, capabilities, and other informa-
> tion with each other to create a unique value proposition
> in the marketplace through the value chain.

This is a key concept on which the future of B2B and Net Markets will be based.

CEO's Playbook for the Boardroom

Remember the context: one of your most prominent investors has read an article about a Net Market in your industry, and she wants to know why your company is not mentioned as a participant. One of the board members, trying to be helpful, speculates that the Net Market in question doesn't have liquidity. You observe the furrowed brows of the other board members. You would like to speak to the issue to demonstrate that you have solid understanding of the trade-offs facing your company in deciding to join, build or abstain from participating in a Net Market.

Observation: The success drivers in your industry may or may not be conducive to joining or organizing a Net Market.

Here are the important issues and questions to present to your team:

- Is a private exchange an appropriate strategy as opposed to being a participant in an existing public horizontal or vertical Net Market? Does our organization meet the key criteria for the applicability of private Net Market success?
- Has our industry developed the industry-wide standards for transaction processing? Have the appropriate XML standards (such as RosettaNet equivalents) been created that we could quickly utilize to join or create a Net Market? Would it be prudent for our senior management team to assemble a team to lead the creation of the industry standard or to participate in any existing initiatives in the industry?
- Does our IT department possess the requisite skills to deploy EAI, XML and related communications technologies to connect our business to a Net Market?
- Have the existing Net Markets in our industry sufficiently matured and begun to integrate among themselves to create exchange-to-exchange Net Markets and increase the value proposition of our organization becoming a participant?
- Is our organization sufficiently prepared through the optimizations of our current internal processes to truly become a 24 x 7 business? Have we looked at key processes and determined the impact of becoming a collaborative business with key suppliers and customers?
- Do we have the intellectual capital in our business to move from a functionally managed business to a process-driven business? Do we understand the key success processes in our value chain and the value that we provide in relation to our suppliers, our customers and our competitors?
- Have appropriate ancillary service providers been driven to service the specific needs of our industry? Can we effectively manage risks and obtain insurance and related performance guarantees on the market for the transactions we contemplate executing on a Net Market?

Once you have answered these questions, you can determine the best course of action and initiate some analysis of the value of joining a Net Market.

Each of the trends may have a unique perspective in your industry and the application of the MIDST and MaRCoT frameworks should be evaluated.

In Chapters 6 through 11 we will dissect these seven trends using the three frameworks. Our goal will be to use the frameworks to provide a deeper understanding of whether these seven trends will, in fact, move from being trends to becoming B2B icons. Having a means of understanding whether a trend has a chance of becoming an industry icon will allow you to assess the reasonableness of investments in the areas where the B2B market is trending.

6

The Rise of Private Net Markets

OVERVIEW AND GOALS OF THE CHAPTER

In this chapter we will explore the concept of private Net Markets. Using a simple case study, we will consider the objectives of a private Net Market, how a private Net Market works and where value is created. Using our MIDST and MaRCoT frameworks we will also assess this trend in terms of drivers and value. In addition, we will critically assess this trend and provide insight as to whether this trend may in fact take substantial hold in the market or die a quick death, as many of the failed Net Markets have in the past few years.

What Is a Private Net Market?

In order to define a private Net Market, we must look at how one is created. In a large vertical industry, the aerospace industry, for example, there are a few very large participants that create the largest portion of the output of that industry. In the case of Airbus Industries, this organization has substantial influence and output. Airbus is a multi-billion-dollar business with hundreds of thousands of employees, and hundreds of thousands of suppliers. Hypothetically, as a major player in the industry, Airbus might assess the various public Net Markets and many of the current independently operated vertical Net Markets in the industry (Exostar, AeroVantix, aviationX.com) and determine that their value propositions (in terms of MaRCoT) are not substantial enough to make it worthwhile for Airbus to participate. Either the number of potential suppliers, the quality of the suppliers or the complexity of Airbus's specific purchasing processes may not be met by the existing exchanges.

Concluding that they have a unique competitive advantage with their current supply chain and the related business processes to support the chain, Airbus may decide that the best way in which to capitalize on this chain and increase its yield is to build a private exchange. They could accomplish this through a specific project to integrate all processes and transactions throughout the supply chain, from the customer back through to the very large number of raw materials and component suppliers.

Determining that there would be significant value in cost efficiencies, risk efficiencies and time efficiencies, Airbus could invest in a project to build a private Net Market linking Airbus and its internal business systems to its customers and suppliers. By invitation, Airbus would ask customers and suppliers to participate (and in some cases share the cost). Airbus would pitch the project as follows:

To customers:

> We can improve upon our delivery time to you by reducing the product development cycle with a process for collaborative design of the product and forecasting of demand, through tailored and customized information including product specifications and pricing, to allow your purchasing agents to efficiently and effectively deal with our organization in real time. The benefits to you will be reduced costs of procurement, faster delivery time, and a better fit of our product to your exacting specifications. Our post delivery service will also improve, as we will provide extensive applications which your operations group can use to log product issues, track service requests and identify product improvement opportunities. We will

use standard technology so that we eliminate the high costs
and risks of technology incompatibility. What do you think?

To suppliers:

> We are building a system to allow our organizations to
> collaborate on effectively planning inventory needs and
> to allow you to better predict needs for component parts
> and raw materials to meet our customer demands. With
> this system you will be able to see demand through our
> private Net Market right through to the end customer's
> order systems. Our private Net Market will allow informa-
> tion to be exchanged in real time regarding orders,
> parts, invoices, payment, logistics and delivery requests,
> backlog, and full inventory management. In addition, we
> will extend this private Net Market to your key suppliers
> so that they may be fully aware of your needs, our needs
> and the customers' needs. Finally, we will build function-
> ality into this system to allow all participants in the
> private Net Market to share information surrounding
> product issues, future trends, and industry needs across a
> wide variety of topics. The technology platform will be
> standardized so that we eliminate the high costs and risks
> of technology incompatibility. What do you think?

With this type of pitch, both customers and suppliers could find
the prospect of participation very compelling.

A private Net Market can, and has, provided this level of integration
and supply-chain efficiency for a number of organizations, including
Wal-Mart, Cisco and Dell.

Private Net Markets are the best example of the concept of collaborative commerce. We reiterate our definition of collaborative
commerce from Chapter 5:

> A means of leveraging new technologies to enable a set of
> complex, cross-enterprise business processes to share
> decision-making, workflow, capabilities and other informa-

tion with each other to create a unique value proposition in the marketplace through the value chain.

To further illustrate our definition of a private Net Market, we compare and contrast private and public Net Markets in Table 6.1.

Table 6.1: COMPARING PUBLIC AND PRIVATE MARKETS

Public Net Market	Private Net Market
Ability to participate:	
Generally up to the Net Market maker, which has the responsibility to prequalify and organize potential market participants. Due to the use of the Internet and its openness and the near-zero cost, all market participants may be included.	By invitation only. Meets the needs of a broader audience as through the use of tiered solutions, suppliers are able to choose between server, PC, Java, client or browser-based options that provide connectivity and different levels of functionality.
Development process	
In some cases suppliers, distributors and other value chain participants are invited to help provide input into the development and running of public and consortium Net Markets; in others, they are not invited to participate in the development but do help determine functionality and product offerings.	To ensure back-office integration and flexible collaboration features, the organizations designing and building the private Net Markets will seek the input of other participants.
Focus and desired benefits	
Though public and consortium-based Net Markets allow for the potential for collaboration, initially there was a misplaced focus on the e-procurement of non-strategic goods and services, which does not exploit the full potential of the opportunities created by Net Markets. Some public Net Markets have partnered with SCM vendors in an attempt to exploit the opportunities, but few have.	Private Net Markets deal with specific needs around direct materials, not just indirect, which is where the real value is. Private Net Markets also provide the framework for the ultimate form of collaboration, with opportunities for demand forecasting, product design and customized information. Only private exchanges provide for total supply-chain visibility, communication and inventory reduction.

Public Net Market	**Private Net Market**
Costs (design, build and run)	
Public Net Markets and consortiums share the risk and infrastructure building costs to design, build and run the shared Net Market.	The costs to design, implement and run the private Net Markets are incurred by the individual organizations. A cost that is estimated to be anywhere from $50 to $100 million according to AMR research. It is also expensive for all trading partners due to the need to build integration to all parts of the value chain.
Adoption and acceptance rates	
Full potential for public and consortium Net Markets will take time to develop. Due to factors such as technology integration issues, trust and security concerns and adoption rates, business cases are harder to develop and time lines are usually too long to be considered feasible by upper management.	The business case for building private Net Markets is easier to develop and more compelling for senior management to embrace, as they see a ROI in a much quicker time frame and the value proposition is easier to understand.
Standard settings	
Public Net Markets and consortiums in particular can help develop and implement uniform standards for transmitting data, describing goods and for business processes.	Companies that do not participate in the development process of public and consortium Net Markets may find when the models mature and they do want to participate, that their IT infrastructure does not support existing industry standards.
Governance and control	
In the case of public Net Markets (consortiums excluded), they are seen as offering a third-party, neutral trading platform free from political influences and hidden mandates. In the case of consortium Net Markets, governance issues are large, and must ensure that they balance everyone's interests, while allowing for the flexibility necessary to dodge the treacherous shoals of external competition.	Consortiums face many governance issues around participation and control, whereas private Net Markets can be perceived to be either working with all partners in collaboration or forcing and creating switching costs with suppliers through the development and implementation of proprietary technology and protocols.

Public Net Market	Private Net Market
Effects on companies' purchasing abilities	
There is just not a lot of margin in commodity goods. Large companies have already done all they can to negotiate with their suppliers to achieve the best possible discounts. Similar companies that couldn't traditionally negotiate discounts with suppliers can achieve greater benefits through consolidated and bulk purchasing.	Allows for the Net Market maker to retain potential strategic advantage they may currently have in their existing supply chain. Organizations that have created a competitive advantage through the size of their purchases and the discounts they receive from their suppliers will not lose this to smaller companies achieving the same discounts through aggregated purchasing. Standards will also make it easier for companies all along the value chain to have greater choice of who they do business with and organizations who once had locked in their suppliers with the use of proprietary technology may lose this advantage on the Internet.
Risk concerns	
Potential for increased risk to organizations which now may trade with new unqualified suppliers, in a time where reliability is more critical due to increased inventory levels, and more important company information available over inherently insecure networks.	Offers the advantage of doing business with known, trusted and preselected companies.
Trust, security and privacy concerns	
Public and consortium Net Markets are facing the issues of anti-trust, lack of trust and security concerns head-on. They are working to alleviate participants' fears and develop strategies, policies and the technology infrastructure necessary to make them successful, in order to realize their true potential such as joint purchasing, sharing of emergency inventories and logistics coordination.	Conduct transactions between a single buyer and several suppliers, but does not alleviate the participants' fear of mis-trust or promote collaboration.

Public Net Market	Private Net Market
Life cycle	
Though many public Net Markets are now non-existent, they are relatively still low in maturity in the adoption life cycle. Public Net Markets are still seen as indirect material markets with limited collaboration functionality.	Private Net Markets have taken a successful mature model founded within EDI and VANs and have adapted it to the Internet.
Value added third-party services	
May have an agreement with or offer themselves other value added services such as financing, escrow services, distribution and insurance.	Organizations either need to complete such value added services on their own, strike up their own relationships with third-party companies or put the burden on their suppliers.

The Purpose of a Private Net Market

Table 6.1 included the key goals of a private Net Market, defined in relation to those of a public Net Market. Typically, the private Net Market maker (such as Dell) is attempting to wring the most value and yield out of the supply chain. In Dell's case, the ability to extensively manage the component parts' supply chain and ensure delivery of components to meet buyer orders in a very short time frame is a key competitive advantage. The advantage is leveraged off of the unique combination of suppliers and integrated information-sharing and seamless logistics that Dell has created to be able to deliver the exact goods to the customer quickly and at an exceptional price. The combination of price and delivery gives Dell the unique value proposition that has driven their growth, profitability and success.

Private Net Market makers are attempting to address their primary value concerns with public Net Markets. These concerns include:

- public Net Markets are less secure in that they are open to any participant and controlled by an independent party, leaving the organization's data potentially vulnerable since the intentions of the public Net Market maker cannot always be monitored

- public Net Markets generally provide limited sources for indirect and direct materials and so may not provide as much value in improving the sourcing of key production materials
- the risks associated with dealing with new suppliers (see Chapter 5) may be higher than dealing with known existing suppliers
- the ability to integrate and share information may be more difficult in the public exchange offering only limited data-sharing capabilities or integration points
- the public exchange may require different technology or the custom development and support of specific integration software

For the most part, public exchanges are limited to purchases and sales, and other collaborative commerce opportunities, such as sales support, post sales support, product design, and vendor management, may be restricted because of the cost entailed in creating their complex features, along with the wide variety of unique needs that individual participants would also demand.

Table 6.2 provides a high-level view of the potential collaborative commerce opportunities that a private Net Market maker could implement, depending on the strategic objectives that they are pursuing.

Table 6.2: COLLABORATIVE COMMERCE EXAMPLES

Function	Basic Capabilities	Advanced Capabilities
Value chain collaboration (visibility)	• Multi-tier forecast visibility and integration • Multi-tier inventory visibility and integration • Forecast modification and collaboration (retail)	• Multi-tier CPFR • Vendor managed inventory • Multi-tier capacity and production synch • Logistics planning and management • Integration with order management, collaborative product commerce
Vendor management	• RFQ/RFI • Vendor selection analysis	• Contract negotiation • Contract adherence and management • Integration with order management, indirect procurement

Function	Basic Capabilities	Advanced Capabilities
Order management	• Transmissions of order-related documents (PO, CO, ACK, ASN, DN, RN, INV, etc.) • Management of order-related documents (tracking, changes, alerts, reporting, etc.) • Collaboration on order-related documents	• Payment, settlement, billing, finance, credit • Order aggregation, splitting, allocation • Integration with vendor management, value chain collaboration
Collaborative product commerce	• Engineering change notices • Engineering release • Product view	• Program management • Collaborative design • Product data management • Component and supplier management • Integration with vendor management, value chain collaboration
Indirect procurement	• Catalog segmentation • Buyer segmentation • Workflow/rules/approvals • Punch out to suppliers/marketplaces	• Integration with vendor management
Sales support	• B2B CRM • Catalog management	• Channel management • Promotion management • Configuration • Pricing collaboration • Integration with value chain collaboration, collaborative product commerce
Post-sales support and service	• Tech publications • Tech support • Warranty management • Returns management	• Maintenance planning • Services management • Parts/repair management

An Example:

Wal-Mart When we look at the example of Wal-Mart as the creator of a private exchange, we must first understand what is driving Wal-Mart in this initiative.

The strategic goal of Wal-Mart is to be the largest retailer in the world with an everyday low-price strategy. To achieve this goal they need to be the lowest-cost seller of goods in the industry while maintaining a profit margin that is at the top of their industry class. In order to deliver lowest costs of sales, Wal-Mart must do three key things correctly:

1. it must source goods at the best possible prices
2. it must reduce inventory-carrying costs by ensuring that goods are purchased and delivered to stores at the right time to eliminate out-of-stock and overstocked situations
3. it must ensure the right supply of a very wide range of quality goods and services is delivered to widely different retail markets to meet the demands and changes in retail shopper preferences (the goods purchased in many parts of the same country, or for that matter in different countries, can vary dramatically because of local tastes, economic conditions and demographics)

Achieving these objectives throughout 4,200 stores in nine countries day after day is not so simple. Wal-Mart employs over one million people and engages 10,000 suppliers, who must interact in real time to ensure that goods are ordered, delivered and merchandised to sell, and sell fast.

With over $165 billion in sales, Wal-Mart continues to be the envy of every other retailer in the world. What they envy is Wal-Mart's supply chain. And what Wal-Mart has, that most others are struggling to achieve, is an extensive network of vendor collaboration, a network founded on EDI and communications.

Wal-Mart's B2B initiatives, while initially EDI-based and now being moved to be more reliant on the Internet, have an exceptionally strong value proposition. In terms of the MaRCoT Value Framework, the integrated supply chain delivers:

- *Risk efficiencies,* through ensuring that participation is limited to only approved and qualified suppliers who can provide the information and deliver the goods as required to meet the inventory management objectives. By knowing intimately whom they are dealing with and being able to monitor the performance record of the supplier, Wal-Mart can reduce risks of non-delivery, quality, and security and privacy.

- *Cost efficiencies,* delivered through reduced inventory carrying costs because goods are only delivered when needed at a specific location. Most of Wal-Mart's fleet of trucks is managed through a tracking system, which determines vehicle location, loads, weights and routes through on-line transmitters. A private satellite communication system links the whole system together. Cost associated with obsolete goods is also reduced. Overall, these reductions have an impact on reduced capital costs for the company. In the area of transaction costs, by ensuring that all suppliers can receive and deliver electronic documents for purchase orders, shipping notices, invoices and payment, costs associated with transactional administration are significantly reduced for all parties.

- *Time efficiencies,* garnered via electronic communication of store sales, forecasted demand and replenishment requirement by product, by store. The ability to manage inventory, sales and forecasts at that level allows Wal-Mart and its suppliers to react to shifts in demand and changed delivery times and the merchandise mix to meet the needs. This ability to react in a much faster time frame to changes in market demand are essential to inventory management and reduced carrying costs.

Overall, Wal-Mart's private Net Market scores very high in delivery of MaRCoT value (see figures 6.1 and 6.2).

Figure 6.1: WAL-MART'S MaRCoT VALUE

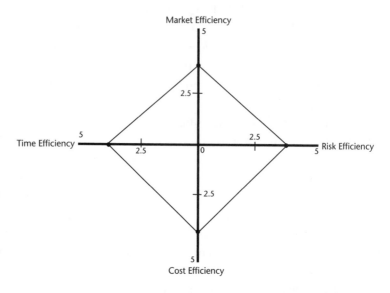

Figure 6.2: STRATEGIC OBJECTIVES AND BENEFITS OF SEVERAL B2B INITIATIVES

	Strategic Objectives	Strategic Benefit
Hewlett Packard	Simplify their business structure while becoming more efficient and effective	– Order cycle time reduction – Direct materials cost reduction – Improved supply reliability
Cisco Systems	Use data networks to revolutionize its business model	– Virtual supply chain model drives improved supply chain efficiencies and responsiveness – Infrastructure allows effective integration of new acquisitions
General Electric	Support virtual business model focusing on time to market and customer satisfaction	– Reduced average order cycle times – Decreased time to market for new products – Improved operating efficiences
Dell	Manage a "configure to order" business model that is customer-centric	Effective planning and collaboration across virtual supply chain allows: – Minimal working capital, rapid fulfillment and improved reliability – Improved decision-making to balance supply and demand
Wal-Mart	Be the largest retailer in the world with an everyday low price strategy	– Improved in-stock performance – Dramatically lower working capital and operating costs – Suppliers benefit from improved information flow

Figure 6.3: **MIDST SUCCESS FRAMEWORK FOR WAL-MART**

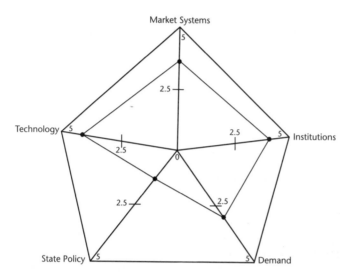

As we will discuss later, a key value and objective of a private Net Market is to shift the ownership of pieces of the business to other trading partners. The emergence of the private Net Market has fundamentally changed the primitive flows of the retail industry. In the case of Wal-Mart, the Net Market has primarily shifted the management of inventory and the associated risks flow back to these suppliers. It has also improved the information flow to allow for significant benefit to flow to the suppliers (see Figure 6.3).

What Is Driving This Trend?

The MIDST Success Driver Framework provides a means for determining which external forces outside of B2B are driving the need for private Net Markets. We will consider each of the dimensions of MIDST and evaluate where the key drivers are likely to take this trend.

Market Systems

As discussed in Chapter 2, a key dimension is that of the *Market system*. This dimension is driving private Net Markets for many of the reasons pointed out earlier. If we ascribe to the concept that businesses wish to achieve productivity gains and re-orient their activities to a more productive use, then a private Net Market can be seen as the ideal means for achieving these goals in a closed system.

In effect, private Net Markets are the creation of closed markets for all of those inputs the organization needs to execute its economic activity. It fully integrates the make-or-buy decisions that a business has made and then focuses on delivering the efficiencies for the business and the market. It creates efficiencies in the business by digitizing and integrating the communication of key make-or-buy criteria such as demand, inventory supply, production constraints and forecasts instantly, to all parties, to allow for fast adjustments to the whole supply chain to respond to changes in end-user demand.

The transaction costs associated with the market systems in a private Net Market are also reduced as the tight integration of the back-office systems of the Net Market participants significantly reduces or eliminates the costs associated with processing transaction data.

The ability to reach and adjust in the whole closed market system of a private Net Market also creates the efficiency gain in the market. Supply and demand is better matched on a real-time basis. Information is also much more accurate and allows for the acceleration of decisions.

Finally, because a single Net Market maker controls and manages the market, the maker's detailed understanding of the impact on all market participants can be applied to optimize the private exchange processes, and technologies designed to deliver the value of most importance to key players can be specifically engineered for the market system.

We see a strong driver from the *Market systems* dimension of the MIDST Success Driver Framework with a private Net Market.

Institutions

Among the greatest drivers of this trend is the *Institutions* dimension.

The key institutions that private Net Market makers are attempting to retain include:

- privacy of information about their operating practices
- avoidance of co-operation or interaction with key competitors, unlike the situation in a public Net Market
- relationships with known suppliers and customers

- current billing and collection processes
- current technology platform

Essentially, private Net Market makers are trying to both keep business institutions as recognizable and comfortable as possible, and keep the benefits of additional collaborative commerce to themselves.

Companies that implement private Net Markets are telling the market that they want to collaborate only with people they know and trust and don't want to share any information about their business or their supply or demand chains with a competitor or any potential competitor.

They also do not want to expose themselves to significant dynamic pricing (for example, auctions) even though it could result in a net reduction in production costs. They believe that the unique value of their supply chain is in controlling it to guarantee quality, availability and delivery of raw materials. In their eyes, this value is higher than the overall benefit of lower costs.

All of these perspectives are accurate and frequently justified. Therefore, we see *Institutions* as a key driver of private exchanges in the foreseeable future.

Demand

A private Net Market is the ultimate in serving the *Demand* dimension of the MIDST Success Driver Framework. As discussed, demand is influenced by the cost and time associated with acquiring needed inputs for the consumption aim as well as the "precision" or fit of the products found on the market.

When we look at the benefits of private Net Markets against the demand dimension, we see that they provide a "direct hit" on the key components of demand. Private Net Markets are organized specifically for the purpose of reducing the time and costs associated with acquiring the inputs of the Net Market maker.

In the case of Wal-Mart, they have created their Net Market to specifically deliver three key benefits. The Net Market:

- eliminates the need to search for products, reducing the costs associated with finding goods for their stores

- secures a steady flow of goods to their stores, reducing the costs and risks associated with searching for multiple suppliers in an open market
- reduces the costs of transacting with trading partners, as the private Net Market fully automates the flow of transaction information using a standard technology platform.

By delivering these benefits to the Net Market maker (Wal-Mart) the private Net Market also delivers a steady flow of demand to the market participants (the Wal-Mart suppliers).

The *Demand* dimension is a high driver of success and will have a significant influence on the success of the trend to private Net Markets.

State Policy

To date, it is not evident that the *State policy* dimension has played a role in the rise of private Net Markets.

However, some industries may be driven to create private Net Markets based on government legislation that could challenge their ability to operate in an open environment. In some countries, Canada, for instance, the government control of the health care industry, combined with the high level of sensitivity to privacy and security of individual patient data, would almost force this industry to be one that would only succeed as a private Net Market. The risks associated with delivering value in any other public type of Net Market would be met with significant opposition from both political and constituent circles.

Conversely, state policy may be a significant barrier to creation of private Net Markets in the slightly less private but still closely held consortia vertical Net Markets. Examples in the United States of the Federal Government conducting investigations into the alleged unfair competition created by a variety of industry consortia, particularly Covisint (the automobile manufacturers exchange), are more common than not.

By wielding huge purchasing power and industry influence over thousands of small participants, these consortia Net Markets are attracting significant attention. Concerns include the high concentration of industry information (such as pricing, costs, demand and supply) of a significant number of industry trading partners in the hands of one organization. Controls over access to this data, its sharing among the owners of the Net Market and the potential loss of competitiveness due to that concentration, were among the primary concerns of the U.S. Federal Trade Commission and Antitrust Division of the U.S. Justice Department.

While an investigation determined Covisint was not involved in any unfair competition practices, many of the consortia Net Markets will be required to ensure that adequate "Chinese walls" are created and security and controls are in place to segregate supplier information. Controls and policies over both the intended use and the potential users of this information will also be necessary to ensure that information that could jeopardize competition and unfair trade practices around pricing and costing are eliminated.

Technology

Technology is a strong driver of the private Net Market trend.

The challenge of a public exchange is to be technologically versatile in a world where there are millions of companies with thousands of combinations of technology platforms employed. And while the challenges associated with maintaining security and privacy of data are recognized and being addressed in various ways, on a public exchange participants are still reliant on the market maker (with whom they may not have a prior relationship) to implement and maintain this security. Finally, the costs of providing seamless integration of the Net Market data with the participant back-office systems are currently very high due to the lack of industry-wide standards for transaction processing, and these standards may not be in place quickly enough to meet the needs of larger corporations. Private Net Markets, by ensuring that the issues of integration, security and technology-platform compatibility are addressed as part of the underpinnings of the initiative, offer significant value and control to the participants.

The closed by-invitation-only nature of a private Net Market makes it possible for the whole system to optimize the technology platform to deliver all of the benefits of collaborative commerce.

The *Technology* dimension of the MIDST Success Driver Framework gives significant momentum to this trend.

MIDST Success Map for Private Net Markets

To recap, Figure 6.4 illustrates the external drives of private Net Markets: Institution, Demand and Technology. State policy is a lesser driver, though it has potential influence when an industry is heavily controlled by government or security concerns.

Figure 6.4: MIDST SUCCESS DRIVER FRAMEWORK FOR PRIVATE EXCHANGES

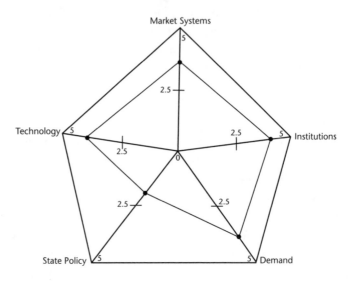

Where Is the Value?

Let's review the value proposition from the perspective of our MaRCoT Value Framework. The framework provides the means to determine how value is created.

Market Efficiency

Our treatment of market efficiency as outlined in Chapter 2 is a gauge of how well a market performs as an allocation mechanism, and it would include the improvement in liquidity and the stabilization of prices. Market efficiency also rises with information diffusion among the participants: the better informed the participants, the more likely prices will stabilize. But if there is only one guy on the other side of the market (a dominant player like Wal-Mart or Dell), then market efficiency suffers a little—possibly, at the expense of enhanced liquidity—because the other players may have to pay higher prices for products they want to procure or get lower prices for products they want to sell.

A private Net Market provides the participants with a stable flow of goods and revenues, generally at predetermined prices. Relatively few transactions take place on a private Net Market that are variable in price (auction, reverse auction, and so on). Most participants would negotiate contracts at set terms and prices in exchange for a stable supply or demand for that product. In addition, liquidity, though not being improved for the whole industry, is all but assured for the private Net Market participants, who can be certain that they will transact for a known product, at known prices, for a period of time.

Because of their closed nature, private exchanges are not "market efficient" at a level that public Net Markets might achieve. While liquidity is assured, it is only assured for the very small number of participants.

We do not see significant improvements in market efficiency from private Net Markets. While some improvements are possible, this efficiency dimension does not generally drive private Net Markets.

Risk Efficiency

The value delivered by private Net Markets in the area of risk is moderate. Effectively, risk is managed to levels that existed under traditional circumstances and beyond, as the participants are all known to each other and the invitation-only nature of the market-place allows for effective screening of the participants for delivery performance and quality, prior to trading.

Opportunities for hedging and speculating are relatively low, although counter-party risk (risk that the fellow you are transacting with will default) is also fairly low.

The control and agreement surrounding security and privacy ensure that the concomitant risks are effectively negated. And because these-risk management processes are created specifically to meet the needs of the participants, it is likely that the costs associated with risk protection are lower than those individual participants would incur by putting these controls in place themselves.

Cost Efficiency

Private exchanges have an inherent cost-efficiency value. For the market maker, the private exchange improves costs for:

- acquisition of raw inputs for production
- research and development (where collaborative design takes place)
- transaction processing, by integrating buyer and seller back-office systems
- inventory carrying
- risk management

For the market participants cost efficiencies are garnered from:

- reduced selling costs
- reduced inventory costs
- reduced delivery costs (shipment size is optimized)
- reduced customer turnover costs (costs of switching are high)
- reduced transaction processing costs, through integrating buyer and seller back-office systems
- reduced post-sales customer support costs
- reduced pre-sales costs
- reduced risk-management costs

Overall, private exchanges improve the yield of the specific supply chain they service, providing significant cost efficiencies.

Time Efficiency

Measured against the market level definition of time efficiency as a system that incurs minimal waiting costs, private Net Markets contribute positively to time efficiency. The private Net Market's goal is to reduce overall waiting time and the time required to process transactions and conduct business. The improvement in the timing, accuracy and completeness of information regarding the demand and supply in the chain provides the participants with opportunities to reduce the time needed to both respond to and process business transactions.

However, because of their closed nature, private Net Markets do not allow for the virtual trading of goods in the form that, say, public stock markets allow. Supply is only met when a specific demand triggers a request. In the stock exchange, stocks are traded whenever the stockholder makes a decision to trade. His timing of the trade is not restricted by the need to identify a purchaser for the stock. This disconnection of interdependencies in the public stock markets is the highest form of time efficiency. Neither party incurs waiting costs: both can buy and sell at any time they choose, given they are prepared to accept or pay the price.

Private exchanges are not as time-efficient but can have significant impact and improvement on waiting time and costs when implemented effectively.

Value Map for Private Net Markets

Figure 6.5 illustrates the value that the efficiencies contribute within the exchanges of the private Net Markets.

Figure 6.5: PRIVATE EXCHANGES' MaRCoT VALUE

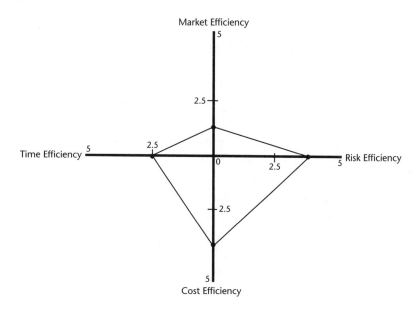

Business Implications of Private Net Markets

The essence of the impact of private Net Markets is the impact that they have on the primitive flows of an industry.

In Chapter 4, we identified the five primitive flows as product, information, payment, property rights and risk.

A private Net Market's primary objective is to shift ownership of some of the business process out to the suppliers of the Net Market maker. Functions such as product development, logistics, inventory management and, potentially, demand-forecasting and post-sales customer support could be moved outside the organization.

When Net Market makers make the explicit decision to outsource these functions to another party, they have decided to "buy" these functions instead of "making" them. This economic decision is not without significant potential risk to the business. The *product flow* necessarily has a direct impact on the other primitive flows of information, payment, property rights and risk.

We have seen that a private Net Market affects the *information flow* by significantly increasing the timeliness, accuracy, reliability and availability of value-chain data to a much wider audience of suppliers and customers. By exposing the information flow to a wider set of users *and* providers, the organization both increases the *risk* of that information flow *reducing* competitive advantage and potentially *increasing* its competitive value, as the quality of the data is likely to improve with the quantity and quality of the information provided across the value chain. Private exchanges should focus on the information primitive flow to ensure that the potential risks are managed and the competitive advantages achieved.

Payment flows can be affected, although to a lesser degree than the other flows, by the potential shift in production of sub-assemblies and the outsourcing of aspects of logistics and shipping that enable the increase in yield from the value chain. Wal-Mart provides an example, as suppliers across the chain begin to assume some of the responsibilities for managing smaller suppliers unable to deal directly with Wal-Mart. In effect, aggregators of products become the key supplier to Wal-Mart, reducing Wal-Mart's need to deal with these smaller vendors. Explicitly or implicitly, Wal-Mart is driven to conduct business only with players of a sufficiently large scale, because smaller scale players cannot produce sufficient product and payment flows to make it worthwhile for Wal-Mart to do business with them.

Property rights flows are impacted as the right to use, transform and alienate are changed through the shifting of business functions outside the organization. In many cases, because business functions are not performed collaboratively (product development, logistics, and so on), the rights that an end purchaser may have on a company such as Wal-Mart may be blurred due to the execution of these functions by a wider audience of players. The ultimate rights of an end user to seek legal recourse on any one player may no longer be easily identified, as the product and information flows in the industry make this situation much more difficult.

As a case in point, Wal-Mart, because of its market power, can acquire rights to alienate property in the form of a product (sell or transfer property to customers) and earn income from doing so without necessarily acquiring all rights to the product—leaving the manufacturer or supplier liable in the event of product failure. Wal-Mart may also be in a position to capture the right to transform a product (break bulk or, possibly, reconfigure it), but chooses not to do so because that would expose it to a liability or responsibility it would prefer to avoid. So, Wal-Mart really just resells a lot of stuff—captures or acquires only limited property rights from its suppliers.

The *risk flow* in any market system derives from the variabilities in the other four flows. In some sense, private net markets are organized to control the product, payment, and rights flows so that they vary minimally. Information flows are a little harder to control, as they cannot be completely contained within the boundaries of the private net market. Nevertheless, a motivation for organizing a private market could easily be to dampen risk, hence to control the risk flow carefully without introducing new players into the market system.

Success Factors of a Private Net Market

The private Net Market trend is growing due to the inadequate value being delivered by e-procurement and public exchange technologies.

However, some success factors have been identified that will ensure this B2B initiative delivers on its key value proposition.

One important success factor is the need for the private Net Market to offer ancillary services to the participant that increase the overall value and potential switching costs. Those listed in Table 6.2 are examples of the types of services that could be provided. In addition, services around insurance, financing, logistics and business process outsourcing are some that can significantly improve upon the overall commitment of the participants.

Industry consortia and large vertical public Net Markets generally provide services that are tailored only to the largest participants, leaving the wider audience of medium and small customers and suppliers all but ignored. A successful private Net Market will consider the needs and be tailorable to the wider audience of the various categories of customers and suppliers that could participate. This factor is significant since the concept of liquidity in a private Net Market is directly related to the extent to which the "whole" supply chain for a business can participate. If a large portion of the population of trading partners is left out, the value derived from cost, risk and time efficiencies will fall dramatically.

With the need to offer the Net Market's services to a wider audience comes the need for the Net Market technology to be scalable to deliver on the demands that will be placed on the infrastructure. Information exchange and business process integration can create a logarithmic growth in transaction volume and significantly stress the system. As the responsibility for supporting the technology falls on the Net Market maker (who may not have scalability and availability of Web services as a core competency), it would be quite easy to destroy significant customer and supplier goodwill through the launch of a Net Market that does not scale to volume.

With the wider audience participating, the opportunity to build communities of interest now has real potential. Collaboration surrounding the key aspects of the supply chain will allow for the participants to increase value in participation and derive further benefits that will continue to increase switching costs. The key to building communities of interest, however, is the need to manage content and provide a means for it to be monitored and moderated, two aspects most organizations have struggled with in the past. This commitment is an additional factor in the overall operating costs of private Net Markets.

Suitability of a Private Net Market Initiative

While the opportunity and promise of private Net Markets is strong, the specific characteristics of the types of organizations that can currently see the value in implementing such a large-scale project are very specific:

- have significant influence and control in the industry
- can build-in high switching costs for participants
- are able to leverage current investment in supply chain technology
- already have competitive advantage

Significant Industry Influence and Control

The first characteristic of a private Net Market maker is that they must have significant influence and control in the industry in which they operate. Major players such as Wal-Mart, Dell, Hewlett Packard, General Electric and Cisco are among the behemoths in their industries. They not only can afford these initiatives but also can create the compelling economic argument to their key suppliers to play ball. As adoption of these technologies is still the single most difficult issue in the B2B, clout is necessary to drive compliance.

Built-In High Switching Costs

The second characteristic is that the private Net Market maker is keenly interested in building in high switching costs for both suppliers and customers. By tightly integrating systems, decision-making and all key business functions on both ends, the private Net Market maker can ensure two major business objectives are met:

1. Sources of main and sometimes short-supply raw materials are secure, since it would be difficult for suppliers to sell their output to another industry player, even at a higher price. The costs of unplugging from the integrated, collaborative supply chain would likely be more expensive than the additional net revenue.

2. Customer loyalty is increased because the added value of the variety of new services and collaborative information exchange would make it difficult for the customer to switch suppliers. Switching could have a significant impact on the customers' ability to service the downstream customer in the distribution channel.

Ability to Leverage Current Investment in Technology

The third characteristic of a private Net Market maker is that they must be able to leverage the current investment in existing supply chain technology. With a strong foundation in supply chain technology, the extension to a broader audience of customers and suppliers with an incremental increase in functionality would be less risky. Since adoption is the largest barrier to success, knowing that a component of the trading partners already finds value in collaboration would provide the basis for further investment.

Competitive Advantage

Finally, those companies that already have competitive advantage in the supply chain would be strong candidates for a private Net Market. Wal-Mart and Cisco began their initiatives on the foundation of a unique supply chain that was created independently of the technology enablement of that chain.

Overall, we see that these characteristics, coupled with the cost of building and maintaining a private Net Market, would make this type of B2B initiative feasible for all but the largest global organizations, or at least those with revenues in excess of one billion dollars.

Will This Trend Survive?

When we assess the value proposition of the private Net Market against the MIDST and MaRCoT frameworks, taking into consideration the estimated costs, at time of writing, to build these applications ($10—100 million), our conclusion is that this form of B2B initiative cannot be supported by any but the Fortune 2000 companies worldwide.

Considering this trend in light of the competing industry consortia vertical market exchanges, which would attempt to commingle the largest players in their respective industries into a semi-private Net

Market, we believe that this trend will continue and be relevant to approximately 1,000 companies worldwide.

While this is significant both in terms of scale and competitive advantage, the bulk of businesses worldwide will not see significant value in the short-term implementation of a private Net Market at the size and scale currently being undertaken by very large organizations.

We do, however, believe that a much larger portion of organizations globally will be compelled and find significant value in the implementation of one or more of the collaborative commerce initiatives as outlined in Table 6.2. These initiatives could be implemented to address key business drivers and create competitive advantage for any organization in their respective industry.

Will this trend survive? The real answer is yes *and* no. The trend will survive but not be so pervasive as to permeate the largest population of businesses globally.

In the next three to five years, our prediction could be significantly altered by the delivery of new software applications that could prebundle private Net Market features and functionality and significantly reduce the overall implementation costs of building these Net Markets. We have seen this general trend in other technology arenas such as ERP and CRM. However, given that the strategic advantage will be in the unique coupling of businesses with processes and data, we would not see cost reduction as being highly likely.

Summary

1. Private Net Market makers are attempting to address their primary value concerns with public Net Markets. These concerns include security, lack of access to a full range of raw materials and inputs, performance risks, limited functionality and lack of consistent technology standards.
2. Private Net Markets are the creation of closed markets for all of those inputs the organization needs to execute its economic activity. It fully integrates the make-or-buy decisions that a business has made and then focuses on delivering the efficiencies for the business and the market.
3. The related transaction costs associated with the market systems in a private Net Market are reduced as the tight integration of the

back-office systems of the Net Market participants significantly reduces or eliminates the costs associated with processing transaction data.

4. The ability to reach and adjust in the whole closed market system of a private Net Market creates the efficiency gain in the market. Supply and demand are better matched on a real-time basis. Information is also much more accurate and allows for the acceleration of decisions.

5. Because a single Net Market maker controls and manages the market, the maker's detailed understanding of the impact on all market participants can be applied to optimize the private exchange processes, and technologies designed to deliver the value of most importance to key players can be specifically engineered for the market system.

6. Private exchanges are significantly influenced by the *Market system*, *Institutional* and *Demand* dimensions of the MIDST Success Driver Framework. *Technology* is also key to success while *State policy* has only moderate influence.

7. Most of the value of a private Net Market comes from risk and cost efficiencies.

8. Private Net Markets are suitable, today, for companies with annual sales in excess of one billion dollars. As the technology matures, the ability to rapidly implement private Net Markets may reduce the costs and might therefore increase the value to smaller organizations within the next five years.

CEO's Playbook for the Boardroom

Imagine you are about to attend an executive committee meeting and your VP of Logistics is going to propose that your firm create or join a private Net Market. How should you prepare for the meeting? What questions should you be prepared to ask? What answers do you need to make a reasoned decision? Here are some starting points for your discussion:

- Are our goals in this project consistent with the goals of private Net Markets?

- Can we not obtain the value and objectives from participation in a lower cost public or vertical Net Market?
- What are the competitive advantages in the supply chain that our organization possesses that we could leverage into a private Net Market initiative?
- Are there any specific MIDST Success Driver dimensions that will positively or negatively impact this initiative? Have we done an assessment and scoring of this initiative against the MIDST and MaRCoT frameworks?
- Do we understand the factors that predict success in a private Net Market?
- Does our organization fit the characteristics of private Net Market makers? Do we have the industry clout to ensure our customers and suppliers will join?
- Is there a less expensive means of achieving the corporate objective of improving yield in the value chain and increasing customer loyalty and retention?

7

The Formation of Exchange-to-Exchange Net Markets

OVERVIEW AND GOALS OF THE CHAPTER

This chapter continues the case study of the aerospace industry to illustrate another of the seven key trends in B2B, the formation of exchange-to-exchange, or X2X, Net Markets. The drivers for X2X are quite different from those driving the private Net Market phenomenon. We will explore where value is created in X2X Net Markets and where significant business impact may arise, and consider whether this trend will take hold in the market.

What Is an X2X Net Market?

An X2X Net Market is not a single Net Market on its own but a network of Net Markets connected to each other to provide benefits to all participants.

Figure 7.1 is an example of how a variety of unique exchanges, which three years ago would not have been considered a collaborative approach to the market, now work proactively to integrate their Net Markets and offer a broader audience of participants a broader suite of services.

Figure 7.1: EXAMPLE OF AN X2X NET MARKET

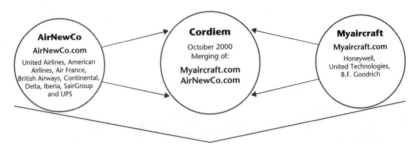

- Provide buyers and sellers with on-line catalogs, reverse and forward auctions, inventory and supply chain management tools, and transaction support features.
- Combined venture will be managed separately from the two constituent exchanges, while ownership will be shared between the independent Myaircraft.com Net Market and the consortium-backed AirNewCo.

This trend is, in effect, an admission by the B2B industry that a *single* B2B solution cannot provide all of the value or answers that efficient businesses demand. A horizontal public marketplace cannot provide the same value as a vertical public Net Market. A vertical public Net Market cannot provide the same value as a vertical industry consortium Net Market. A consortium cannot provide the same value as a private Net Market.

Each of these B2B models has different value propositions, different focuses (indirect materials, direct materials, integrated, nonintegrated, and so on) and differing degrees of value as defined in their approach to MaRCoT efficiencies.

It is not that one type of Net Market is better than another, but that each provides a unique set of services to create a different value. Therefore, they need to be considered, and potentially implemented, as a suite of solutions. A *portfolio* of B2B initiatives is needed to mix and match against the variety of needs an organization will bring to its search for the holy grail; a truly optimized value chain.

Given that any enterprise might be obliged to participate in more than one B2B option, the question is whether an enterprise should let some supra-market organizer stitch together multiple B2B Net Markets, each oriented to delivering different value propositions, or whether the enterprise should just do this for itself.

In Figure 7.2, we have summarized the key values and differences that are provided by the myriad of Net Market options. With X2X

Net Markets, we see the opportunity for an organization to pick and choose the solutions most relevant to serving their specific needs surrounding value chain problems.

Figure 7.2: KEY VALUES AND DIFFERENCES PROVIDED BY NET MARKET OPTIONS

Value Drivers	e-Procurement	Public MRO	Public Vertical MRO	Public Vertical Materials	Consortium Vertical	Private Exchange
Market Efficiency						
• Reaches wide audience of participants	H	H	M	M	L	L
• Allows for dynamic pricing	H	H	H	H	M	L
• Creates high liquidity	?	?	?	?	M	H
• Build competitive advantage of the supply chain	L	L	L	L	H	H
Risk Efficiencies						
• Minimizes security and privacy risks	L	L	L	L	H	H
• Minimizes payment risk	L	L	L	L	M	H
• Eliminates non-repudiation	L	L	L	L	H	H
• Risk of non-use (liquidity poor)	H	H	H	H	M	L
Cost Efficiencies						
• Open view of full industry supply and demand chain	L	L	M	M	H	L
• Meets needs of all participants through wide variety of participants through wide variety of ancillary services	L	L	L	L	M	H
• Maximizes supply chain yield	L	L	L	L	H	H
• Barriers to switching	L	L	L	L	H	H
• Cost to participate	L	L	L	L	H	H
• Delivers value across all procurement needs	L	L	M	L	M	L
• Functions to key business process of participants	L	L	L	L	M	H
• Full integration to all back office applications	L	L	L	L	M	H
• Minimize technology platform compatibility problems	L	L	L	L	M	H
• Leverages current investment	L	L	L	L	M	H
Time Efficiencies						
• Reduces decision time	H	L	H	L	H	H
• Reduces transaction processing time	H	H	H	H	H	H
• Reduces production times	L	H	H	H	H	L
• Reduces delivery times	L	L	L	L	L	H

The Purpose of an X2X Net Market

By connecting an exchange to another exchange and growing a network of such exchanges, the X2X Net Market is attempting to address some of the most fundamental issues in B2B:

- How to increase the transaction volume passing through their Net Market by increasing the number of buyers and sellers that provide and procure goods and services in an industry. This objective is directly tied to the need to increase *liquidity*.
- How to ensure that participants obtain value by ensuring that the market system provides opportunities to *hedge and speculate*.
- How to expand the types of services offered, including core and ancillary services to a broad industry. This objective is directly tied to the need to capitalize on core competencies that a Net Market has built in an industry and *spread fixed operating costs over a wider audience of participants*.

As we can see from these objectives, the key issues are to address the drivers on the dimensions of *Market system* and *Demand*, thus driving the value of the Net Market in the areas of market efficiency and cost efficiency.

An Example of X2X: The Aerospace Industry

The aerospace industry has been the subject of significant initiatives in B2B in the past few years. Extensive writing about initiatives that span the spectrum of B2B has left analysts wondering if these initiatives could survive a shakeout. As we explore each of these Net Markets, we begin to understand how they can form an intricate web of value propositions and, potentially, co-exist in harmony with a fine balance of interdependency as they attempt to service the same constituent market.

As of June 2001, there were at least 17 unique Net Markets serving the aerospace industry.

Our review of the various Net Markets in the aerospace industry is provided to identify:

- imminent consolidation and coordination
- potential consolidation and coordination and
- attempted consolidation and coordination that would create X2X models

These examples clearly highlight the need for the X2X business model. We also believe that while our example is clearly aerospace-based, it is a harbinger for many other industries that have not yet reached this maturity or saturation of Net Markets.

We will briefly explain the focus of each initiative and identify the value it brings to the market.

CORDIEM

In October 2000, two cooperative Net Markets, Myaircraft.com and AirNewCo.com, merged and created a new identity—Cordiem (Figure 7.3). Cordiem is a good example of a seller vertical Net Market partnering with a buyer vertical Net Market. Cordiem is the aviation industry's first B2B exchange and application services provider jointly owned by buyers and sellers. By the two independent exchanges coming together they can now achieve value chain synergies, avoid duplication of effort and accelerate the establishment of individual customer and supplier relationships.

Figure 7.3: **SELLER VERTICAL TO BUYER VERTICAL**

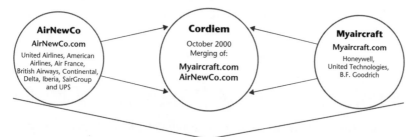

- Provide buyers and sellers with on-line catalogs, reverse and forward auctions, inventory and supply chain management tools, and transaction support features.
- Combined venture will be managed separately from the two constituent exchanges, while ownership will be shared between the independent Myaircraft.com Net Market and the consortium-backed AirNewCo.

Cordiem's members include participants from the two founding Net Markets: Honeywell, United Technologies, B.F. Goodrich, Air France, British Airways, Continental, Delta, UPS and others. Twelve Technologies will provide the Net Market with its supply chain management (SCM) abilities, while Ariba has been chosen for its e-procurement platform.

Cordiem will focus on providing its members with supply chain management and e-procurement services to drive efficiencies across the industry's specific operational and major spend categories: maintenance and engineering, fuel and fuel services, catering and cabin services, airport services and general procurement. Cordiem, whose name is derived from the Latin "core," meaning the central or most important part, and "diem," for day, plans to sit in the center of aviation's supply chain, providing a Web-based network where aircraft operators, suppliers and repair centers can gather to conduct business in a neutral arena.

Cordiem's integrated service solutions have four pillars—supply chain management, procurement and trading, engineering, and value added services—and each is customized to serve the five industry-specific operational areas.

Buyers that choose to go through Cordiem will have the ability to source and purchase products and services from catalogs and new and serviceable parts inventories and through reverse auctions. A supplier directory service will help buyers search for new sources of supply. Launch functionality also supports on-line negotiation through a variety of request-for-proposal and request-for-quote (RFP/RFQ) capabilities, multi-site inventory visibility, and the ability to dynamically collaborate on order fulfillment. Participants on the sell side can post their customer-specific catalogs and inventory, receive RFP/RFQs, participate in reverse auctions and initiate forward auction. Sellers can also receive, confirm and track orders.

EXOSTAR

Exostar.com is a global industry consortium Net Market that is owned and operated as a separate company, and originated through the collaborative efforts of Boeing, Lockheed Martin, Raytheon, and British

Aerospace (BAE), along with technology partner Commerce One. Exostar.com provides its participants— suppliers, manufacturers and customers of all sizes—with the ability to trade on a global basis.

Through Exostar's SupplyPass 3.0, participants can manage incoming orders and standardize processes that streamline how they accept, respond to and plan orders. Exostar's Publisher 3.0 allows participants to build a fully Internet-capable electronic catalog, using their existing content, and to store it on Exostar to be made available to all subscribing buyers. With Auctioneer 4.0, participants have a real-time auction pricing mechanism available.

To leverage existing systems, both Boeing and Raytheon have expressed interest in integrating two of their own independent Net Markets, MyBoeingFleet.com and everythingaircraft.com respectively, into the new Exostar structure (Figure 7.4). This integration effort would allow both organizations the ability to expand their offerings, while utilizing some of their existing infrastructure investments.

Figure 7.4: EXOSTAR

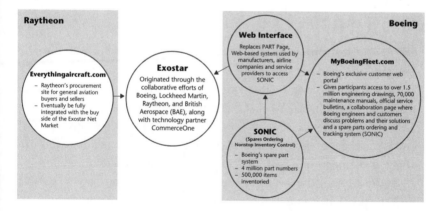

Exostar plans to connect over 250 procurement systems currently used by the five founding partners in 20 countries over the next two years. To date, approximately 4,000 suppliers have been activated and they have implemented exchange interoperability with Commerce One.net

EVERYTHINGAIRCRAFT.COM

Everythingaircraft.com is an aviation industry portal for general aviation buyers and sellers. Everythingaircraft.com offers a variety of B2B transaction capabilities, such as giving buyers, both domestic and international, the ability to locate and purchase airplane parts from numerous suppliers through one-stop shopping, with no subscription fees.

Everythingaircraft.com displays to the buyer prices of parts from numerous manufacturers and distributors, eliminating the costly and time-consuming process of parts purchasing.

Everythingaircraft.com offers such services as credit card transactions, credit verifications, account settling and timely payments to the suppliers. The site also provides account reconciliation and extensive advertising for participating aviation suppliers.

Raytheon plans to fully integrate everythingaircraft.com with the buy side of the new global industry consortium Net Market of which it is an originating partner: Exostar (Figure 7.4).

MYBOEINGFLEET.COM

MyBoeingFleet.com is a Boeing-exclusive private customer Web portal that was launched in May 2000.

The portal has over 8,000 registered participants, including mechanics, procurement administrators and contract administrators. The portal gives its participants access to over 1.5 million engineering drawings, 70,000 maintenance manuals, official service bulletins, a collaboration page where Boeing engineers and customers discuss problems and their solutions (Fleet Resolution), and a spare parts ordering and tracking system (SONIC).

The first achievement of MyBoeingFleet.com was to reduce the amount of paper exchanged between Boeing and its airline customers. Boeing's Spares Ordering Nonstop Inventory Control (SONIC) system contains the company's spare part inventory and allows its users access to over four million part numbers and 500,000 inventoried items. Users currently access the system through PART Page, a non-Web interfaced process. Boeing plans to replace PART Page with its link to Exostar and provide its users with a Web-based system to access SONIC (Figure 7.4).

PARTSBASE.COM

PartsBase.com is a third-party public independent Net Market for the aviation industry. PartsBase.com was created in 1996 with the objective of streamlining the aviation supply chain using the Internet. Participants of the Net Market include Boeing, Honeywell, Federal Express, Airborne Express, United Airlines, Saab, Southwest Airlines and others.

The global Net Market provides the arena for participants operating in the aviation industry the ability to buy and sell new, refurbished, or used aviation parts; to list products, services and catalogs; and to operate as an on-line auction house.

At year-end 2000, PartsBase.com estimated that its Net Market utilized a database of approximately 2,500 suppliers, containing over 23 million line items of inventory. Participants of the Net Market are charged a fee to join and a percentage of all transactions that occur within. To decrease the risk of poor liquidity and ultimately no revenues, PartsBase.com has included other revenue-generating features, such as advertising and employment services.

AEROXCHANGE.COM

Aeroxchange.com is a global consortium Net Market for the aviation industry (www.aeroxchange.com). Founding members include Air Canada, All Nippon Airways, America West, Scandinavian Airline System and Singapore Airlines. With its open architecture, Aeroxchange claims to have the capability to interoperate with other Net Markets and will do so as strategic opportunities arise.

Aeroxchange breaks its service offerings into five categories: exchange, cooperative supply chain management, purchasing intelligence, Internet procurement and system integration services. The exchange provides the capability to build and search interactive catalogs, to conduct on-line auctions and reverse auctions, requests for quotations and marketplace research. Key features of the site's cooperative supply chain management service will be cooperative supply and demand forecasting, global inventory visibility, and cooperative order promising, strategic planning, vendor inventory management and transportation planning.

E-SPARES

e-Spares is Pratt & Whitney's private Net Market that sells aircraft engine parts and services to business customers on-line. e-Spares will sell 300,000 new, refurbished and used aircraft parts. The private site is being slowly rolled out to large Pratt & Whitney customers. Pratt & Whitney is also participating through United Technologies in Myaircraft.com, now part of Cordiem to hedge its risk of restricting itself to a single public or private Net Market.

Pratt & Whitney chose the solutions provider SpaceWorks (www.e-spares.com) to provide the platform for their Net Market.

JET-A

Aeroxchange and AirNewCo (now Cordiem) announced in January 2001 that they would create a public sub-exchange focused on the jet fuel supply chain. The result was jet-a.com, an independent, Internet portal designed to improve the efficiency of the entire jet fuel supply chain.

Participants in this new exchange would come from various industries including the airline industry, oil companies, and intermediaries within the jet fuel supply chain.

Jet-a offers its participants supply chain management, invoicing and contract management solutions.

In May 2001 Jet-a announced that the first tenders had been placed on the Web site where all the major participants had earlier posted requests for quotations on jet fuel at the time of the site's launch.

By requesting and posting quotation tenders, Jet-a allows airlines to select suppliers at each of their locations to participate in the RFQ. Once the suppliers enter their bids, the buyers are able to see normalized bids for easy comparison. Jet-a then prepares a contract schedule for the buyer and the selected winner.

Jet-a is backed by some of the world's largest oil companies: BP, Chevron, ExxonMobil, Shell, Texaco and TotalFinaElf.

A MODEL GONE WRONG: AVIATIONX

aviationX.com was a third-party independent public Net Market for the aviation industry, and after only a few months of existence, changed its business model to become an e-business solutions provider.

aviationX.com is a private company that was founded in 1999 by former aviation executives to fill the needs of aerospace manufactures and aircraft maintainers. In May of 2000 and with $1.6 million in financing, aviationX went live; then, one month later, aviationX reportedly laid off at least one-third of its 30-person staff and announced it was no longer a Net Market.

Why? aviationX's Net Market was not seen as being able to bring the right participants (large buyers and numerous suppliers) to its marketplace, which led to its demise and change of direction. aviationX also discovered firsthand that the task of managing and storing all the needed content was huge. Each airplane model required tens of thousands of parts, designed by a multitude of suppliers.

For aviationX to have been successful, they would have had to track all the required part numbers and support this information for its participants. The independent third-party piece did not sit well with the airline industry. Federal regulations require each manufacturer and airline to maintain meticulous records for each part, serial number, manufacturing date and other details. The airlines and parts manufacturers were not eager to let a third party manage such information, for fear that federal regulators could come back later and determine that records were not properly kept by the marketplace. Moving to an electronic Net Market also meant that the airlines were required to use new workflow processes—purchase orders and invoices posted on the Web, rather than business conducted by phone, fax, or secure electronic connections—at the time, something they were not ready to do.

Now aviationX has turned its attention to developing software for regional airlines. Leveraging the expertise developed from its failed Net Market attempt, the company offers procurement, workflow, and knowledge-based applications.

Bringing It All Together: Exchange-to-Exchange Commerce

Figure 7.5 looks at the current and potential future state of the aerospace and airline industry and what may start to take place as the rate of X2X integration increases.

Figure 7.5: CURRENT AND FUTURE X2X INTEGRATION IN
AEROSPACE INDUSTRY

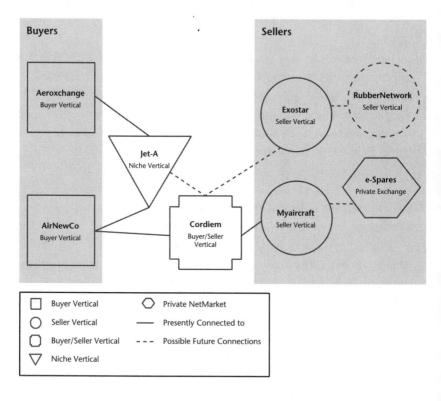

Cordiem is a good example of two independent Net Markets, one a buyer vertical (AirNewCo) and the other a seller vertical (Myaircraft.com), partnering to achieve a greater set of benefits and increase their chance of survival.

Jet-a, a Net Market devoted to the jet fuel supply chain, was created by two buying verticals (AirNewCo and Aeroxchange). Jet-a leveraged the buying verticals' knowledge of the industry and Net Markets in general to create a sub-Net Market with a niche focus. Other Net Markets, such as Cordiem, would be a good fit for an X2X integration with a niche vertical such as Jet-a in order to boost both volume and liquidity and leverage specific capabilities and domain expertise around the jet fuel supply chain. This potential linkage would then save the two Net Markets from the exercise of individually reinventing the wheel in an attempt to satisfy niche requirements, and keep them from going head to head in competition.

Instead of continuing to invest time, effort and resources to build redundant capabilities and compete for market share, buyer and seller Net Markets seek a win-win. They aim to develop complementary capabilities—in effect, co-investing in an infrastructure that transforms trade and interaction between their members. Such a relationship could form between Cordiem (a buyer and seller cooperative exchange formed by the merging of AirNewCo and Myaircraft.com) and Exostar (a seller exchange made up of Boeing, Lockheed Martin, Raytheon, Airbus and others). If these Net Markets were to link to each other, they could achieve value chain synergies, avoid duplication of effort and accelerate the establishment of individual customer and supplier relationships.

e-Spares, Pratt & Whitney's private exchange, builds a good case for X2X integration with Cordiem, as its parent (United Technologies) was a founder in Myaircraft.com, now part of Cordiem. Pratt & Whitney is trying to hedge its risk in the Net Market arena, as it can achieve superior collaborative benefits with its customers and suppliers through its own private exchange.

Another potential example of a future buyer vertical to seller vertical Net Market fit could be a relationship between RubberNetwork.com —a seller vertical made up of the seven major tire companies—and Exostar. This relationship would help enable many-to-many interactions that support and enhance one-to-one trade.

Another Fairy Tale Destroyed

Clearly, in the early days of X2X, as in the early days of the railroad and electric power industries, many players attempted to "corner the market" and go it alone, hoping for greater than normal returns. This phenomenon in the B2B market can likely be attributed to the huge advantage that was created by Netscape as the first major Internet play to be listed on the public stock exchange. The most common writing in technology journals was that the B2B race was all about "a digital land grab" and that once each major industry had its Net Market created and operating, the rest would be history.

It was quite premature to conclude that a single player in any industry would solve the problems and meet the needs that exist and continue to evolve. The fundamental flaw was the assumption that a *single* B2B initiative or business model would and could be the whole *value* proposition to an industry.

The single biggest message of this chapter is that B2B requires a series of potential solutions, service providers and business models to deliver the total requirements and value that a participant expects.

There is no single right answer. E-procurement is not an answer in itself. Joining a public Net Market will not crack the secret supply chain optimization code on its own. Creating a vertical Net Market or a private Net Market will not deliver the total answer to the problem. Any business that wants to take advantage of B2B will require a suite of solutions to succeed.

What Is Driving This Trend?

The example of the aerospace industry is representative of the trend that is as common and pervasive in other industries, including manufacturing, retail and high technology. We have used the MIDST Success Driver Framework to provide insight in assessing the drivers for this trend.

Market Systems

The drive to connect independent Net Markets together is clearly based on the needs of the market system. Recalling the key aspects of the *Market systems* dimension we can see that X2X Net Markets address efficiency gains in the firm and the market, and productivity gains.

Efficiency Gains in the Firm

By allowing an organization to deal through a single interface point to multiple Net Markets, significant savings in time and costs associated with creating linkages to a variety of Net Markets can be obtained.

In addition, if the X2X Net Market makers have done an effective job of seamlessly integrating their transaction-processing engines, then the participants can effectively garner the benefits of multiple exchanges without incurring the costs associated with learning how to use multiple exchanges, or potentially having to know or understand the relationships of the X2X Net Market players.

For the X2X participants, efficiencies are achieved as they find ways of offering higher value services without incurring higher operating costs. They benefit from being associated with other Net Market makers with special services that increase end customer loyalty.

Efficiency Gains in the Market

It is quite clear that X2X Net Markets are attempting to resolve the issues associated with a lack of liquidity by increasing the availability of products, services, buyers and sellers in their respective industries and by improving the pricing mechanism. In the aerospace industry the connection of vertical exchanges such as Jet-a.com with Exostar or PartsBase.com would provide a mutual benefit to the Net Market makers in increasing Jet-a's exposure to a wider variety of potential buyers.

The connection of PartsBase.com with other net markets specializing in the aerospace market, such as TradeAir or ILSmart.com, would provide each of these organizations with greater access to buyers and sellers with the potential to bring further liquidity and price stability to the marketplace. The prospect of more buyers bidding on a wider variety of products is significantly more appealing to all parties, particularly when dynamic pricing models are employed (auction, reverse auction, and so on).

By leveraging their investment in a unique set of technology infrastructures, industry expertise and a focus on a particular stream of products and services, these exchanges attempt to increase liquidity without significant increases in marketing and customer acquisition costs.

Productivity Gains

Productivity gains are defined as the ability for a firm to produce more at given cost levels and are a key goal of X2X Net Market participants. The increased liquidity allows for a more efficient market, which typically lowers acquisition costs for raw material inputs.

Where **P** is the population of potential exchange partners, **T** is the propensity of the potential exchange partners to transact, and **R** is the rate or intensity of the transactions of the parties, we gauge liquidity by the formula:

$$P \, x \, T \, x \, R$$

X2X Net Markets clearly focus on increasing **P**, the population of potential exchange partners, or as a minimum attempt to increase **R**, the rate of intensity of the transactions. Exposure to more buyers and sellers has a direct impact on **P** and **R**.

Institutions

It is not apparent that the *Institutional* dimension plays a role in driving the formation of X2X Net Markets. We do see, however, that the shift from the fixed price institution prevalent before the Internet to the dynamic pricing model of auctions and spot pricing of a wider variety of inputs may be driving a part of this trend. This constitutes a change in business practices for a whole industry. Linked closely to the *Market system* dimension, the pricing institution and its effectiveness may be driving market participants to force Net Market makers who are not liquid to seek other ways of ensuring that they are not victims of bad prices in an illiquid market. Their demand for efficient market pricing will force Net Market makers to deliver a wider audience of suppliers and bidders.

We also saw in the case of AirNewCo.com that institutions can have a negative effect on a Net Market. Industries, such as aerospace, because of the direct tie to the airline industry, have significant *State policy* implications and therefore have built strong institutional customs to deal with the state policy requirements of reporting and control.

Demand

For the Net Market makers, X2X is primarily driven by the need to substantially increase demand or face the economic reality of failure. For many of the same reasons as outlined in the *Market System* dimension, *Demand* drives Net Market makers to connect to each other.

But the issues of neutrality and industry ownership have been recognized and will be essential prerequisites for a successful Net Market, regardless of industry sector. John Watson, director general of SITA, quoted in an industry article on **www.airlineinfotech.com**, explains: "Unmatchable neutrality and vital industry-wide ownership is an essential foundation for future business success and the rapid growth of e-business across our industry" ("Linking the B2B Chain," February 12, 2001).

State Policy

State policy does not appear to be a driver of this trend. However, there are two key areas where state policy will have a significant *impact* on this trend.

First, the greater the X2X integration and the wider the sharing of information and collaboration between independent marketplaces and market makers, the more unlikely it will be that government competition agencies will focus on the potential conflicts, which are their primary concern regarding private Net Markets. Wider sharing of information, reduced control of key market data, and the greater access of buyers and sellers in an industry all reduce oligopolistic or monopolistic tendencies.

Second, as with the aerospace industry, state policy has a significant impact on most industries. In the auto industry, consumer safety is a significant government concern. In the food industry, government regulations exist to control quality and food preparation. Most major industries, including pharmaceuticals, retail, technology and manufacturing, have aspects that are significantly influenced by the state. These industries are bound by levels of control, reporting and ethics that directly impact how they process information and how they manage that process.

This fact, coupled with the first issue of competition, will be important drivers in X2X Net Markets. As the commonality of the state policy requirements grow, we will see *State policy* and the high costs of conforming and reporting as being a key driver for Net Markets to cooperate. They are bound by a consistent need and will be driven by that need to reduce the costs associated with compliance.

Technology

Technology is considered a driver of the X2X trend. With participants being required to connect to a wide variety of Net Markets using differing technology standards, the X2X trend is driven by the need to simplify these connections and reduce them to the fewest possible, given the huge hurdle that a lack of industry standards currently presents. Access to the larger populations of Net Markets is facilitated by X2X Net Markets through the reduction or elimination of the need for participants to deal with incompatible technologies.

The ongoing progress being made in search and retrieval technology is also driving Net Markets to connect and allow for standard search engines to take advantage of the rich content now spread across hundreds of servers, potentially in dozens of countries.

The need to post and bid in an industry requires an ability to update and maintain catalog and inventory position information. Technology that allows for X2X will allow for the management of the content to be assembled once, yet accessed, updated and shared across multiple marketplaces, thereby increasing the timeliness and accuracy of the data.

All of these are strong technology arguments for the continued connection of Net Markets to each other.

Ludo Van Vooren, Senior Vice President Business Development, PartsBase.com, quoted in "Linking the B2B Chain" (Industry article, February 12, 2001, **www.airlineinfotech.com**), explained that

> ...no exchange will be able to satisfy 100 percent of a buyer's needs, [and] each will offer a seamless integration of the other...[Net Markets'] features within their own interface. To achieve this connectivity on a global scale, our industry needs two important technical developments.
>
> Most importantly, we need a standard message set to communicate requests and responses between marketplaces. To work with today's latest Web technology, this must be defined in XML. An updated version of the EDI

standard Spec2000 expressed in XML would be ideal. All the required data structures needed are already defined in this standard and it has been tried and tested for at least 20 years...Alternatively, each marketplace will develop...[its] own XML standard or use a commercially available one like cXML. There would then be a need for translation hubs which companies like CommerceQuest and Ironside already provide.

The other technological requirement is to have universal user identification across the networked marketplaces. Indeed, a buyer could not truly benefit from the exchanges' collaboration, if, at each jump across the network, she had to login with a different username and password. We need an independently controlled and managed mechanism to issue unique digital certificates or tokens that can be recognized by all industry exchanges...

The connection of ancillary service Net Markets, such as insurance and credit providers, to horizontal and vertical industry Net Markets would significantly improve upon a participant's ability to process and confirm transactions. By providing a means for a transaction to be executed, validated, confirmed and returned to the participant, without the need to use multiple marketplaces, is a strong value proposition. The technology to allow this—middleware, XML and translation hubs—exists today and is allowing and driving Net Market makers to connect in an X2X Net Market.

Overall, while the *Technology* dimension and the X2X Net Market trend appear to be in a chicken-and-egg battle of influence, it is clear that they are linked, and their mutual success can be seen as symbiotic.

It is also clear that the X2X Net Markets trend is a driver of the trend to the creation of industry-wide transaction-processing standards; more on this to come in Chapter 9.

MIDST Success Map for X2X Net Markets

Scott M. Clements, Myaircraft's vice president and general manager, has asserted that the Net Market's success will require a

...crystal-clear focus on solving complex customer problems by delivering in three areas:

1) Providing a sustainable value proposition. Simple e-procurement cost based benefits will be short-lived and quickly commoditize. At Myaircraft, we have focused our design criteria and early efforts on building a platform to deliver sustainable value to customers by reducing supply chain and information inefficiencies in the $50 billion aerospace aftermarket for aircraft parts and maintenance services. Dynamic supply chains that react to changing market conditions can repeatedly generate value.

2) Delivering a broad and deep technology foundation. As aircraft operators and their suppliers evaluate the benefits of using e-marketplaces, they first want to know they are connecting to a robust technology platform. They know this requires more than cutting edge point solutions in a field where the technology is often immature. Long-term customer value creation will be fostered by technology providers that have deep experience in core applications, a broad solution set that minimizes the complexity of integrating basic marketplace services, and the financial strength for ongoing aggressive investment in its platform.

3) Integrating customer-centric solutions. E-marketplace customers require integrated solutions that map to specific business problems. When an aircraft is on the ground, the maintenance organization wants technical information tools that not only identify the necessary replacement parts, but that also give supply chain visibility to multiple sources for the parts. The tools must also initiate and track the purchase process, issue work instructions to the maintenance station, and automatically update inventory records and demand forecasts. Successful customer-centric e-marketplaces will create their own intellectual property by integrating multiple best-in-class applications into value added services that increase aircraft availability while lowering inventory levels and

reducing the burden of managing technical information. (Quoted in "Linking the B2B Chain," Industry article, February 12, 2001, **www.airlineinfotech.com**)

Figure 7.6: MIDST SUCCESS FRAMEWORK FOR X2X
NET MARKETS

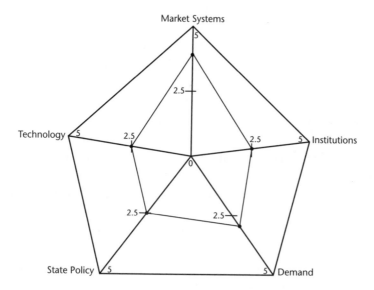

Where Is the Value?

Market Efficiency

As the examples and previous discussion have outlined, X2X provides a strong value proposition in the market efficiency dimension. When done effectively, X2X can increase liquidity. That is, by increasing the number of buyers, sellers, products and dynamic pricing options, it is likely that market clearing prices are more easily established. So long as the net market organizers inform market participants in a timely manner of transactions and positions of the participants, then market efficiency is likely to rise and prices will tend to become relatively stable.

Risk Efficiency

Risk efficiencies may not be improved through X2X initiatives. While the opportunity exists, X2X requires most industries to operate outside the current box of thinking. It also requires specific ancillary service providers to invest in understanding the special needs and institutions of an industry. In effect, ancillary service providers must become *vertical* ancillary service providers.

The opportunities for hedging and speculating on X2X are no greater than for other Net Markets, unless there is something to be said for dynamic pricing that encourages participants to take positions well in advance of their need to deliver or consume. In addition, counter-party risk doesn't seem to be any greater or any less with X2X than with other forms of Net Markets.

At this point of maturity of the ancillary Net Markets providers, we do not believe that they are well positioned to deliver value to a specific industry. They are horizontally focused and must meet the challenges of creating value vertically.

For this reason, we do not rate X2X as a high-risk efficiency provider. We do, however, reserve the right to change this rating when the trend of risk management service providers to go vertical is in full swing.

Cost Efficiency

Cost has the potential to be a strong value provider in five key areas:

1. *Technology connection costs.* When X2X Net Markets are created, they provide participants with the opportunity to connect to all marketplaces through a single marketplace, thereby reducing the overall costs of creating integration points to the variety of other Net Markets. These costs, as discussed in Chapter 9, can be substantial.
2. *Product acquisition costs.* The costs associated with acquiring needed inputs can be reduced as they relate to the time efficiencies of searching for, and finding, needed inputs. If the X2X Net Market is properly integrated, then the ability to put out a single request for a specific good can be communicated throughout all relevant Net Markets where the good may be available. Reductions in cost come from the reduced time it takes to search and acquire, *and,* as discussed below, from the reduction in *failure to procure* costs.

3. *Prices of goods acquired.* With more buyers and sellers, and with a wider variety of goods to purchase, the overall price of goods should fall or at least remain stable over time. For the buyer, a wider selection of sellers and products should drive costs down in the short term.

4. *Prices of goods sold.* Prices for goods sold should stabilize over time as market efficiency is achieved. This is good news for the seller, as wild fluctuations in prices impact decisions over production and ultimately result in a mismatch of production to demand. Therefore, for the seller, cost efficiencies are achieved as the costs of production (including carrying costs for excess inventory and obsolete inventory) are reduced.

5. *Costs to market and sell.* For the seller, X2X Net Markets also reduce the overall costs to market and sell goods. By reaching a wider audience of targeted prospects, the seller can spread the costs of the B2B initiative to a wider audience. While the costs of creating the integration to an X2X Net Market may be high, it is ultimately much lower than the costs associated with attempting to create connections and provide catalog content to a series of technically incompatible marketplaces.

Time Efficiency

On the time dimension this trend will drive two specific improvements in value and efficiency:

1. *Reduced acquisition costs.* This reduction will come through an absolute reduction in search times for products. In the example of the aerospace industry, the ability for participants to find parts faster in the integrated market, as illustrated in Figure 7.5, as compared to using each of the five or more individual Net Markets, is obvious.

2. *Reduced waiting costs.* If search time drops, then wait time drops and therefore the value of X2X also comes from the lower costs associated with reduced waiting.

The magnitude of time efficiency should not be undervalued, particularly in an industry such as aerospace. Within the complex airline "system," each flight scheduled to depart is dependent on the arrival of another flight. Jets generally do not sit on the ground, they are turned around and sent to another destination, perhaps flying as many as ten flights a day. The cost associated with a plane on the ground is not the cost of a single flight, but the chain reaction of multiple lost flights and the revenue associated with that plane, in addition to the other flight revenue for the segments that the passenger cannot fly *and* that the plane cannot complete. The replacement cost for a defective part could be as little as $500, but the revenue lost in not being able to procure that part quickly could be $100,000. When we frame the costs associated with wait time and search time, we should not only consider the costs of the individuals who are doing the search, but also the downstream costs of *failure to procure.*

The most important value in X2X is the value created in reducing *failure to procure costs.*

For this reason, we would rate time efficiency as the highest value of X2X Net Markets.

Value Map for X2X Net Markets

Overall, we see the Value map for X2X as illustrated in Figure 7.7.

Figure 7.7: X2X NET MARKET'S MaRCoT VALUE

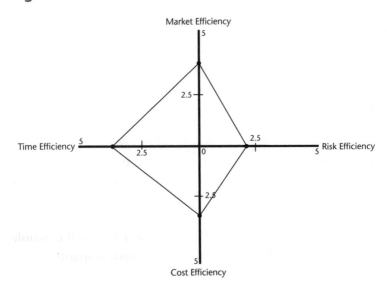

Key Success Factors of a X2X Net Market

The success factors for an X2X Net Market have five key aspects:

1. The initiative should ensure complementary Net Markets are connected to expand value along the MaRCoT value dimensions. The connection of Net Markets with similar value propositions may not necessarily provide value. Tying two horizontal marketplaces together may not add enough value for participants to garner any change in market liquidity.
2. The increase in liquidity comes from the network effect of increasing the number of buyers and sellers. An increase in the types of dynamic pricing models will also positively affect overall market liquidity because it makes it easier to arrive at market clearing prices.
3. The initiative should ensure that adequate technical integration of the exchanges creates a strong, seamless face to participants. When the participant is able to effectively deal with the X2X Net Market as though it were a *single* exchange, then significant value will be garnered by all parties. Creating this seamlessness may be a challenge, because the complexities of compatibility of technology platforms and software applications may be very expensive. However, the reduction in wait time and search time *must* be achieved in order for the initiative to create real value.
4. Risk efficiencies must be addressed in order to create adequate value over and above the individual offerings of the X2X initiative.
5. The addition of ancillary service providers such as insurance, payment, verification and product quality validation will add value. Institutions for the industry must be understood and either strictly adhered to or embellished through the initiative. An X2X initiative should *not* attempt to create value or change the primitive flows of an industry. Attempts to circumvent institutions are usually going to provoke resistance, since, though institutions can and do change, they do so slowly.

Effectively, successful X2X initiatives attempt to create the "whole product solution" for both the industry and the participants.

What Is the Whole Product Solution?

The whole product solution, a phrase coined by Geoffrey Moore in *Crossing the Chasm: Marketing and Selling High-Tech Products to Mainstream Customers* (HarperBusiness, 1995), is the need for a solution for a customer to have all of the key pieces as an integral part of the value proposition.

In the case of the aerospace industry, we could see that in order to improve upon risk efficiencies, additional Net Markets would be added to the X2X Net Market for:

- business validation (e.g. Dun & Bradstreet)
- credit validation (e.g. Equifax)
- identity verification (e.g. Identrus)
- product verification to meet industry specifications (e.g. World WideTesting.com)
- payment processing (e.g. Citibank)

Each of the ancillary service providers could contribute significant value in delivering the whole product for the aerospace X2X industry.

By creating an environment where trading partners can effectively buy, sell, and make payment, all within a risk-managed process, the X2X for an industry such as aerospace would go a long way toward creating a truly optimized supply chain. The industry would be able to greatly increase its yield from the whole supply chain.

By way of example we will predict that the aerospace industry will look something like the following in three years' time, containing some of the needed solution providers shown in Figure 7.8.

As the diagram depicts, we have extended the marketplace we envisioned previously when discussing the aerospace and airline industries. As Net Markets realize that participants are requesting solutions to their problems, or clusters of related activities in order to satisfy their needs, Net Markets will bring together diverse providers. Questions of trust will need to be answered: how does a buyer or seller know that the participants in the Net Market are authentic and authorized to participate? What assurances do participants have that they will receive what they have ordered, or will be paid for what they have sold? These are questions relating to specific activities that the Net Market will be responsible for addressing. We envision a combination of third-party authenticators (such as Identrus), open ratings (such as openratings.com), satisfaction surveys (such as conducted by eBay), security tools (for example, Public Key Cryptography) and others that will need to be integrated into the existing Net Market.

Figure 7.8: **THE FUTURE OF THE AEROSPACE X2X**

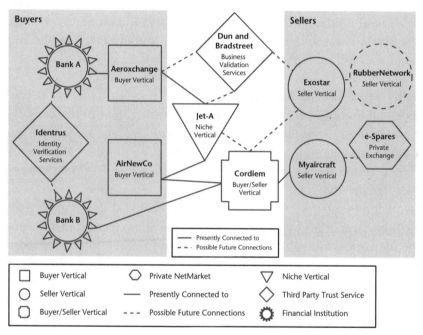

For example, before Net Market Aeroxchange decides to link with Net Market Jet-a or even conduct business with Jet-a, Aerox-change will require some form of assurance that Jet-a has a sustainable credit history and that there is a high degree of possibility bills will be paid. For this to happen Aeroxchange may decide to link with Dun & Bradstreet, a provider of credit reporting services and business and financial information, to acquire this information so that they can formulate a decision to conduct business together or not.

Another activity that will need to be addressed as part of the total solution involves the real-time verification of cash payments. In this particular scenario, prospective trading partner Aeroxchange banks with Bank A, while prospective trading partner Cordiem banks with Bank B. As there is no present means for real-time verification, neither Net Market can debit its account for the cash amount of the transaction, nor can an amount be transferred to the trading partner's bank account. The participation of a third-party service such as Identrus (consortium of major global banks that acts as a Certificate Authority) and the deployment of a Public Key Infrastructure (PKI) might solve this problem. By using digital certificates and digital signatures Identrus could validate the identities of both banks in real time, providing the needed assurance that both parties were authentic, and could complete the cash payment transaction in real time.

Will This Trend Survive?

The drivers of this trend are very strong and in light of the ongoing failures of high-profile and low-profile Net Markets, we foresee the trend of the formation of X2X Net Markets continuing. What is left to determine are the ultimate benefits of these connections. Too few Net Markets have had sufficient experience and time to assess the net value of moving in this direction. This trend will, in fact, lead to further consolidation in the market, as Net Markets without a unique value proposition will be consolidated, and to an end state where a smaller number of larger participants providing unique products and services are connected, bringing significant value to participants.

Each major industry will acquire a similar look to that of the aerospace industry. Ancillary services, such as credit management, payment, risk insurance and others, will be added to complete the full business cycle of needs, delivering the "whole product solution" to the industry.

Finally, we see the trend of X2X Net Markets contributing to the validation and continuation of the seventh key trend (discussed in detail in Chapter 11), the maturing of Net Markets to become market-efficient.

In a sense, the X2X trend is quite consistent with the trends preceding it that contributed to the increasing scale of retailing and wholesaling operations. Some smaller players will either cease to exist or be absorbed into larger consolidated, integrated Net Markets (X2X), but some will survive to serve relatively well-defined niches or pockets of specialized demand.

Summary

We would encourage CEOs to heed our message and ensure that not only their boards, but also their executive teams, understand this point. Once engrained in the leadership, this concept will make life in a networked economy much easier—or at least, slightly less stressful. The single biggest message of this chapter is:

B2B requires a *series* of potential solutions, service providers and business models to deliver the total needs and value that a participant expects.

The second message is that *the* most important value in X2X is the value created in reducing *failure to procure costs.*

CEO's Playbook for the Boardroom

In hearing about the failure of a Net Market in your industry, and the consolidation and alliance of two other industry vertical Net Markets, a board member challenges you when you suggest that the current e-procurement project is not the answer to the B2B needs of your company. You suggest that connecting to one or more Net Markets in addition to implementing e-procurement software may be the right strategy. The board member contends that Net Markets are failing and that the current initiative is more than risky, and adequate to serve the needs of the company.

Before you respond, remember: there is no holy grail, there is no single right answer, and any business that wants to take advantage of B2B will require a suite of solutions to succeed. E-procurement is not an answer in itself. Joining a public Net Market only will not crack the secret supply chain optimization code. Creating a vertical Net Market or a private Net Market will not deliver the total answer to the problem. *Never* expect that your business will be an e-business with a single B2B initiative.

You need quick questions and knowledge to address the board member's concern. Your approach :

- Ask who are the parties that have consolidated or formed a strategic alliance: is this move one that will improve the value of both parties and the value to your company *and* industry as participants?
- You suggest that this move may, in fact, reduce the company's overall costs of connecting to two different Net Markets to get the value each separately offers. Reduced costs could be a good thing for the company.
- You explain that the value proposition of e-procurement is substantially different from that offered by the Net Markets that are seller-focused. E-procurement offers the company an opportunity to reach new markets. E-procurement is directly focused on cost reduction on the supply side of the business and has very little in common with a seller-focused Net Market.
- You refer the board member to Chapter 1 of this book and suggest that the failure of the Net Market in question may have more to do with its business model than with the value of the concept it was attempting to deliver.

Overall, your message is that there are a variety of Net Markets and B2B initiatives that need to be evaluated by the organization for applicability and value.

8

The Business Process Implications of B2B Net Markets: Process Relationship Management

OVERVIEW AND GOALS OF THE CHAPTER

If we were to follow the evolution of technology and its progressive infiltration into an organization, it would become evident that one of its most significant values has been the integration of various aspects of business systems. Up to this point businesses' efforts have tended to center on the integration of data systems that varied across the entity, accomplishing integration through the introduction of applications designed to reduce redundancy and the errors and costs associated with keeping the data. Enterprise resource planning (ERP) systems promised to deliver this integrated view of data. Through the use of workflow technologies, ERP systems do address a level of process integration, but ERP functionality has not yet matured enough to meet the full challenge of ERP-to-ERP integration of both data and processes.

In this chapter we will explore the implications of moving from an internal focus—integration focused on data only—to an external focus—the *integration of processes*, the central requirement in B2B collaborative commerce. As we will see, while technology has a primary impact on B2B, processes are often more important and less frequently addressed by initiatives.

Business process integration has two important steps:
- the re-optimization of internal business processes for a 24 x 7 business, the first step to create a collaborative commerce environment
- the creation of optimized value chain processes between all trading partners, to capitalize on the value proposition of collaborative commerce

Business Process Re-Engineering

Business process re-engineering has been the subject of many books and many multimillion-dollar consulting projects in the past five years. The primary goals of these projects have been to drive efficiencies *within* the organization through a structured process to reduce the administrative time and costs associated with performing basic business functions. Driven by a functional view (optimize cash collection, reduce inventory purchasing time and cost, reduce invoice processing costs), these projects often spanned many phases and many years. Their value and benefits, while sometimes questioned, had two primary impacts; they focused the organization on:

- understanding the value and benefits of integrated data and on eliminating redundancies and inefficiencies associated with keying, rekeying and validating data gathered across various departments of a business. Companies became data-efficient.
- taking a hard look at the value and costs of all internal processes, to reduce the time and effort required to deliver the basic administrative operations of a business. Companies become internally administratively cost-efficient.

The early view of the Internet as a new channel of distribution and a vehicle with which to communicate with suppliers and trading partners led organizations to explore the use of Web sites as storefronts, customer relationship self-serve sites, and as a more efficient way of sending transaction data back and forth. These projects had two pitfalls. They:

- were driven as technology projects designed to implement Web-based applications and provide broader access to data but with little consideration given to the value of these technologies
- did not consider the impact of business processes within the organization or with trading partners

As a result, businesses made substantial investments in Web-based technologies without receiving corresponding returns on investment. After a flurry of investment and activity in building Web sites and the implementation of a wide variety of software and hardware, businesses have begun to pull back and re-evaluate their approach.

Fundamentally, as with any business systems project, these projects were functional initiatives, not technology initiatives. B2B projects add the twist that these projects belong to everybody, and nobody.

B2B integration projects are everybody's project for the primary reason that they are not function-based (accounting, operations, finance, logistics, sales) but process-based (order to cash, procurement to payment) and so touch every function in the business. In most organizations, nobody other than the CEO "owns" the whole *process*, only individual functions. This failure to understand the pervasive impact of B2B projects as processes has been a hallmark of most B2B initiatives up to now.

The issue of process ownership is magnified in a B2B collaborative world. While it is clear that nobody inside the business owns the whole process, in a situation where outsourcing production, collaborative product design and other joint functions are executed by an organization and its trading partners, the question of "who owns the process" becomes almost impossible to answer.

Of course, business cannot survive without some level of responsibility and ownership being assigned. Therefore, a drive to revisit and re-optimize internal process must occur. A focus on integrating and optimizing internal processes with external trading partners must also occur, with a clear focus on ownership and accountability.

We can therefore predict a renaissance for business process re-engineering and transformation in the next five years, with a combined external and internal view.

The Drivers of Collaboration

There are a variety of drivers of the trend toward the re-optimization of internal processes and the re-engineering of external processes, including:

1. *Competitive drivers:* The need to reduce customer "churn" (turnover), increase revenue per customer and create higher switching costs (a tighter bond) between an organization and its customers.

   The need to lock in customer loyalty is based on the low costs associated with growing revenue from an existing customer compared to the costs of acquiring a new client. By providing a means for customers to communicate and collaborate with suppliers, the bond is facilitated and customer loyalty can be strengthened. The linking of business processes (as in private Net Markets) between customers and suppliers makes it more difficult for customers or suppliers to switch out without substantial cost.

2. *Strategic drivers:* The need to differentiate offerings and provide a unique, non-replicable value proposition in the market.

   Tied to this driver is the focus on operational and process excellence, which drives the outsourcing and strategic alignment of organizations to reduce overall cost through focusing on their expertise. A good example is a company such as Southwest Airlines who have created a unique value proposition surrounding air travel costs and on-time delivery. By delivering a collaborative means of executing commerce, a firm may create a unique business model in an industry to its strategic advantage (as is the case with Wal-Mart).

3. *Technology drivers:* The advancements in the Internet and the creation of tools that allow for ERP systems to be integrated across the supply chain, coupled with the development of XML standards.

As the costs of technology fall and the costs of human capital rise, there is a drive in business to increase the use of technology and reduce human intervention costs in most processes.

4. *Global drivers*: The need to expand global reach and to increase utilization of plant and equipment and fixed costs, directly requiring an organization to move to 24 x 7 operations.

Going global obliges almost any firm to collaborate with new partners or with existing partners in new ways, to both optimize the use of existing plants and equipment and to allow for 24 x 7 operation to continue, through the linkage of manufacturing, financial and customer support activities around the globe to support a single, global customer base. The challenge is to move to this level of operation without a direct corresponding increase in costs.

Each of these four drivers points to a need to shift organizations away from a functional view of business to a process view. As organizations outsource key functions and move away from human intervention and toward 24 x 7 operation, collaboration and clarity regarding the ownership of processes and data become of paramount importance to success.

The move toward *process relationship management (PRM)* is the key to B2B collaborative commerce. At a simple level, most organizations in the late 1980s and early 1990s went through a process of implementing business software and systems that allowed information from different business functions (finance, marketing, sales, operations, human resources) to be shared between departments. Before then, each department within a business had its own spreadsheets, databases and word processing files with which to keep track of essentially the same information as held by another department for another use. The sales department, feeling it was the owner of the customer, kept its own database of customer information. Accounting kept detailed records of customers and the account receivable balances. Marketing, of course, had its targeted customer mailing lists for specific campaigns. "Integrated" software allowed simple efficiencies, such as a single customer database, or an up-to-date inventory system to be maintained and used across the functions.

At a second level, in the mid 1990s, organizations turned to enterprise resource planning systems to provide a higher level of integration of business functions across different geographic units and different business units. Management could then see information about any customer who dealt with the entity, no matter whether the customer was purchasing goods from the transportation division or from the power train division. A single view of the customer extended to all business units in the corporate entity. At this level some form of process re-engineering occurred, although only in the larger, more complex businesses. A relatively small percentage of businesses achieved this level of process and data integration, and they did not achieve significant benefits from process re-engineering.

Through the late 1990s, the concept of reaching out to customers as well as to suppliers began with the introduction of widespread use of the Internet as the communications vehicle. In well-publicized cases such as Dell, Cisco and others, suppliers now had the ability to improve upon the timely delivery of component parts and to allow all parties to more effectively manage inventory through the use of timely information. The concept of customer relationship management and the "self-serve" applications now available to customers with which to check on inventory availability, order status and accounts receivable data become more popular. Although these initiatives were effective, they were executed with an internal view and did not consider the processing issues of the external parties (the supplier or customer). They were limited and executed via remote access to data, this access generally being initiated by the supplier or customer. Proactive and continual data sharing and integration of this information into supplier and customer back-office business systems were rare and generally ignored. The collaboration was missing.

In the early years of the 21st century, a new focus on significantly improving the extent and timeliness of data sharing is taking hold. Systems are being designed and technologies such as XML are being created and propagated to allow for the data to be transferred between suppliers and customers across the value chain. The focus will be not only on data sharing but also on streamlining the processing of this information. With the addition of "processing commands" to the data in an XML transaction, technology and systems can now begin to do something with the data that are received. No longer will a supplier need to determine what steps it needs to take with the data. The XML record received from the customer will now be able to "execute" by itself the processing of this information in the supplier's system and, in most cases, return the results of that processing back to the customer's system for further processing. This is the beginning of collaborative commerce: the interaction of trading partners, in real time, to make things happen.

In the years 2005 and beyond, this interaction will be both much more extensive, in the types of data and processing instructions that can be processed, and pervasive, in the number of organizations that can actually accept this information into their systems and execute the related process requests received.

In this world of inter-enterprise communication, businesses will need to work very closely with customers and suppliers alike to clearly define who will perform what processes and the protocols for executing these processes. A whole new world of inter-enterprise process optimization will need to take place.

Figure 8.1: INTER-ENTERPRISE COLLABORATION

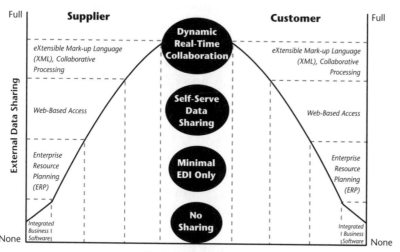

Value and efficiency in the supply chain will focus much more on process efficiency than in the data sharing that was typical of the late 1990s.

Getting more out of the supply chain (increasing the yield) will be the goal: creating more products and services with less effort. Reducing the huge burden of processing information, sharing information and acting upon information will be the shared and consistent goals of an organization, if not of an entire industry. This type of process redesign will also require changes to industry institutions, which otherwise would pose barriers to increasing yield. Changes to the tradition of paying for goods on "terms" is one example of an institution that might change. Holding orders for credit authorizations (a process that can take days) will have to disappear as an institution. These changes will force other changes and broaden the need for collaboration, data sharing and process sharing to be critically evaluated and modified to include other ancillary service providers (credit agencies, banking, insurance), so that these processes are fully automated, in real-time, with appropriate security and authorization controls in place.

Process Relationship Management

Much has been written about customer relationship management and supplier relationship management, yet when we look at B2B, Net Markets, e-business and all of the surrounding drivers in demand and supply chains, the ability to manage all of these relationships must have as their foundation the ability to dynamically model, configure, control, tailor and support business processes.

An Example

Let's explore a simple example of a common B2B process to further understand the issues of collaboration.

We will assume that Buyco is a continuous manufacturer of petroleum products. Its plant runs 24 hours per day, seven days a week. A smaller company ($500 million in sales), it has agreements with customers to ensure appropriate delivery of products on demand. Its business processes are matching inventory to orders and ensuring adequate product to meet customer delivery times.

Table 8.1: POINT-TO-POINT PURCHASE VERSUS COLLABORATIVE PURCHASE

Point-to-Point Purchase	Collaborative Purchase
1. Buyer from Buyco. reviews inventory status reports that show a need for key raw material based on minimum inventory status. Buyer performs a search of the web to determine which of 3 key suppliers has the required material for production. Search provides result that Sellco. has the product in inventory at a reasonable price based on buyers "knowledge" of the market.	1. Sellco. a strategic supplier to Buyco. has online connection between its order system and Buyco.'s inventory system. Given predetermined inventory levels, Sellco.'s system determines that an order for a product is required and initiates a purchase order process out of the Buyco. ERP system.
2. Buyer calls Sellco. to confirm details and to place order. Conveniently, Buyco. and Sellco. have an EDI connection and therefore purchase order document is sent electronically.	Sellco. has agreement that price will be based on best spot price on the open market, less 2% volume discount. This gives Buyco. guaranteed access to this key raw material.
3. Sellco. receives EDI order, prints it and re-keys order into order management system.	2. Sellco. ERP system receives purchase order electronically, validates credit through D&B.com and Buyco bank and posts order directly to its own ERP system.
4. Sellco. verifies credit through call to third party credit company. Credit is O.K.	Sellco. also updates Buyco. ERP with order delivery details to enable production scheduling
5. Sellco. prints picking slip, picks order, and call logistics company to schedule pickup.	3. Sellco prints picking slip, picks order and electronically sends logistics company all relevant details. Sellco sends electronic invoice to Buyco ERP system for payment.
6. Buyco. receives the order, creates a receiving ticket and sends to accounting for payment. This process could be electronic. Buyco. updates ERP system inventory status.	4. Buyco receives goods, scans receiving information to validate delivery and update inventory status.
7. Accounting verifies and 3 way matches purchase order, receiving report, and invoice, then schedules payment. This could be done electronically by the ERP system.	5. Buyco. ERP runs daily routine to validate delivery, match to purchase order and invoice and sends electronic payment through agreed upon banking partner.
8. Payment sent via EDI to Sellco.	6. Sellco. runs daily process to match cash to outstanding invoices, reconcile and post information.
Total time from procure to payment 3 days.	Total time from procurement to payment 2 days.
Total human effort in hours to execute total processing for all parties: 1	Total human effort in hours to execute total processing for all parties: 0.2

The above example, while hypothetical and simple, is indicative of the type of process and time savings that could result from a relatively straightforward integration of the inventory systems of Buyco with the order management systems of Sellco. If Sellco integrates credit checking and logistics with its suppliers it can significantly reduce its processing costs and time to deliver on orders.

In this example, many issues of ownership and control surface. Some of the questions that get posed in this collaborative world include:

- Who is in control of the inventory levels at Buyco?
- What is the role of Buyco's purchasing department?
- What is Sellco's responsibility if Buyco experiences a stock out situation?
- What steps have been taken to ensure that both Buyco's and Sellco's ERP systems are available 24 x 7?
- Can Buyco or Sellco make quick changes to the interfaces if either organization changes or upgrades its ERP system?
- Who pays the costs of disconnecting Buyco and Sellco if one of them decides to change the relationship?
- How easy is it to change the operating processes due to any business circumstance? How much IT effort is needed? What is the process for negotiating these changes?
- What are Sellco's rights surrounding the use of Buyco's inventory position data? Can Sellco share it with their suppliers? Can Sellco use it to predict needs for new manufacturing facilities or to evaluate best practices in Buyco's industry?

Our simple case provides a strong backdrop for some of the most important and fundamental issues of the collaborative process. We can imagine the magnitude of the challenges that would need to be addressed within a sophisticated industry, with a much more complex process, as summarized below.

Challenges and Requirements of Process Relationship Management

As the central strategic focus of an organization, process relationship management can deliver a strong value proposition. However, the move from a functionally led and managed business to one of process entails a number of challenges new to most organizations. Among those challenges (explored below):

1. Current business software embodies organizational processes and institutions.
2. The internal view is prevalent.
3. Data ownership is blurred.
4. Process ownership is blurred.
5. Business functions are central to management.
6. IT is challenged to deliver.

1. Current Business Software Embodies Organizational Processes and Institutions

In the 1990s, most enterprises were driven to re-engineer processes, standardize these processes, and embody them in a structure of control to drive consistency of application.

This embodiment was the foundation and key ROI of ERP systems. Vendors of ERP drove their value off the message that their systems could be tailored and configured to be the enablers of re-engineering. With new tools such as workflow management and automated configuration of software to match required business processes, ERP systems have become the de facto controllers of business processes. Business processes have been codified and enshrined in ERP applications over the past 10 years. The benefit, of course, is that significant control has been established and costs have been reduced. The bad news is that these processes are so tightly embodied and so internally focused that most organizations' ability to move to a collaborative relationship with trading partners through the management of process relationships will be compromised without changes being made to the ERP and the addition of new tools to enable process relationship management.

2. The Internal View Is Prevalent

ERP and re-engineering were, by definition, focused internally: Let's get our own house in order before we deal with our customers and suppliers. Again, this approach was appropriate and successful in meeting the objective. It all happened pre-Internet, pre-e-business, pre-Net Markets and pre-collaborative commerce.

The required view for collaborative commerce, based on our drivers, is an external view. An external view requires an external understanding, an understanding of options for collaboration, how others achieve results and what is needed to deliver value. Those who control internal processes do generally not possess this knowledge and understanding.

In fact, most organizations have been extremely successful at building cultures and institutions upon which their businesses have achieved success and created value. These cultures and institutions are nonetheless the main barriers toward change and toward the move to an external process orientation. In a collaborative world an organization may be required to share and work through an industry vertical Net Market one day, and compete for business with a key customer the next day. In a business environment thick with analogies to war, and where business battles are fought each day, *co-opetition* is interesting, but not consciously acknowledged in most organizations. Co-opetition can be adopted as policy but it is going to happen anyway, because customers will choose to also be competitors and, in some instances, may approach a competing firm to be a partner. Co-opetition has been a part of the struggle to not only form vertical Net Markets, but to get them liquid. Culture is a very difficult, long-term thing to change.

3. Data Ownership Is Blurred

Our experience in most organizations is that the challenge of implementing any new process or technology pivots on a discussion regarding data ownership. The question "Who owns the data?" in a customer relationships management system usually degenerates to an argument between sales ("We own the customer"), marketing ("We own the target market, which includes all customers"), finance ("We own the accounts receivable and invoicing systems that store all customer data") and customer service ("We own the relationship"). Of course, the answer is once again everybody and nobody. Each function has specific responsibilities that require specific access to and mining of the data and processes but none has control.

Consider this issue in a collaborative commerce environment. In our simple example of Buyco and Sellco, who owns the data on inventory? Buyco's operations manager, purchasing manager or forecasting manager? Where does Sellco's customer service manager fit in? If the process is totally electronic, without human intervention, does anyone really own the data or have responsibility for it?

All of these are important questions, yet are commonly the ones that organizations either ignore or assume are much less important than a question such as "Will the server box handle the volume of transactions we expect?" Technology vendors clearly drive the discussion toward hardware and software. Functional managers drive the discussion to functional processes. Most leaders avoid the whole messy discussion of ownership of and responsibility for data and processes.

4. Process Ownership Is Blurred

When an automobile company completely outsources the production of engines, is it still responsible for the process, or has it totally abdicated responsibility for that process? When Buyco outsources the monitoring of key inputs to Sellco and gives Sellco the ability to query, order and fill raw material needs, does it transfer ownership and responsibility for the fulfillment process to Sellco? Where does Buyco's purchasing department stand?

Even using an example as simple as that of Buyco and Sellco, it is clear that the answers to the questions of process ownership are not. There are no right answers to the questions. The answers are determined by situation. Nonetheless, in most cases the questions are not even being asked!

Collaborative commerce requires that the questions be asked, answered and then embodied in the software and technology implemented to enable the process. Particularly because of the significant reduction in human interaction, the need to clearly agree upon process ownership and ensure that management controls are implemented becomes a foundation of B2B success.

A key insight for the CEO is that a much better understanding of the key business processes in both the organization and the whole value chain must be achieved. An understanding of how they relate to each other, and especially of how they relate to external parties, is essential to collaboration and value creation. The corollary to this is that the CEO must recognize the broadening span of responsibility, especially as it relates to B2B Net Markets and the inherent collaboration requirements for success. It is no longer enough to clearly understand how one's own organization works and fits into the value chain, the CEO must now begin to understand how every other player interrelates, adds value, and is impacted by collaborative commerce.

Most executive teams are not well equipped to gain this understanding, as B2B is not a responsibility of any single function in the business. This fact further amplifies the need for a role of process relationship management monitor in the organization.

5. Business Functions Are Central to Management

The time-tested implementation of functional management (finance, sales, marketing, operations, production) and its related hierarchy structure do not lend themselves well to process relationship management. The management of process relationships—an external view we have established is a requirement of collaborative commerce—will require either a change in business structure or a form of matrix management and new functional responsibility within the business to deal with the ownership and management of processes. These structures will also, by implication, require a broader audience and authority through the co-opting of trading partner resources into the overall management process. The objective of this management is to leave the lines blurred between organizations, to, in effect, promote collaboration and sharing. It is also to ensure the controls and ownership of key pieces of the process are clearly articulated and assigned.

6. IT Is Challenged to Deliver

Finally, in most organizations, IT is challenged to deliver on this mandate. It must attempt to unravel the tight integration of processes within the ERP and other business systems and allow for matrix management. If this cannot be accomplished, IT is faced with the challenge of dealing with an increasingly growing number of "shadow processes," skunk-works systems, and ad hoc processes that will be created in and among the functions and the trading partners in an attempt to put the right management processes in place to support collaborative commerce. This unraveling leads to a spiraling loss of control and an increase in overall costs, as IT departments chase their tails in an attempt to keep control over a wider and wider audience, many of whom are not direct employees of the organization.

CEOs are then challenged to direct IT investments into a wider set of possible projects. In most organizations a continued focus has been on internal systems. Improvements in the value derived from ERP implementation continue to be a focus. Internal projects, however, add incremental value and do not attract the attention or the focus from IT that most CEOs would hope.

Recent forays into external, Web-based projects such as on-line sales and e-procurement have also faced huge challenges in meeting expectations. These projects are exciting because they use new technology, but IT organizations are missing the mark on value. The projects appear to fail to meet expectations of management because:

- IT departments are ill equipped to technically or operationally deliver these projects and therefore underestimate the needs for change management, trading partner input, process re-engineering and most other aspects of B2B projects. Yet, these projects have been mandated as "technology projects."
- These projects generally focus on the wrong target audience and drive at the most complex aspects of B2B, back-office integration. Most organizations look to obtain ROI by implementing collaborative commerce for the largest of the trading partners. While this does represent the largest dollar volume, these relationships may already be relatively efficient and therefore not provide the level of ROI when evaluated against the most complex and expensive aspect of collaboration, integration.

We therefore see that IT must continue to play a key role but not to drive the collaborative aspects of the project.

The Requirements of Collaborative Commerce

Executive leadership of an organization will be required to bring focus to process relationship management and position it in the forefront of the strategic planning process, an approach new for most organizations and one requiring significant senior leadership and change management to ensure success. The elements of this initiative, as outlined below, are:

- process integration and optimization approach
- change management
- EAI integration skills
- disaster recovery and security
- *scalability* and availability
- management and monitoring

Process Integration and Optimization

Process excellence must become a core competency of the collaborative organization. The functional orientation of most organizations will not allow process relationship management initiatives to succeed through assigning them to the current leadership team. Leadership of process optimization and the collaborative commerce project should be accomplished through a new, independent team that could be empowered with the role of process ownership. This new function of process relationship management would have responsibility for and ownership of the key processes of the organization and the trading partners. With the goal of optimizing business processes across the whole demand and supply chain, the process relationship management function would have the authority to strategically plan and manage the processes. Whether the initiative was centrally controlled (through a single unit) or decentralized (through a committee of functional leaders), its role would be the same, to create a collaborative organization. Acting as a knowledge management function for the entire supply/demand chain of processes, this team could also manage the translation between functional needs, process needs and technology needs to deliver on the mandate.

Change Management

Change management, as with all change imperatives, is a challenge. The effective CEO will lead through measured change and step-wise investments in the area of collaboration. Projects that start with analysis of the impact of collaborative commerce on a specific process or trading relationship should be undertaken. The knowledge gained should be cataloged and shared to begin to build a repository of process-based skills. To drive a process culture, each B2B initiative should have an impact analysis on process as a key deliverable of the business case process. Management should ensure that all IT initiatives have a process component to the business case as a mandatory deliverable.

EAI Integration Skills

IT organizations need to significantly increase their core technical skills in XML and *enterprise application integration* tools. Current EAI tools have begun to incorporate many of the needed functions to deliver and effectively manage interorganizational processes. As discussed in the next chapter, the drive to create industry-wide transaction processing standards is a fundamental trend and enabler of collaborative commerce. The tools to deliver this capability are inherently about process as well as data integration. Therefore, IT organizations will need to have a much broader business perspective as it relates to key processes in the industry and in their constituent business.

Disaster Recovery and Security

The needs of collaborative commerce by definition move the flow of information from inside the organization and its inherent security and control processes to outside the organization, where data is shared, processed and moved between a much broader stakeholder group. As process and data ownership is shared, the security of access becomes an issue that requires the organization to expand their view of security and understand a much broader set of risks in the stewardship of this data. Coupled with the broader security issue is the need to ensure that the hardware infrastructure, across the supply/demand chain, has been designed to ensure availability and to ensure that the organization's business processes are executed as intended, regardless of trading partner issues. The ability to create redundant and controlled hardware infrastructures becomes much more complex as it requires tight coordination and joint investments in technology architecture designs to be effective. Proper disaster recovery planning would also ensure that fail-over procedures for critical processes would be designed into the overall process relationship management framework.

Scalability and Availability

Tied to disaster recovery and security are the concepts of *scalability* and availability. Collaborative applications dramatically increase the load on conventional IT systems, and the effective planning of the technical infrastructure to ensure that it can scale to the volume of data and processes and ensure availability 24 x 7 is critical to long-term success.

Management and Monitoring

The drive to reorient the organization to process relationship management and collaborative commerce will require executive leadership to look for new means of managing the organization and measuring effectiveness of the initiative. As discussed, the creation of a team to own and drive process change will be a first step. To drive change and performance, new mechanisms to reward appropriate behaviors at all levels will be required. Individuals, departments, divisions and trading partners must see a clear tie between performance and rewards. It will be incumbent upon management to ensure that these performance systems are implemented and monitored to ensure success.

Many tools and technologies have recently been developed to assist in modeling and driving a process view of business. Products from companies such as ProVision, CaseWise and Meta Software have the ability to perform simulation, value-chain analysis and optimization to assist in the implementation of collaborative commerce initiatives.

What Is Driving This Trend?

The drivers of this trend were discussed earlier in the chapter as competitive, strategic, technical and globalization drivers. When we look at those drivers in the context of the MIDST Success Driver Framework, a different perspective on this trend is revealed.

Market Systems

We will reiterate the four key drivers of market systems:

- to create efficiency gains for the firm
- to create efficiency gains for the market
- to create productivity gains for the firm
- to allow the firm to reorient its activities to a more productive use

These are the four ways a technology advance can be exploited—all relate to the market system—but the system has both a horizontal and vertical dimension. Activities within the system may be characterized by primitive flows and by the role each player assumes in enabling the flows. The horizontal dimension addresses competition and collusion; the vertical dimension addresses distribution, commonly the dimension on which collaboration takes place. The system evolves through a collection of make-or-buy decisions connecting the external processes to the internal processes of a firm.

The trend to re-engineer internal business processes and enable collaborative commerce is being driven by the *Market systems* driver. The efficiency of the supply and demand chain is driven by a need for organizations to improve productivity, become more efficient in execution of the business and to look for ways to reorient capital to more productive uses. When executed properly, collaborative commerce will support those desires and therefore will be driven fairly strongly by the *Market system* driver.

Institutions

The *Institutions* dimension is a strong influencer of this trend. The embodiment of culture and institutions in an organization is typically strong and requires significant change management efforts to shift. This trend could be driven by a need for a new institution surrounding the delivery of products or the servicing of customers, which is required for a business to remain competitive. The *Technology* dimension and the *Market system* dimension do, however, influence the impact of the *Institutional* dimension on this trend. We can see that by ignoring the technology or the demands in the marketplace for improved service, pricing and delivery, an organization would be ignoring the influence and shift in institutions in its industry surrounding acceptable levels of all of these items.

The *Institutional* dimension has a moderate influence and drive on this trend.

Demand

As discussed in Chapter 2, the *Demand* dimension is one that entails the successful completion of a buyer making a decision to actually buy. This decision is influenced by a number of factors, including the time it takes to purchase goods, the availability of a wide range of relevant products and the costs associated with executing the transactions (that is, the transaction processing costs).

In this regard, we can view the trend to re-engineer internal processes and create a collaborative commerce environment as one that assists in sustaining demand, and therefore the *Demand* dimension is a relevant driver of this trend. By enabling the processing and exchange of data, this trend reduces the time required for an organization to execute a make-or-buy decision.

By making the processing of this transaction seamless, instantaneous and accurate, the purchaser will experience a reduction in the overall costs associated with executing the transaction.

While this driver is important, it is not as significant to this trend as it is to others, due to the need for it to be enabled by the technologies of EAI and XML. We would rate its influence as moderate.

State Policy

State policy is not an inherent driver of this trend. State policy, however, could impact on the full value to be derived from this trend in specific industries where government regulation could have an impact on the level of collaboration allowed and the nature of regulatory reporting required. Areas such as health care and pharmaceuticals could have stringent regulations regarding process control, reporting and data ownership and make this collaboration more difficult to achieve with cost efficiency.

Technology

Technology is not a significant driver of this trend but a significant enabler. The key technology drivers appear to be the technology vendors who are promoting the value and benefits of EAI technology, instant access and the significant reductions in the costs of communications and bandwidth to support collaborative commerce. As the cost of these technologies continues to drop, the net impact on ROI of collaborative commerce initiatives will increase. However, we would caution that the complexities and costs of true collaboration on processes and data are not to be underestimated (see Chapter 9). This technology is relatively new and therefore has a long way to go before it is mainstream.

The impact of *Technology* as a driver of this trend is moderate.

MIDST Success Map for Collaborative Process Optimization

Figure 8.2: MIDST SUCCESS DRIVER FRAMEWORK FOR COLLABORATIVE PROCESS OPTIMIZATION

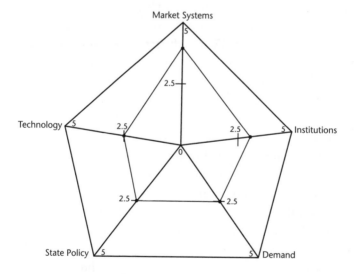

Where Is the Value?

By re-engineering and optimizing both internal and collaborative processes, organizations will be responding to the drivers of this trend. If a corporation can reorient its strategy, information technology and management processes to one that is process-driven rather than functionally driven, it will begin to see value from the re-engineering process.

With regards to the MaRCoT Value Framework, this trend provides significant value along all of the dimensions. It is readily apparent that an organization that is truly process-driven and has embraced the need to manage process relationships will increase the yield in the supply chain.

Market Efficiency

At its core, market efficiency (liquidity and price stability) requires improved timeliness of data and improved sharing of larger quantities and a better quality of data. As discussed in Chapter 2, market efficiency requires that information be readily available and timely. Collaborative commerce and the optimizations of internal and external business processes can contribute to making markets more efficient. The value of this trend is directly tied to its enablement through technology to deliver industry-wide transaction processing standards. In and of itself, this trend cannot continue, nor value be realized without the technology enabler. This trend has moderate impact on market efficiency on its own.

Risk Efficiency

The value in optimizing collaborative business processes has a strong risk efficiency value. As discussed, the devolution of the clear ownership of processes created by the outsourcing and sharing of business processes significantly increases the risk that an organization will lose control of its competitive advantage and be unable to deliver on its key value proposition.

As collaboration increases in the supply chain, risk increases. Therefore, optimizing collaborative business processes delivers high value in managing, mitigating and controlling risk. Organizations that do not pay attention to this component of collaborative commerce face the possibility of significant sub-optimization or potentially catastrophic failure of their value chain.

Collaborative processes also reduce risk through providing an additional ability for the organization to reduce the variability in the primitive flows (as discussed in Chapter 4). Collaboration reduces uncertainty in the primitive flow areas of product, information and payment by improving on the timeliness and accuracy of the information provided in each of these areas. Therefore, the risk efficiency value provided by this trend is high.

Cost Efficiency

The opportunities for cost efficiency created through collaborative business processes have been legendary in companies such as Cisco, who, it was reported, had achieved a five-percent saving (on revenue) or $500 million in savings in a single year through the implementation of collaborative business processes and technologies. Wal-Mart's most significant strategic advantage appears to be its collaboration with suppliers to drive cost efficiencies. However, these savings are fully predicated on the creation of industry-wide standards for transaction processing. Without these standards, it would be practically impossible to achieve any level of collaborative process integration and consequently any value from this trend. Therefore, we would see the cost efficiencies from this trend as being very high, but fully contingent on standards for its enablement.

Collaboration is not without risk as both Cisco and Dell have experienced in recent times. Tight collaboration in the electronics industry has become much more problematic in an economic downturn. As smaller suppliers and customers are financially challenged, the costs and risks associated with managing collaboration expose the chain to risks associated with financial failures. Both Cisco and Dell have had experience with this type of risk in the downturn of 2000 and 2001.

Time Efficiency

The time efficiencies to be garnered from collaborative business process optimization are directly tied to the effective delivery and implementation of industry-wide standards for transaction-processing through the widespread use of XML, middleware and translation hubs by an organization. At the highest level of integrated collaborative commerce, the time efficiencies achieved in terms of conducting commerce become logarithmically large. Processing time, delivery time and decision-making time drop dramatically through the effective integration of trading partners and the automation of transaction processing between them.

In combination with the delivery of industry-wide transaction processing standards, this trend will deliver a very high time efficiency value. However, without these standards, we do not believe that sufficient value can be achieved through collaborative process optimization to justify the costs associated with implementation.

Value Map for Collaborative Process Optimization

Overall, we see the value map as follows in Figure 8.3.

Figure 8.3: MaRCoT VALUE FOR COLLABORATIVE
PROCESS OPTIMIZATION

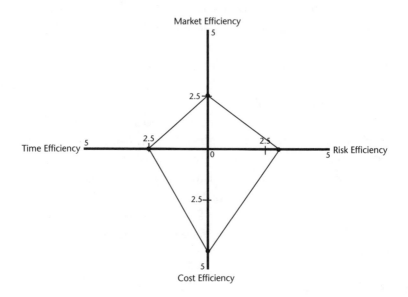

Will This Trend Survive?

Our premise is that collaborative commerce extends an organization's processes along the whole of the value chain in order to improve yield in the supply chain.

If we accept this premise, and we clearly understand the overall needs of a business when it enters into a collaborative relationship with customers and suppliers, then the trend to revisit and re-engineer processes that affect the organization's touch points with customers and suppliers will continue for the next five to 10 years.

The key enabler of this trend is the creation of industry-wide transaction processing standards, which are the subject of the next chapter. Without this enabling technology, collaborative process optimizations cannot be achieved. As we will see, the promise of these collaboration technologies and potential value is very high, and the issues, costs and challenges are also significant.

Over time the tools, technologies and business management processes to effectively implement collaborative commerce will become well defined, broadly implemented and fully supported by the major players in key industries of the global economy. This trend will remain and become a foundation for the successful businesses of the 21st century.

Summary

The underlying theme of this chapter is that to know his or her business the CEO must know its key processes, how they relate to each other and especially how they relate to external parties. The corollary to this is that the CEO must recognize the expanding span of his or her responsibility, especially as relates to B2B Net Markets and the inherent collaboration requirements for success.

The messages of this chapter are:

- The aspects of business process integration that must be revisited during a B2B project include a re-optimization of internal business processes to create a 24 x 7 business and the creation of optimized value chain processes between all trading partners.
- Business processes are generally "orphaned" in a business in that they are critical to all functions in the business, yet generally not "owned" by any person or department, leading to a major issue in B2B projects, since ownership and optimization of processes are key.
- Process relationship management (PRM) must be a senior executive team-led initiative and is essential to creating a collaborative commerce environment.

- Creating a process relationship management culture is difficult due to the embodiment of business processes in organizational systems and cultures. An internal view is much more prevalent than an external collaborative view of processes. Data ownership is generally blurred in most organizations.

The six elements of creating a collaborative commerce environment are:

1. Process integration and optimizations approach
2. Change management
3. EAI integration skills
4. Disaster recovery and security
5. Scalability and availability
6. Management and monitoring

Applying the MIDST Success Driver Framework, the drivers of this trend include the *Market System* and *Demand* dimensions.

The value being created by this trend is strongest on the dimensions of time efficiency and market efficiency.

This trend will become the foundation for business practices in the 21st century.

CEO's Playbook for the Boardroom

During a board meeting, the CFO presents a request for funding of a project to review key operational processes in conjunction with a Web-selling initiative. This comes on the heels of a very large re-engineering project in the finance department that has just been completed. A board member objects to the request, stating that the benefits of re-engineering are questionable based on the experience of the recent project and that the company should not continue to follow every trendy consulting suggestion it hears. Your response:

- You ask the CFO to present the implications of the Web sales project on 24 x 7 operations.

- You ask that the impact on key supplier and customer processes be understood and a project team of multi-functional managers be created to clearly document these processes and the impact of Web-selling on them.
- You suggest that the team be externally focused, unlike the current re-engineering project that was exclusively focused on internal finance processes, which did not touch external trading partners.
- You suggest that all processes along the value chain be documented for future reference if and when the company embarks on a Net Market initiative.
- You clearly explain that future projects will require a process focus and that multi-functional teams will lead projects that are B2B in nature, as the organization must increase its appreciation of the role it plays in the value chain. This cannot be accomplished by any one function of the company.
- You suggest that senior management begin to understand the key processes, which will be competitively advantageous to the corporation in the future.

9

The Technology to Deliver Industry-Wide Transaction-Processing Standards

OVERVIEW AND GOALS OF THE CHAPTER

This chapter explores the basic technologies that will enable true optimized value chains and collaborative commerce. We begin with a review of the EDI standards to provide a clear understanding of not only the limitations of EDI but the drivers for the emergence of new technologies with which to manage the complex data and process interactions demanded by collaborative commerce.

Collaboration and B2B integration make use of the entire spectrum of software and technology to support the exchange and processing of data between different organizations, *without human intervention*. In most cases, the organizations will be using different and incompatible technology platforms and software.

The need for collaborative technologies applies to all levels of business integration:

- *internal integration*: the need to tie internal systems such as legacy, custom and ERP together to better share data and processes

- *private Net Market integration*: the need to tie companies in a supply/demand chain together, when the technologies and software being used are consistent
- *B2B integration*: the need to tie data and processes of different organizations together, especially when the technologies and software are inconsistent

Most integration requirements are made necessary because an external transaction is received by a business. A variety of examples include:

- a request for inventory availability
- a request for order status
- an order submission
- an invoice from a supplier
- a request for accounts payable or accounts receivable balances
- a product design change request

These are a few of the hundreds of unique information and process requests most businesses receive in a single day. Each of these requires that the requester and supplier of the information perform specific processes to find and present that information. Some of these processes are simple, some complex. In order to deliver on the request without human intervention, technology must be able to determine the nature, timing and reasonableness of the request, as well as the security of the requester, and then to process the request accurately and return the results. As we will see, this objective is by no means straightforward or easily achievable. We will review the various aspects of technology that drive this objective and explore the challenges organizations will face to achieve them.

Electronic Data Interchange (EDI): A Brief History

The origins of EDI are difficult to trace, but date back to the mid-1960s when the use of IBM computers began to seriously infiltrate larger organizations in the United States. In those days, the time a buyer needed to create a purchase order, mail it to the supplier, and wait for processing, picking and shipping was generally estimated as a 10- to 14-day exercise *at the very least*. The most time-consuming stage was the time the postal system took to deliver purchase orders, on average three to five days. Driven by major players in the automotive, retail and petroleum industries, EDI began as an initiative with three main goals:

- to reduce errors in the processing of orders, invoices and payment transactions
- to increase speed in the communication of this information between businesses
- to reduce human interaction and intervention in acquiring data regarding inventory positions, orders and shipping of orders between organizations

As the movement continued into the 1970s and the types of computer technology mushroomed from one (IBM) to dozens, corporations found that EDI was much more complex, as the types of hardware coupled with the types of business software and communications protocols being employed were so varied. Every combination of transactions needed to be uniquely mapped from the purchaser's system to the supplier's system. The cost associated with creating these "maps" were high and maintaining these maps was even more expensive. Many companies had specific and unique ways to capture, store and communicate data that were incompatible with those of most of their trading partners.

It was clear that there was a need for "standards" to govern the structure of each type of transaction as well as the means for communicating these transactions among a growing number of trading partners. In 1979, a guiding body called the American National Standards Institute (ANSI) created the Accredited Standards Committee (ASC X12) and gave it the mandate to create and manage the standards for the structure of these various transactions. This standard, which is generally accepted in North America, is ANSI X12.

In 1986, in other countries outside of North America, a different standard was created, called the United Nation's Electronic Data Interchange for Administrators, Commerce and Transport (UN/

EDIFACT). ANSI X12 and EDIFACT are not seamlessly compatible, although an international effort has been made to integrate the two standards into a single standard.

EDI and Web-Based Collaborative Commerce

One factor that is important in the understanding of Web-based collaborative commerce is the significance of the underlying technology of the Internet and the Web overlay. The adoption of TCP/IP as a foundation for data communications over the Internet removes or diminishes all kinds of per user costs that are otherwise incurred in building and running EDI. There is a trade-off, though, as users of Web-based collaborative commerce are effectively using a public infrastructure rather than a closed proprietary or dedicated infrastructure (even if it is closed in the sense of a virtual private network). For the Web-based collaborators, some security has to be introduced, and even though some of the integration is accomplished intrinsically by the architecture of the Web, some additional integration has to be accomplished by connecting disparate enterprise systems to the Web. The installation and operating costs associated with the two collaborative routes (EDI and Internet) are vastly different, because in the Internet case, most of the costs are shared across countless users of the infrastructure, whereas for EDI the costs are shared among a relatively small number of users in a closed system.

Components of EDI

There are three standard components required to use EDI:

1. A standard ANSI X12 or EDIFACT transaction type. There are at least 16 standard types of transactions. The more commonly used are: purchase order, purchase order acknowledgement, order status inquiry, shipping notice, invoice and payment order.
2. A communications ability to connect with your trading partner. This ability can be achieved through
   - a direct connection to a trading partner
   - the use of a Value Added Network (VAN) service provider
   - the Internet
3. Software to translate information into standard ANSI X12 or EDIFACT format and these standards into the business's own

internal format. There are wide varieties of software products that are sold commercially to perform this translation.

VANs can provide a full suite of translation software, secure connections and redundant back-up to ensure that communication is always reliable. There are many VANs, and trading partners can subscribe to any service, as VANs have established connections and protocols to route transactions between them and their respective customers.

Phases of EDI Sophistication

As larger corporations progressed, the need for electronic data interchange became more apparent based on the cost of processing very large volumes of business transactions. However, the level of integration of the company's systems with their trading partners through the VAN was varied. Those companies that used EDI had to choose whether to fully integrate their EDI system with their business systems or manually rekey information from their systems into an EDI electronic form for transmission through the VAN to the trading partners.

Figure 9.1 COST EFFICIENCY OF EDI VS WEB-BASED
                COLLABORATIVE COMMERCE

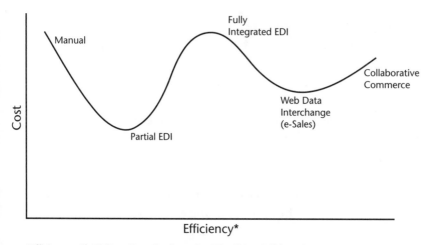

*Efficiency = Flexibility + Data Sharing + Data Quality + Collaboration

Of course, the costs associated with full integration are substantial. The number of different transactions types, combined with the number of trading partners and the need for "maps" of each transaction to each trading partner, makes the whole process costly to develop and maintain.

When we chart the relative costs of EDI and Web-based collaborative commerce against the efficiencies provided, fully integrated EDI appears more expensive than Web-based collaborative commerce and provides less value in terms of efficiencies. (See Figure 9.1.)

Here our definition of collaborative commerce could include EDI:

> A means of leveraging new technologies to enable a set of complex, cross-enterprise business processes to share decision-making, workflow, capabilities and other information with each other to create a unique value proposition in the marketplace through the value chain.

Costs in this case would be the overall costs associated with hardware, software, map creation, maintenance and processing costs. Efficiency is defined as the full ability to collaborate, share data and processes, manage relationships and integration of data and processes, and do so in an easy manner.

The Benefits of EDI

The benefits that businesses have realized in the implementation of EDI include:

- reduced transaction execution time from the point the purchase order is created through to the time the goods are delivered
- lower keying error rates than with manual systems on all transactions
- lower transaction-processing costs than those associated with manual data entry
- improved inventory availability and reduced "stock out" situations due to timely matching of ordering to demand

While the benefits of EDI have led to its use in the largest organizations in key industries, it has not been widely adopted by medium-sized and small organizations. It is typically estimated that less than five percent of businesses worldwide use EDI. Unless mandated by an industry, such as automotive or retail, its adoption has been generally lower than those rates. The reasons for these poor adoption rates are directly related to the limitations of EDI, which include:

- *No collaborative processes.* With EDI all data is batched and sent to a trading partner for processing. Once processed, responses are batched and sent back to the originator. The ability to access data in real time, make changes to it and query the systems of a trading partner does not exist.
- *Technical complexity.* The standards for EDI transactions are currently managed by at least two organizations (ANSI X12 and EDIFACT) and the number of transaction types continues to grow. Yet, because of the very rigid standards set for the transaction types and the long process for the creation, approval and rollout of any new transaction type, the flexibility trading partners need to create unique transactions and processes does not exist. Therefore, trading partners are limited to the currently approved list of transaction types supported by the standards bodies. If any special needs exist, trading partners must create direct links and special transaction processes to meet their needs, which increases their overall costs for maintaining transaction maps across the value chain.
- *Cost.* The costs associated with building and maintaining maps for each type of transaction for each trading partner are high. In addition, costs to connect to a VAN are substantially higher than using an Internet option. These costs are the greatest deterrents to EDI's adoption by a greater number of businesses and have a negative impact on its ultimate value to a whole supply chain. The availability of connections (universal access) is limited to a small number of VANs, which also has a direct impact on adoption.

Small and medium-sized companies find it difficult to invest the large sums needed to get an EDI solution up and running because they do not generate the sufficiently high volumes of use or transactional revenues to realize a returnable ROI. Web-based solutions, on the other hand, require a relatively low upfront investment.

While EDI has been a significant advantage for many industries, it is primarily a cost and time efficiency value. It provides little if any value on the dimensions of market efficiency and risk efficiency. Therefore, we see the drivers of *Technology* and *Market systems*, along with the need to increase value on all dimensions of market, risk, cost and time efficiencies, combining to drive the creation of industry-wide transaction-processing standards with a specific view to delivering a collaborative environment.

The Needs of a Collaborative Business

With the Internet facilitating low-cost business communication, and the underlying drive of *Market systems* to deliver continually higher levels of efficiency and improved yield in the supply chain, firms are driven to collaborate. Market, cost and time efficiencies are the key drivers of collaborative commerce.

Technology is often thought to be the key element of collaborative commerce. However, companies that have focused exclusively on technology in these projects have delivered little in terms of ROI. In addition to all of the issues outlined in Chapter 8 regarding process relationship management, collaboration projects that attempt to deliver value must have several components:

- integrated, automatic system-to-system exchange of data with all trading partners
- the ability to integrate data and process interactions seamlessly with in-house applications and processes to provide end-to-end control
- the ability to adapt to changes in market conditions through efficiently locating new products, services or partners, quickly leveraging their specific capabilities and forming a rapid connection to them
- a high quality, reliable and secure means of exchanging messages over the Internet, ensuring guaranteed delivery and integrity
- the ability to accommodate the unique aspects of each trading partner's method of interfacing
- intelligent management of all interactions, allowing both control and the ability to change them dynamically

Let's look at a simple example of how difficult transaction sharing could be without standards for the exchange of data and process information among trading partners.

WRITECO: TRANSACTION SHARING WITHOUT INTEGRATION

In our hypothetical company, Writeco wants to purchase four raw materials to make its key product, pencils. They require wood, lead, metal and eraser material. For each of these four materials the company has two main suppliers, in order to ensure availability of the material at all times. Woodco supplies the wood in a processed form so that Writeco only need insert the lead and attach the eraser with a metal fastener. Woodco has two sources of raw wood product. Leadco supplies the lead in a processed form so that Writeco only need insert it into the wood holder. Leadco has two key sources for pencil lead. Metalco supplies the metal fastener in a preshaped form to hold the eraser and Eraserco supplies the material in a preshaped form to fit the metal holder. Metalco and Eraserco have two sources each for raw materials.

We will assume that each of the suppliers uses unique business system software but the same technology hardware. In order for the seamless movement of transactional and process information to occur, Writeco would need to build four unique integration points, one to each of its four suppliers. In addition, Woodco, Leadco, Metalco and Eraserco would each need to build two integration points with their suppliers, for a total of eight, in order to send and receive information needed to manage production and inventory.

In total, 12 unique interfaces would be required. Assume that each company would like to electronically trade information about four key business documents: purchase order, shipping confirmation, invoice and payment. There would now be a total of 48 unique types of data and formats to create and share among the five trading partners.

Remember that in this example the trading partners all use the same technology hardware. If the partners were using different technology hardware platforms, the illustration would be complicated significantly.

At a very conservative cost of $10,000 per transaction type, the total cost for Writeco and its suppliers to integrate four transaction types across five partners would be $480,000.

Of course, we know that each of these companies would have hundreds of suppliers and dozens of transaction types and potentially hundreds of customers that could see value in sharing information across the value chain, making the potential cost calculation logarithmically large: potentially tens of millions of dollars to fully integrate the key pieces of data.

Enter XML...

Let's now consider the possible impact of XML (extensible markup language), a standard for the storage and transmission of data and processing instructions across the chain, on the pencil industry of the example above. XML could allow the pencil industry to develop standards for sharing purchase order, shipping, invoice and payment data *regardless* of business software or technology. Instead of 48 unique types of data and transactions, there would be four, one for each type of transaction: invoice, purchase order, shipping notice and payment. If the group funded the development of the four standards, then their cost would be the equivalent of developing one, or $10,000. Conservatively, the cost of integration could be reduced by 90 percent compared to the cost the value chain would have incurred without XML in this simple situation.

If the XML standard for the purchase order, shipping confirmation, invoice and payment could be shared among a variety of industries, then Writeco could also integrate its office supplies trading partner, its shipping company trading partner, its dealer network and any other trading partner in the value chain through the same means. The cost would then drop from 1/10 to 1/1000 or 1/100,000 as the broader use of the standard would allow Writeco to send and receive data in *one* format only, knowing that it was readable, translatable and usable by *all* of its trading partners.

With this magnitude of cost savings being possible—based on eliminating the costs of building the technical integration points—the *transactional efficiency* value of B2B alone will demand that industry-wide standards for data and process communication continue and be rapidly adopted.

Follow-on benefits would include the ability for a trading partner such as Writeco to also have flexibility to connect to one or many Net Markets for wood, lead, metal and erasers without incurring significant costs to do so. Writeco could then choose which markets to participate in and in which it would cease to participate. Writeco could provide liquidity or move it around as it saw fit, based on market conditions for its products and those of its suppliers.

Exchanging Data: The Challenge of Collaborative Commerce

In order that any two organizations may exchange data, these agreements need to be in place:

- parties must have decided what format a message will take so that both parties can interpret the information they receive. With differing business systems (SAP, J.D. Edwards, Oracle and others) and with differing technology platforms (IBM, Microsoft, Sun) the challenges of formatting and sharing information among thousands of trading partners can be daunting.
- parties must be agreed on what information will be shared and how it will be used and processed when it is received. The common business objects such as invoices, purchase orders and other related business documents, in addition to the actual data such as customer names, supplier numbers and so on, will differ significantly between trading partners. How the documents are processed (including the type of software being used to process the data) will also differ.

The challenge of exchanging data is the "language issue" that all businesses face.

The Language Issue

In human terms, the agreement to speak a particular language is an institution. Many countries have chosen English as the commonly accepted means of communication. Others have agreed to speak French, Chinese, or Hungarian. In all cases, the language is a legitimate, acceptable language that has been created with a set of standard sounds that have meaning. The agreement of which sounds mean what has been established over thousands of years of convention and literary validation. These languages evolve as new words, expressions and usages are introduced and older ones fall into disuse.

With business communications, we are attempting to get to the same level of understanding. In order to exchange information, businesses or industries must first agree on the language they will use. One cannot use Spanish when another uses German. Both languages are valid, yet understanding will not occur in the transaction. Once the language "system" is agreed upon, users of the language have to agree as to the individual meanings of individual combinations of sound. English speakers have agreed that the word water refers to a liquid that humans need to sustain life. It could have been defined as the shining ball in the sky that provides light and warmth, but it was not. In B2B terms, standards are needed for both individual words and their meanings *and* the system of language to be applied in translation. This is where new technologies such as XML are being created to solve the communications issue.

Figure 9.2 depicts the complexities of connecting a variety of systems together through traditional means without the benefit of EAI tools and standards.

Figure 9.2 CONNECTING SYSTEMS THE "TRADITIONAL" WAY

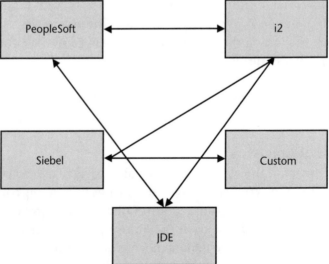

The Emergence of New Technologies and Standards

To meet the challenges of collaborative commerce head on, technology vendors have developed a vast array of hardware and software solutions. Business executives need not focus on the "how to" aspects of these technologies, but should focus on the "what and why" aspects of these technologies. The new technologies can be grouped into three areas:

- extensible markup language (XML)
- middleware and Enterprise Application Integration (EAI)
- translation hubs and exchanges

Each of these technologies works with the others to allow an organization to create collaborative commerce solutions. We will explain these basic collaborative technology components, their impact on a business and the value proposition that each delivers.

Extensible Markup Language

In its simplest terms, XML is a standard set of tools to create the equivalent of a communications "language" that companies agree to speak when passing information between them. It defines the syntax of the language and its basic structure. In addition, it provides a means for creating a common lexicon to define each of the words. The meaning of "invoice" for companies in the retail industry is different than the meaning it holds for companies in the professional services industry, and the same is true for "terms," "item number," "invoice number" and "customer id."

With XML, an individual company's "words" can be defined and mapped to the company's trading partners' words and meanings, without the need for one-to-one or complex software and processes.

How Does It Work?

To understand the basic mechanics of XML is to understand both its simplicity and power.

XML has two components, the data itself and the Document Type Definition (DTD) that defines how the data is structured and how it will be used. The DTD component is known as meta data. Meta data is data about the data. The meta data is given a name, or "tag," as a form of shorthand. As an example, one company may use the tag **<Customer ID>** to signify the field in an accounting system in which the customer's number is stored. "**<Customer ID>**" is the data about the data. In another company, the meta data could be called **<Customer Number>**. Additional meta data about the customer could include the length of the customer number: **<Customer Number length>6</Customer Number length>**.

The ability to specify information about a piece of data in a system allows the users to create a wide variety of formats for data and a way for another system to read and interpret the information without having to ask anyone else for assistance in interpretation, since the interpreter (the "lexicon") is sent along with the data in the form of meta data and the Document Type Definition.

Here is an example of how an invoice's data might be tagged in XML:

```
<Invoice>
<Number>12345</Number>
<Date>01012002</Date>
<Amount>456.66</Amount>
<Customer_Number>171177</Customer_Number>
<Due_Date>02012002</Due_Date>
</Invoice>
```

With this simple example, we can see that an invoice can be described in any way a company wants, and with any number of data elements in any order. By tagging the field with the appropriate name, data can be retrieved from any location in the XML record.

A Document Type Definition (DTD) describes the allowable structure of the XML document. While use of DTD is not mandatory, DTDs are the accepted means for translating the data contained in an XML record. In our example, the following DTD may be used in association with the XML invoice transaction.

```
<!ELEMENT Invoice (number, date, amount,
customer_number, due_date)>
<!ELEMENT Number (#PCDATA)>
```

```
<!ELEMENT Date (#PCDATA)>
<!ELEMENT Amount (#PCDATA)>
<!ELEMENT Customer_Number (#PCDATA)>
<!ELEMENT Due_date (#PCDATA)>
<!ELEMENT Number (#PCDATA)>
```

This example illustrates how data can be defined and some structure given as to how the data is allowed to be stored and structured. DTDs can also specify information, such as the number of times a field can be repeated, or constraints on the elements.

In more sophisticated examples of XML and DTDs, information about the *processes* to be executed on an XML record can be created and sent with the data. The power and flexibility of XML thus allows a company to define and exchange data through the combination of raw data elements, meta data and Document Type Definitions.

Varieties of "sub-languages" of XML have been created in attempts by software developers, industry leaders and others to more precisely define the unique needs of business. Some of these sub-languages are ebXML, cXML and xCBL.

Therefore, not all XML is created equal. Since XML requires an understanding of the specific data elements to be exchanged between trading partners, it still requires companies to agree that they are going to speak Japanese, say, rather than Italian. Both are recognized, legitimate forms of language and both parties will understand each other, if they agree to speak the same language. Organizations that exchange XML documents need to know how the data should be used, how it maps to their internal systems and if it conforms to the conventions set out for the type of transaction. Therefore, translation and interpretation are essential and have led to the development of standards for specific industries to ensure consistent standards of definition for all of the data elements and process elements of those industries.

Standards Groups for XML and EAI

Here is a brief review of some of the major standards and standard-setting bodies that are in existence to create the language of B2B.

OAGI

OAGI is a non-profit consortium of many of the major vendors of business process software. It was comprised of the major industrial, telecommunications and systems software companies with the goal of creating a group of business processes based on XML content that will extend beyond the current boundaries of corporate industry and geography. The OAGI provides content development, architecture and XML leadership to the industry and is considered the single largest content developer in the XML space.

RosettaNet

RosettaNet was formed to focus on developing interoperability standards for the electronics industry, including the electronic components and information technology sub-industries. This group's goal is to optimize the cost savings and productivity gains of B2B commerce for the industry. Starting as a vertical solution for data integration, it has moved to ally itself with OAGI for content standards, and with ebXML for transport framework standards. RosettaNet's own transport framework is known as RosettaNet Implementation Framework (RNIF).

BizTalk

BizTalk is a Microsoft initiative for defining a transport framework. BizTalk is already working with OAGI and RosettaNet toward common standards. BizTalk is also an XML repository that makes standardized XML definitions widely available. A significant portion of the content on the XML.org site is provided by OAGI.

Commerce One

Commerce One is a company working on its own proprietary framework (xCBL) for content, framework and business processes based on XML. Commerce One is an e-procurement and Net Market software developer specializing in complex transactions among organizations using a variety of pricing models.

Ariba

Ariba is another software company working on a proprietary framework (cXML) across all levels. It specializes in Net Market and e-procurement software. Ariba is harmonizing its transport framework with BizTalk.

EbXML

EbXML is a United Nations initiative working with European EDI groups to formalize a framework that will serve both EDI and XML standards. CEFACT (an associated U.N. organization) creates policy and technical development in areas of trade facilitation and e-business, and OASIS, a non-profit, international consortium, is dedicated to product-independent data and content interchange.

WfMC

WfMC (Workflow Management Coalition) is part of ebXML and is working on a meta-standard for trading partner agreements.

XMLEDI

XMLEDI group is working on interfaces that accommodate both EDI and XML.

BPMI.org

The Business Process Management Initiative (BPMI.org) is attempting to standardize business processes that span multiple applications. It is attempting to create a Business Process Modeling Language (BPML) and Business Process Query Language (BPQL).

As can be seen from the examples above, the concept of standards in XML embraces a series of standards, highlighting institutional issues of B2B commerce and the complexities and unique needs of various industries that are attempting to capitalize on the value in increasing supply chain yield.

EDI to XML

The reality of XML use is that it will take a long time to replace the full breadth of EDI functionality, and consequently a number of organizations have taken the time to create tools that can translate EDI and XML back and forth. New Era of Networks Inc. (NEON), for example, has created a product to provide connections between XML formats such as BizTalk and RosettaNet to the ANSI X12 and EDIFACT EDI formats. Other companies have also begun to develop software to help automate the conversion from EDI to XML. The needs of organizations and the long history of EDI will require some level of translation between XML and EDI formats for many years to come.

Middleware and Enterprise Application Integration (EAI)

The definition of middleware has changed over the very short life of the concept. Middleware is a suite of "packaged" software tools that connects various business applications together to allow them to exchange data. The applications can be internal to a business or span a variety of trading partners in the supply/demand chain. Before middleware tools were prominent, this connecting was accomplished through custom software programming that had to be created for each connection and for each type of transaction. The costs associated with this endeavor were significant, particularly because of the complexities created whenever any part of the applications being connected was changed or upgraded. Middleware has been designed to act as a "middleman" or agent that can translate the data requirements independently of the applications, thereby minimizing the issues created where connecting applications differ from each other.

Enterprise Application Integration Tools (EAI) are an enhanced category of middleware that include more robust features to manage the communication of data between enterprises and to more effectively manage the storage and retrieval of this information. EAI tools also play the important role of managing *processes*, not just data, as well as the business rules that govern how the data will be handled by the receiving application.

In a collaborative world, EAI tools provide a more robust and necessary feature set; therefore, we will focus our discussion on the needs for EAI, though middleware is important and valuable as a toolset in its own right. Middleware can be used effectively on its own or in conjunction with EAI tools to deliver the right balance between data and process integration.

At a fundamental level, once a vehicle for the packaging and interpretation of data has been established (through XML) businesses need to perform five key technology functions with regards to collaborative commerce:

1. *Business process management,* to model, automate, monitor and analyze complex, multi-step collaborations between internal systems and external parties. Business process management includes creating the workflow processes to move data around and outside a business.

2. *B2B integrations,* to securely tie communication of systems to external trading partners. This includes the basic routing of information based on its content and the rules designed to govern its processing.

3. *Enterprise Applications Integration (EAI),* to seamlessly integrate with internal systems, including ERP, custom and legacy systems.

4. *Message management, storage, transmission and retrieval,* to provide the ability to effectively manage the messages and ensure complete and accurate delivery and execution of the message.

5. *Real-time analysis and reporting,* to provide business managers with a custom status of their business processes and exception reporting. (Source: Vitria Technology Inc. *Executive Overview: Managing Real World B2B Integration,* **www.vitria.com**)

The value of EAI tools can be summarized into four key areas:

1. *Reduced complexity of application integration:* By sitting at the center of the business (Figure 9.3), EAI allows the organization to write a single interface to that application. EAI tools then act as a repository and manager of the data, determining how it will be used by the other applications. A reduced number of interfaces are thus required, and there is a reduced impact of changes to the originating application.

2. *Control.* EAI can store the data to be integrated and ensure that controls are in place to ensure that the data is complete, authorized and accurately processed by the receiving application. In situations where problems with transmission or processing occur by the receiving or sending application, EAI tools can track and identify issues and ensure human intervention occurs to correct the problem.

3. *Improved accessibility.* Since EAI tools can be used to store information for future transmission and processing, EAI can in many cases

be used to allow for 24 x 7 processing of data. As discussed in Chapter 7, the need for a business to operate 24 x 7 days per week is fundamental. However, technology has not been designed to operate 24 x 7. Software needs to be upgraded, maintained and tested. Most systems today still require basic housekeeping and administration to happen at *some point* during the day. Therefore, it cannot be accessible 24 hours a day every day. There is a point of down time. EAI tools can be designed to be the "placeholder" system that can accept the data while the applications are maintained, and then route the information to the applications once they are available. While this may not be satisfactory for a real-time system, it can go a long way toward assisting businesses with the issue of managing 24 x 7 operations.

4. *Trading partner management.* The equivalent of B2C personalization, trading partner management allows companies to keep track of specific information regarding a trading partner, including:
   - the way a transaction is structured (how the data is laid out)
   - the protocol used for communications
   - the specific way a transaction should be processed
   - the specific output formats for the processed transaction

Figure 9.3 CONNECTING SYSTEMS WITH EAI TOOLS

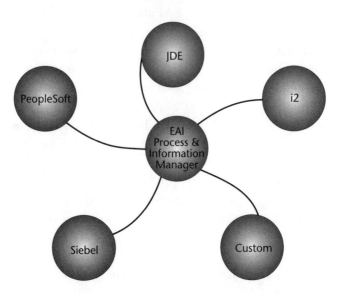

EAI combines the technologies and processes that enable custom-built and/or packaged business applications to exchange business-level information, either internal or external to an organization, in formats and contexts that each understands.

EAI is the combination of technologies to meet all of the needs above. Figure 9.3 recasts Figure 9.2 with the use of EAI tools at the center of the hub to manage all collaborative data and process integration for an organization.

Figure 9.4 shows the relationship between the level of integration (which is directly related to the value of EAI tools) and the costs/complexities of these integration levels. EAI tools do not come without costs and complexities and it is apparent from the chart that the highest value and cost are garnered with the integration of inter-enterprise application integration (integration between applications and between many enterprises or businesses). At this level, all key business processes and data are integrated between key trading partners in the demand chain.

Figure 9.4 RELATIONSHIP BETWEEN INTEGRATION LEVELS AND THEIR COSTS/COMPLEXITIES

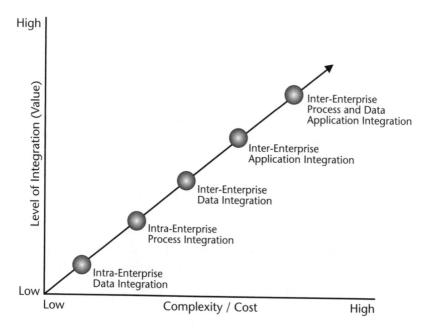

Translation Hubs and Transaction Exchanges

Translation hubs are a new type of business (independently owned and operated for profit) being established to allow companies to store and retrieve information about a trading partner's capabilities, transaction-processing requirements and unique integration requirements. These hubs act as central registries so that any organization can retrieve the requirements and use them to interface with the trading partner on both a data *and* process level.

One such hub, Contivo eService, has been created with the objective of allowing B2B trading partners to dynamically create the trading relationships they need without the effort of working through the definitions and standards required. Their "hosted" service and software offering automates the complex and time-consuming process of constructing the links required for each type of business transaction.

As discussed, the B2B standards such as ebXML, cXML, RosettaNet, BizTalk and others are driving some level of consistency in application integration and communication. However, without a single standard, companies are still challenged by the need to integrate various systems using different standards. Contivo's automated service can translate different document formats (standards) into the required equivalent for the receiving system. Therefore, regardless of the standard being used, Contivo can produce the mapping code needed to translate and integrate one system to another.

In a situation where a company is using a J.D. Edwards back office and a trading partner is using a RosettaNet-based XML application, Contivo will provide the ability to open the J.D. Edwards purchase order, evaluate all of the fields in the purchase order, then open the RosettaNet order system, and automatically map and process the appropriate information to transfer the purchase order to the order system of the supplier. Without a solution such as Contivo, this process would be manual and time consuming and fraught with issues when either system changes.

While Contivo has created extensive libraries of connectors and formats for business transactions including xCBL, cXML, RosettaNet, EDI, SAP, Oracle and others, by allowing companies to submit their own formats for transactions, Contivo is promoting the concept of an open-access repository for customers to create and share these formats and significantly reduce the time and cost of integrating applications.

Through the service, trading partners have access to:

- industry standard maps and interfaces based on the industry demographics
- customized maps and interfaces created from trading partner data that are unique to that industry
- trading partner profiles that include specific trading partner technical and business properties that are stored in a secure, centralized directory
- a central "thesaurus" to allow for the automatic data mapping of trading partners
- expanded content as it is made available from the trading partners or from industry standards-setting bodies

Figure 9.5 IMPLEMENTATION OF KEY COMPONENTS DRIVING INDUSTRY-WIDE TRANSACTION-PROCESSING STANDARDS

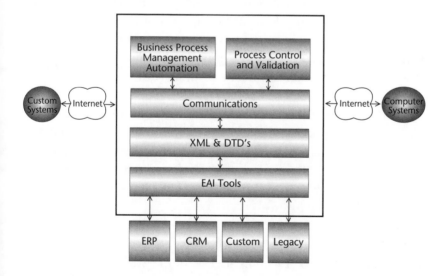

The values and benefits of translation hubs such as Contivo include:

- accelerated time to market of trading partner connections
- increased reusability of business object maps and a decrease in the effort required to create maps for the trading community

- increased quality and decreased administration costs to support the trading community
- increased collaboration between trading partners as expanded capabilities are introduced

Figure 9.5 shows the conceptual framework of the key components of the technology. The implementation must address the coordination of all of the components driving industry-wide transaction-processing standards.

What Is Driving This Trend?

Organizational growth, coupled with the globalization of supply and demand, is causing shifts in the composition of business applications. With the pervasive nature of communications over the Internet, global businesses are required to deal with:

- multiple divisions, locations and languages
- multiple business systems, technology platforms and databases
- new channels to market, including Web-based sales and additional distribution channels in these new countries
- unique business processes, customs and institutions that govern the conduct of business outside of their country of origin

Given these needs, the technology to deliver industry-wide transaction-processing standards will be essential to the success of collaborative, global commerce. When we assess the drivers in relation to the MIDST Success Driver Framework we see that, while primarily being a technology-based solution, this trend has significant impact from the other dimensions.

Market Systems

The hallmarks of market systems are the four key drivers of that system:

- to create efficiency gains for the firm
- to create efficiency gains for the market
- to great productivity gains for the firm
- to allow the firm to reorient its activities to a more productive use

When we assess the trend to deliver industry-wide standards for transaction processing, we can evaluate the *Market systems* driver as a strong dimension influencing this trend.

When effectively implemented, considering the specific needs for process relationship management outlined in Chapter 8, EAI and XML tools and technologies can potentially deliver efficiency gains and productivity gains to the firm and the market. Digitizing processes and information within the firm may allow the firm to save certain costs, such as purchase of paper, archival costs of physical documents, postage and courier expenses, and personnel costs associated with cataloging information. EAI and XML tools contribute directly to these efficiencies and substantially enhance them.

Efficiency Gain in the Market

Digitizing information and communications may also produce efficiencies in markets. If markets become more efficient, then prices for procuring a given set of resources tend to stabilize. In this case, the firm may substitute "making" for "buying." Considerable activity in "e-enabling" procurement seeks to capture the efficiency gains from the electronic market place. Again, EAI and XML technologies contribute substantially to these efficiency gains.

Productivity Gains

If the firm can increase output for a given level of costs or use of resources, then it might rather decide to produce more and simply maintain costs at historical levels. By maintaining costs associated with higher levels of transacting, a firm can increase its scale and be more productive.

Therefore, we would rate the *Market systems* driver of this trend relatively high.

Institutions

Broad adoption of a single data model and process model is unattainable. In any industry, a group of leaders will want to define a set of data and processes for a single transaction according to their own specific needs. Different trading partners in the chain have their own view of the universe and look at information in unique ways. As an example, even in a single industry, such as office fixtures, a chair could be called an administrative chair, a seating system, or a seating unit. The level of description for each item may vary as well, as may all of the other attributes and data elements for an office chair. The institutions that are very specific to individual companies in a single industry are hard to break down.

XML and EAI tools are being designed to allow for trading partners to retain their institutions, yet allow them to map and process the data and transactions in their own way, to provide a solution to the total industry supply chain, with a unique solution for each player. In this regard, XML and EAI can be thought of as beginning new institutions in the B2B industry.

Demand

As discussed in Chapter 2, the *Demand* dimension is one that entails the successful completion of a buyer's decision to actually buy. This decision is influenced by a number of factors, including the time it takes to purchase goods, the availability of a wide range of relevant products and the costs associated with executing the transactions (that is, the transaction-processing costs).

In this regard, we can view the trend to deliver industry-wide standards for transaction processing as one that assists in sustaining demand, and therefore the *Demand* dimension is a relevant driver of this trend.

By enabling the processing and exchange of data, this trend reduces the time required for an organization to execute a make-or-buy decision. By making the processing of this transaction seamless, instantaneous and accurate, the purchaser will experience a reduction in the overall costs associated with executing the transaction.

By facilitating and making the transaction easier, faster, less costly and less risky, EAI tools and XML standards drive a continued support of the Net Market and therefore sustain demand.

While this driver is important, it is not as significant to this trend as it is to others we have discussed. We would rate its influence as moderate.

State Policy

State policy is an interesting dimension that could play a role in shaping the features and functionality of the EAI, XML and translation hub solutions. Consider the issues of cross-border integration of trading partners, coupled with the unique and complex requirements for business processes, reporting and regulatory compliance that exist in the hundreds of countries and industries around the world. The need for industry-wide transaction-processing standards to provide the ability to create compliance to local government business policies could be a significant influencer of this trend.

It is clear that various countries have specific rules governing business reporting, taxation, foreign ownership and transaction reporting and a large number of specific needs. When a business begins to automate the integration of data and processes between trading partners across these state boundaries, it is clear that tools such as XML and EAI will need to have robust features and functionality to simultaneously deal with not only the data and process needs of the trading partners, but the local government's third-party compliance and reporting requirements for these transactions.

When we add the complexities of industry-specific reporting (which may be different in different countries), we can only begin to understand the level of complexity and sophistication that B2B entails. Therefore, the technologies and standards must be broad enough to deliver on these needs.

We therefore see a strong need for state policy to be considered in the assessment of this trend. While not a driver, the influence will be substantial and so we would rate this dimension as being important to this overall trend.

Technology

It is obvious that on many fronts the *Technology* driver is a strong one for this trend. As EAI and XML continue to grow and gain rapid adoption as the standard for communication and transaction processing, firms will be able to substantially improve upon the key aspects of access to information, authorization and authentication of transactions, and search/query capabilities that allow for collaborative commerce.

In addition, these technologies allow for significant improvements in the ability to post/bid, offer/match and clear, and process and confirm transactions. These characteristics are also fundamental to Net Markets becoming market efficient, the topic of Chapter 11.

We would encourage a review of the *Technology* dimension of Chapter 2 so the reader can fully appreciate the importance of this driver on this trend. We would rate the importance of this driver as very high.

Figure 9.6 MIDST SUCCESS FRAMEWORK FOR INDUSTRY-WIDE TRANSACTION-PROCESSING STANDARDS

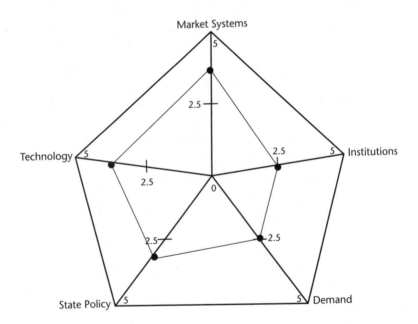

Where Is the Value?

The value created by this trend is among the most significant that we will see in B2B. It impacts on every dimension and provides the foundation for the future of B2B.

Market Efficiency

While this trend is not inherently about improving market efficiency (liquidity and price stability), it does allow for the market to become more efficient through improved timeliness of data and improved sharing of a larger quantity and potentially higher quality of data. As discussed in Chapter 2, market efficiency *requires* access to information and timeliness of information to be pervasive and instantaneous. Through the creation of industry standards for the processing and sharing of data, this trend contributes to the potential of B2B to make markets efficient. The impact of this dimension is relatively high.

Risk Efficiency

As discussed in Chapter 3, risk efficiency is created through the reduction in the variability of the five primitive flows. The key flows that are influenced by the implementation of industry-wide standards for transaction processing are the information flow, the product flow and the payment flow.

Through integrated data and processes, trading partners can significantly reduce risk and uncertainty in these primitive flows through improved timeliness and accuracy of information. In effect, this trend provides for the technology tools to allow for primitive flows to be fully enabled in a B2B environment. The instant access and processing of information enables the efficient flow of products, payment, rights and risk to the appropriate trading partner in the value chain.

Therefore, the dimension of risk efficiency as a key value of this trend is strong. It enables the value chain to increase yield without a corresponding increase in risk. As information about all components of the chain is shared, the risk of producing goods that cannot be sold is diminished. The risks associated with trust are also diminished. Transactional integrity can be ensured, as can the issues of completeness, authorization and accuracy of the transaction.

With these improvements in risk efficiency, we would rate this trend very high in terms of value.

Cost Efficiency

The cost efficiencies of using XML and implementing EAI tools can be upwards of 1500 percent. (Source: Webmethods white paper *The Business Integration Imperative,* **www.webmethods.com**).

Without the cost saving associated with the delivery of these industry-wide standards for transaction processing, we can see a future where it would be practically impossible to achieve any level of B2B integration and therefore any level of value proposition from collaborative commerce. Therefore, we would see the cost efficiencies from this trend as being the highest possible among the seven trends.

Time Efficiency

With the creation of industry-wide standards for transaction processing through the widespread use of XML, middleware and translation hubs, significant time efficiencies can be created. At the highest level of integrated collaborative commerce, the time efficiencies achieved in terms of conducting commerce become logarithmically large. Processing time, delivery time and decision-making time drop dramatically through the effective integration of trading partners and the automation of transaction processing between them.

While it would be easy to overstate the value of time efficiencies, it would be difficult to defend any position that would not rate time efficiencies of this technology as less than a full 5.0.

MaRCoT Value Framework for Industry-Wide Standards for Transaction Processing

Overall, we see the Value framework as detailed in Figure 9.7.

Will This Trend Survive?

Of all of the trends we have identified, this trend is not only the most significant, but also the one with the most impact. While the maturity of the software to deliver truly standardized transaction processing is still in its infancy relative to other business applications, the impact of XML and EAI on the development and delivery of collaborative commerce solutions has been felt in most major organizations in the world. Overwhelming value can be derived from the ability of trading partners to exchange information without human intervention and have this information actually processed by another system and the results returned for further processing by the originating entity. This ability allows for extensive sharing across the whole value chain in microseconds without appreciable increases in processing costs.

Figure 9.7 MaRCoT VALUE FRAMEWORK FOR INDUSTRY-WIDE
TRANSACTION-PROCESSING STANDARDS

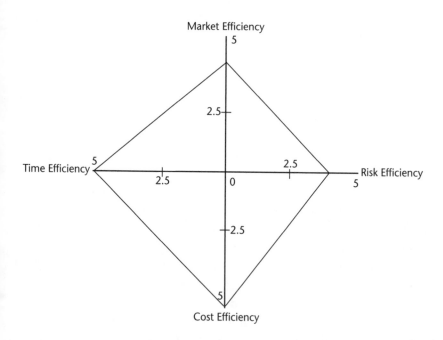

In the next five years we would predict that the rapid adoption of XML, coupled with the implementation of translation hubs and EAI, will drive a snowball effort in collaborative commerce. We see the major ERP vendors adapting their products to be able to be more open through XML and to drive interchange standards for the wide variety of business documents they create. Building capabilities directly into the software and standardizing common business objects will also allow for smaller organizations to adopt the technology and make collaborative commerce more pervasive.

Summary

The importance of this trend cannot be overvalued. A perceptive CEO would ensure that discussion of the technologies of EAI and XML are part of the organizational strategic plan. Points that should be considered include:

- Does our IT department have the skills to critically assess the various EAI and middleware tools on the market and their fit to our business needs and objectives?
- Where are the key opportunities to use these technologies and garner the benefits?
- What are our key trading partners doing and which technologies are they deploying in the areas of EAI, XML and middleware?
- Are there specific industry standards being developed (such as RosettaNet)? Do we have effective representation on these standards-setting teams, and how are we planning to implement the standards once they are finalized?

The CEO who has a clear understanding of the impact and value of this trend will understand that it *must* be part of the organizations' strategy and that investment in skills and use of the tools is essential to enable effective collaboration with trading partners in the future.

Whether the organization takes a slower approach (e-procurement and access to public exchanges) or a more aggressive stance (private Net Market creation), these technologies will be fundamental to the delivery of any value in B2B. Therefore, strong leadership in the organization surrounding the technologies and standards will be essential.

CEO's Playbook for the Boardroom

At a recent board meeting a board member conveys a conversation she had with the CIO regarding a move away from EDI. The conversation was of concern because the board member understood from it that EDI was a well-established technology in use by a majority of competitors in the industry. She did not understand how the company could consider moving away from this to XML, which was new and as yet unproven. Her perception was that the CIO was not sufficiently knowledgeable to make the decision and she suggested that the question was of sufficient importance that it should be put on the next board agenda regarding IT direction. You need quick answers.

- You begin by explaining that new technologies to allow for collaborative commerce in the industry hold promise for significant value over EDI in the next five years.

- You suggest that there are standards being created specifically for the industry and that the company needs to contribute to the team creating these standards.
- You ask the board member to read Chapter 9 of this book to begin to understand the differences between EDI and XML.
- You ensure the board member that there is technology in existence to convert between EDI and XML and that the CIO will consider these.
- You talk to the CIO to understand the internal capabilities of the IT department to embark on any XML or EAI initiative.
- You recommend that any move to XML be reviewed and the value proposition be identified and documented in a value analysis.

10

The Creation of Value Added Risk Management Services

OVERVIEW AND GOALS OF THE CHAPTER

In this chapter we wish to explore the issues of risk and trust in a B2B world, as we look at another of the seven key trends shaping B2B, the creation of value added risk management services. As discussed in Chapter 5, there are essentially six key risk questions associated with B2B commerce:

1. Who am I dealing with?
2. Is the commitment they are making reasonable? Can they perform/deliver? *(Product flow risk)*
3. Will the goods/services meet the specifications agreed upon? *(Rights flow risk)*
4. Can and will they pay? *(Payment flow risk)*
5. How much risk exists that the transaction will not be completed? *(Information flow risk)*
6. Can they be trusted to keep the business arrangement secure and confidential? *(Information flow risk)*

These questions drive the need for, and extension of, trust and risk management-related services associated with the exchange of goods and services in a Net Market.

These questions can be directly tied to the five primitive flows discussed in Chapter 4:

1. Product flow
2. Information flow
3. Payment flow
4. Property rights flow and
5. Risk flow

Understanding the issue of risk flow is essential in the reading of this chapter. The risk flow is, in effect, an outcome of the uncertainties created by the other flows. The risk flow is designed to address and manage the six issues above related to issues of risk in:

- *Product flow*: Will I get the goods that I ordered?
- *Payment flow*: Will I get the money I am owed?
- *Information flow*: Will I receive appropriate information to manage my business relationships and transactions? Will the information be kept confidential and private?
- *Rights flow*: Will I have title and right as promised by the vendor to use the products in an unencumbered way?

CEOs and their delegates continue to ask these common questions, and we see an industry is growing to address these issues in a digital world. These value added service providers are essential to the rapid adoption of B2B in a networked economy.

We also return to Chapter 5's "three overarching tenets" to ensure that transactions are recorded properly for management purposes: transactions must be *complete, authorized* and *accurate*.

A CEO must evaluate these issues from three perspectives: *trust, performance* and *guarantees*. These perspectives are overlaid on the risk flow issues and the six key risk areas discussed previously:

1. Trust: can the parties be trusted?
2. Performance: will the parties perform their commitments?
3. Guarantees: what kind of guarantees are given?

In this chapter we will explore these three key tenets and then discuss the new and emerging service providers that have designed services to manage these three areas. The roles of these service providers will be to substantially deliver on the needs of businesses for trust, performance and guarantees.

Managing On-Line Risk

There are nine key components of risk that need to be managed in a B2B environment, as summarized in Table 10.1. As part of a foundation in managing on-line risk, these nine areas and the related questions posed must be addressed before the CEO can be comfortable that the risks are being managed, that is, the CEO must *understand the definition of risk.* Note that the risks can be managed, *not* eliminated. The costs associated with managing risk follow a "law of diminishing returns" model. Risks cannot be managed to zero; at some point the returns on the investment are not justified to reduce risks the final few percentage points. The second element of risk management is *building trust.*

Table 10.1 COMPONENTS OF RISK IN B2B ENVIRONMENT

1. Authentication	• What is it?
	• Are the users who they say they are?
	• Are we dealing with the right people?
	• To what degree of certainly is identity comfirmed?
2. Access Controls and Authentication	• What are the user's rights?
	• How are the privileges implemented and maintained?
	• Is the user restricted to only authorized data/activities?

3. Application Availability	• Are application services ready when needed? • Are contingency plans in place for disruptions? • Is system performance adequate?
4. Confidentiality and Privacy	• Is stored information protected from unauthorized access? • Are messages (data in transit) protected from unauthorized read/write access?
5. Path Integrity	• Are messages routed only to intended recipients? • Is there confirmation that messages are received?
6. Non-repudiation	• Are parties to transactions accountable for their actions? • Is responsibility for transactions undeniable?
7. Audibility	• Are there appropriate records of transaction and access history?
8. Transaction Integrity	• Are transactions handled as generally or specifically intended by management? • Were authorized activities performed correctly/completely/on time?
9. Data Integrity	• Is the information reliable, accurate, complete and timely? • Do the data elements have quality attributes?

The Implications of Ignoring Risk and Trust

When people refer to the dynamics of risk and trust and their place in the B2B business model, mention is undoubtedly made of the concept of brand image. It is easier to relate trust to something familiar, something one may have grown up with (Coca-Cola), one's family and peers express confidence in (financial institutions) or even a name that is so ubiquitous it is used more often than the generic for the product it describes (Kleenex for facial tissues, Band-Aid for adhesive bandages).

If facial tissues were a hot on-line purchased item, Kleenex would have a large proportion of the market share. But increasingly even well-established, trusted brands find themselves at risk of being destroyed instantaneously because of the inherently insecure nature of the Internet. A good example of such a case took place in April of 1999.

THE BLOOMBERG INCIDENT

Artoo Deetoo, you know better than to trust a strange computer!
—See-Threepio, *The Empire Strikes Back*

April 1999 will go down in history as the April with two April Fool's days. One at the beginning of the month, which most people were prepared for, and a second in the middle of the month when Gary Dale Hoke took it upon himself to fool investors. Hoke was then an-unheard-of employee of PairGain Technologies Inc. of Tustin, California. Hoke created a fake news story, stating that on April 7, 1999, an Israeli company, ECI Telecom, would acquire PairGain for $1.35 billion (US), twice its market value at the time. Hoke posted a message on Yahoo!'s investor memo board, with an embedded link in it. As investors followed the link, they were shown what looked to be a real Web page from Bloomberg, a trusted site. Investors read and swallowed the story, since they had relied on the information presented by Bloomberg in the past, and PairGain stocks rose as high as $11.12-1/2 from a closing price the day earlier of $8.50. When it became apparent that the story was a hoax, the stock price dropped. As a result of the incident, companies such as Yahoo!, Lycos and, of course, Bloomberg, who had all diligently worked to become known as trusted brand names, suffered severe damage to their reputations. A total of $93 million (US) was said to be lost in subsequent transactions.

Defining Risk

What is interesting about the Bloomberg incident is that most businesses do not appear to have really learned anything from this event. How many people download third-party toolbar applets for things such as stock quotes and music players? Can these tools be trusted enough to base business trades on their information? How do companies know that their computers won't be infected with malicious files? In November 1999, RealNetworks Inc. admitted that its software had been secretly gathering and transmitting personal information about consumers' listening habits (Source: **www.ecom-mercetimes.com**). These stories illustrate the real need to identify risk and come up with a strategy to manage its many forms.

Risk comes in many forms, all of which are present when an organization opens its systems to the world at large on the Web. Before we progress through the issues of risk management and the services needed in a B2B world, we should clearly define risk. Some of the more common risks are summarized below.

Business Risk
Business risks include:

- *Fraud and illegal acts*: Companies are dealing with a larger (sometimes unknown) user population and utilizing new technology, resulting in new ways of perpetrating fraud or illegal acts.
- *Data corruption*: As companies open their virtual doors to the world, the chances of data being lost, stolen or corrupted greatly increase.
- *Reputation or company image*: Companies need to deal with their virtual image as well as their bricks-and-mortar image. Their reputation is shaped by their position on privacy and confidentiality and their proactive stance on the use of this information in the business.

Technology Risk
As companies decide to go on-line, the increase in business risk is directly related to risks associated with technology. The inability to effectively utilize technology to address the issues of risk directly correlates to the company's on-line failure. A key issue in this area is the risk of a company not having its Web site provide adequate response time to the users.

Process Risk
In addition to technology risk, processes that support B2B play a crucial role in mitigating business risks. Specifically, the processes that support risk-mitigating efforts include:

- technical processes
- fulfillment processes
- transaction fulfillment

Transaction Risk

Transaction risk is the risk that the hardware and communications infrastructure provider will unintentionally become liable for the business and information transactions between the ultimate buyer and seller of goods and services who contract using the providers' products or services. Infrastructure providers and facilitators include:

- Net Market providers such as eBay
- e-commerce enablers such as Commerce One
- e-commerce transaction management service providers such as Vitessa Credit Risk

Credit risk is the risk that a debtor will be incapable of meeting its obligations to creditors. Credit risk can be experienced from a number of sources, including:

- cash payments, goods or services owed by the debtor
- loans, bonds, credit notes
- supply contracts
- derivatives

The circle continues: for Net Markets to be successful they need to create liquidity, and to do that they must first effectively manage the risks identified above, which means they must be secure and reliable. Therefore, it is important for organizations considering being participants or market makers to take a broad view of the transformation or development process with a focus on risk.

As discussed in Chapter 8, business processes, applications and technology infrastructures are all influenced by elements of credit risk and the impact and associated risks need to be clearly understood and managed in order to make the most of the opportunity. The greater the sensitivity of the information organizations make available to more of the outside world, the more important it is to know with whom exactly they are sharing the information. The appropriate levels of trust, as well as the paths for building trust, will depend on transaction sensitivity and business model risk, which can be expected to evolve.

Transaction sensitivity is influenced by:

- the value of the actual transactions that are exposed to risk
- the confidentiality of the data being exposed
- the business impact of a breach of security and exposure to risk
- the legal/regulatory requirements to manage the data, processes and risk

Business models influence the level of trust primarily by their level of integration with the supply chain:

- A *stand-alone* system has no external interface to any other organization. (An internal system such as purchasing is stand alone.)
- *Buyer/seller integration* moves transactions between a single buyer and a single seller (as in a supplier connected to a customer via EDI)
- *N-tier (supply chain) integration* moves a transaction across and between multiple players in a supply chain (such as in the Covisant automotive exchange)

Figure 10.1 TRANSACTION SENSITIVITY

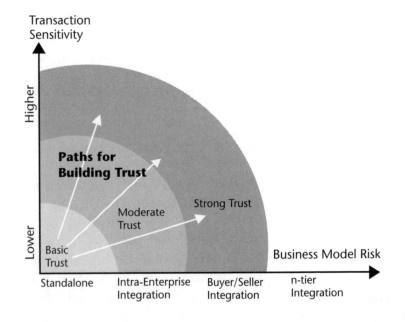

As Figure 10.1 shows, risk expands as the business model becomes increasingly complex. The ideologies and concepts of trust are becoming more important as it is becoming more common that trans-actions and flows of crucial information are taking place with little or no human interaction.

Harness the Power and Tame the Risks

The Internet and Net Markets can provide an organization with real opportunities to increase productivity, grow revenues, create short-term competitive advantage and reduce costs. The statistics related to Internet adoption and usage rates are supportive. In the summer of 2001, the Web encompassed over 1.2 billion pages, which were served from 30.5 million registered Web domains (Neilsen/NetRatings July 2001). During the same time, there were over 420 million Web users worldwide, 41 percent of whom resided in North America (Neilsen/ NetRatings July 2001), and within five years, it is expected that one-sixth of the world population will be using the Web (BizRate, July 2001). The statistics supporting on-line trade are just as compelling: Jupiter predicts that with total on-line trade hitting $1.5 trillion in 2002, $300 billion will be with new partners. By 2005, that proportion will jump to $1.3 trillion out of $5.0 trillion.

Traditionally, 90 to 95 percent of off-line commerce occurs between existing partners. But with the benefits of the Internet, Jupiter predicts that the on-line percentage will jump to 20 percent, a substantial increase in a relatively short period of time, which will require busi-nesses to move quicker than normal when it comes to building new trust relationships.

But in order for organizations to achieve these benefits there must be connections between new and existing participants, connections which not only create boundless opportunities but the potential for significant risks as well. In 1999, 90 percent of FBI-surveyed compa-nies had some form of security breach, with estimated losses in excess of $265 million as a result. Hacking attacks went from 12 per day as of May 1999 to 61 per day as of March 2001 (ICSA Labs, July 2001).

What Is Trust?

Most people place the concept of trust on a continuum where it takes on various degrees or levels. The word trust comes from the stem of true: *trow*. By examining the traditional definition of trust—"a confident reliance on the integrity, veracity or justice of another...A confidence in the reliability of persons or things without careful investigation" (*Webster's Comprehensive Dictionary of the English Language*, Encyclopedic Edition, Trident Press)—or the definition of trust we use in this chapter—"A firm belief or confidence in the honesty, integrity, justice and reliability of a person or entity"—it's clear that rating trustworthiness employs a high degree of subjectivity and a heavy reliance on a person's judgment. Another question that is worth exploring is "What undermines trust?"

Traditional business rules and relationships, which are foundations for the conventional business model, are not as easily transferable to the networked economy and are being replaced by business processes that are mainly electronic. In this new environment, who can be trusted and how does one go about effectively developing and managing trust relationships? Building trust requires that we address the nine components of risk in B2B as outlined in Table 10.1 above. The implications of each are explored in the following sections.

1. Authentication

Net Market participants want to know with whom they are trading and if those people can be trusted. If the Net Market is fraught with cases of misidentification and members being deceived, the market will lose the trust of its members and potential members and will eventually fail.

The B2B marketplace has responded with a series of new services from a combination of third-party authenticators, open ratings surveys and satisfaction surveys, Web trust seals and security tools such as public key infrastructure (PKI), which include the use of certificate authorities (CA) as forces that act in establishing trust. Third-party authenticators include market research analysts, such as Forrester and Gartner Groups, and credit agency partners, such as Dun & Bradstreet. These companies indirectly provide a form of credibility to market participants through their review of them. In addition, sellers and third parties displaying open ratings and satisfaction survey results on their sites provide another means for potential buyers to make more educated decisions in choosing business partners, such as seen in the eBay model. Lastly, CA WebTrust is a unique seal of assurance developed jointly by the CICA and the American Institute of Certified Public Accountants (AICPA) that breaks down barriers to e-commerce by assuring on-line customers that Web sites carrying the seal adhere to standard business practices and controls to reduce risk of error and fraud.

Companies such as VeriSign and Identrus provide digital authorization and certification services. Users and institutions such as banks are more readily adopting technologies such as smart cards and biometrics. A business model like eBay's, which controls whether the auction is limited to registered buyers/sellers, is most of the time relatively simple, as the majority of the auctions run through eBay are open or public auctions. But when the auction is closed or private, participation is by invitation only or participants may require some special qualifications in order to bid.

2. Access Controls and Authentication

Who am I trading with? Net Market membership and validation can be handled in various ways. One way is for the Net Market to sign up, verify and control the participation of its members. Another way is for the Net Market to use a third-party authentication service, which has the benefit of scalability across multiple markets, industries and geographies.

Authentication is extremely important, especially in the Net Market where anonymity is often of use to its members. For example, a party may not want its other customers, especially major customers, to know that it is selling its overproduction goods at a cheaper price through an on-line auction, but still needs visibility to leverage the relationship when a customer posts an RFQ for products.

Authentication policies and systems make up a set of checks and balances for verifying the identity of both Net Market and transaction participants. Authentication systems range from those that provide traditional user IDs and passwords to more sophisticated systems that issue and manage digital certificates. As the value of the transaction and the degree of trust increase so does the need to implement centralized authentication engines.

Access control technologies provide user access permissions for specific application functions and transactions. Basic role and transaction permissions will become more complex and detailed, which may lead to the centralization of access control and administration. It is important to remember that access protection extends security to stored information as well as to the data in transit. Access protection policies are necessary and stipulate how data is to be secured.

3. Application Availability

While organizations can possibly mask a weak internal architecture implementation from consumers and business partners, technical infrastructure deficiencies at an Internet company such as eBay would likely be highly visible and quickly experienced by customers. Moreover, eBay's business model requires high reliability and consistent response time, and competing in the on-line market demands a robust and flexible architecture with flawless execution.

Application availability ensures that application services are available when needed. With the proper use of availability, contingency plans will be put into place to deal with unforeseen disruptions.

4. Confidentiality and Privacy

Confidentiality and Privacy are generally addressed through policies which are posted and adhered to by the NetMarket. In additional, the use of trust seals such as WebTrust and the related "validation and auditing" of compliance to stated policies surrounding confidentiality and privacy provide assurance to participants that NetMarkets will have adequate processes in place to ensure compliance.

5. Path Integrity

Path integrity ensures that messages and bids are routed only to intended parties and are not inadvertently disclosed or transmitted to other bidders. It is important that when a message is transmitted a confirmation is also sent, stating that the intended recipients have received the messages. Path integrity can be achieved through technical software and hardware solutions that are readily available on the market today.

6. Non-Repudiation

Non-repudiation is a way to ensure that bidders cannot deny having bid and the seller cannot deny having accepted the bid. Non-repudiation measures ensure that parties to a transaction are accountable for their actions and that the agreement or contract is securely recorded so parties are precluded from denying their participation and therefore their legal obligation to pay for goods or accept delivery of goods they ordered.

For the Net Market to prove that the specified authorized transaction took place as stated, when stated and between the stated parties, mechanisms for non-repudiation are required, including authenticated participant identification, proof of transaction, data integrity, time stamping and audit trail.

7. Auditability

Auditability puts in place measures that allow the system to reconstruct an event by looking at audit trail information to determine who had access to the records. Auditability, basic application audit logs and data backup will all progress to more robust real-time transaction monitoring and event archival retrieval. Support for detecting spurious bids injected by an auctioneer or seller must also be made auditable by a trusted third party to help protect against acts like shilling (see the eBay example below).

8. Transaction Integrity

Transaction integrity procedures are designed to assess whether authorized activities are performed correctly and completely. These procedures should also make clear which processes are taking place and where, and ensure that the transacted and stored data is reliable and accurate.

Transaction integrity typically requires control points within applications and middleware in risk areas within processes that are open to change. As trust demands increase, end-to-end process controls are required to ensure transactions are appropriately processed across the application chain.

9. Data Integrity

If the Net Market, for example, eBay, is hosting multiple auctions concurrently, issues like reliability and availability of the site become extremely important, as the timing of the auction is crucial in both determining a winning bid and to the participants who may be working within a pre-specified fixed time frame. If the Net Market has a reputation of poor availability, the potential risks of not being able to make a bid or sell the item may be greater than the benefits received from the use of dynamic commerce. Thus hardware infrastructure can play a key role in creating trust as participants clearly relate trust to reliability and accessibility of a B2B site.

Appropriate Level of Trust Varies by Attribute for the Business Transaction

Figure 10.2 maps the importance of the nine key issues involved in establishing trust. In given circumstances, these issues vary in importance and therefore require a different set of focus areas for the participant, the Net Market maker or the ancillary service provider.

Figure 10.2 RELATIVE VALUE OF ISSUES KEY TO
ESTABLISHING TRUST

In an alternative view, we can explore the issue of trust from the perspective of the Net Market maker and identify six foundational areas organizations need to focus on in order to have a successful transformation of their operations into a trusted, secure and controlled environment (Figure 10.3).

Figure 10. 3 THE NET MARKET MAKER'S PERSPECTIVE:
THE FOUNDATIONS OF TRUST

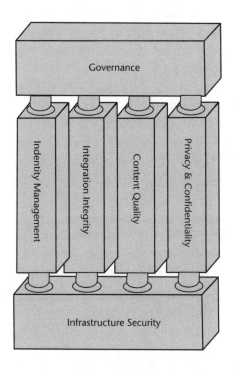

1. Governance

Long-term success will hinge on how well governance structures can guide and regulate Net Market management, balancing the interests of shareholders, members and outside interests. A Net Market must maintain independence from any single player or group of players. Aligning the Net Market too closely with particular groups of buyers, sellers or other stakeholders will stunt the cooperative effort required for growth and success.

How does a Net Market present seller information on the goods and services to buyers? How does it set fees? How such questions are answered can often determine whether buyers or suppliers benefit.

Since the only certainty is change, a Net Market must be flexible enough to respond to internal and external changes. Net Market success will be characterized by the ability to quickly shift direction and to capitalize on innovation. Governance structures must support agility and lightning-quick decision-making (amid what may turn out to be hard-fought boardroom debates). A Net Market must effectively resolve disputes among its members, many of whom may be long-standing rivals and not likely to agree on everything, and must provide venues for effective mediation and resolution of disputes, as well as provide mechanisms and guidelines for addressing competition between the Net Market and its owners.

2. Identity Management

Having trust in the identities of the Net Market participants is critical to the success of the Net Market and its participants. Identity management deals with the establishment of trusted identities by the application of policies, processes, procedures and regulatory compliance.

Identity management requires addressing two fundamental concerns. The first concern organizations have is, "Are we dealing with the right companies and organizations?" Company identity is the first aspect to identity management and requires capabilities such as:

- membership establishment and renewal procedures
- independent, on-line source of supplier/buyer performance and financial condition
- on-line services for members to select partners based on performance, financial criteria and other certifications

The second concern is derived from the question "Do we know with whom we are dealing?" Once company identity is established from the above processes, individual identity is required through solutions based on the three A's.

- Authentication: are users really who they say they are?
- Authorization: is an individual allowed to perform the intended transaction?
- Administration: is the security environment maintained to enable trust?

3. Integration Integrity

In a Net Market, it is very important to ensure that transactions flow accurately, quickly and completely throughout the value chain (that is, from buyers to shareholders to suppliers and/or other stakeholders). Integration integrity ensures that all parties involved fully receive all transaction elements and these are properly processed throughout the extended environment. Delays in processing, missing or incomplete data records, or erroneous data elements related to the flow of data could be very troublesome for any Net Market. Assurances must be in place for the business processes, allowing information to flow smoothly and quickly, so a weak business process in any participant's operation won't hold up transactions.

Integrating applications from the Web through back-end systems requires careful consideration of the integrity of that integration. Specific areas of concern center on:

- Application of middleware: consideration should be given to the integrity of business rules, development standards, and procedures and the ability to execute middle services
- Alignment of integrated applications, business rules, authentication, authorization and standards and procedures
- Controls for end-to-end integration: need to be in place to ensure complete and timely execution of transactions and correction of exception conditions

4. Content Quality

Data is the underlying ingredient in revenue-generating schemes for Net Markets. Data being used in a Net Market transaction must be accurate, timely, pertinent and current for it to be effective. Data quality issues, such as non-current part numbers for supplier participants, could impair the success of the Net Market. Reliable data is needed in order to properly bill for referrals, assess transaction fees and provide marketing data for attracting subscriptions, advertisers and tenants.

Content quality ensures that the information being used to conduct business through the Net Market is accurate and current. Content quality depends on data standards for the entire Net Market environment. As data is used to populate the Net Market, as in a catalog, it must be cleansed and reviewed on a regular basis. The ability to monitor data quality across the transaction chain is also required.

To address content quality issues, agreements will need to be made on responsibility and procedures for the following three areas:

1. *Data quality management*: Will the initial state of the data be analyzed and assessed? How? What data? How will data quality be improved?

2. *Interface and data conversions*: What interfaces and data conversions are planned (content, format, protocol, mergers, re-sorting), either one-time or ongoing? Do interfaces contribute to the level of data quality? Are controls being developed to convert data after its initial quality has been established?

3. *Data monitoring*: Will continuous interfacing and data maintenance require a data-monitoring program? How will it be implemented?

5. Privacy/Confidentiality

Information being used internally and externally needs to be classified and protected to maintain company and personnel confidentiality. Customer and vendor content should be restricted to appropriate individuals only, and steps must be taken to address the fear that unauthorized parties might eavesdrop on transactions. Companies considering Net Market participation want assurance that unauthorized parties cannot view sensitive business information, such as design specifications, pricing and inventories during transactions.

A lack of appropriate privacy and confidentiality within a Net Market may lead to loss of competitive advantage for participants and legal issues related to anti-trust or anti-competitive behavior between members of the Net Market. The following items are considerations in the determination of an approach to privacy and confidentiality:

- number of members transacting within the Net Market
- availability and sensitivity of transactional information
- level of Net Market supply chain integration
- complexity of information flow between Net Market participants
- nature of ownership structure/participant owners
- nature of information available

- cross-border privacy/confidentiality issues for multinational Net Markets

6. Infrastructure Security: Practical, Risk-Based Solutions

As the business-to-business Net Market concept grows in acceptance, the amount of sensitive data in play will increase enormously and rapidly. All these important issues will take on even greater significance, and Net Market participants must work harder to ensure the level of trust all parties need to carry out their business. Not all transactions, however, require the same level of security. As Net Market functionality and supply-chain integration increase, the need for trust builds up from a basic to a strong level. Each level has a range of solutions to be implemented based on the demands of the exchange and its participants.

Infrastructure security provides administrative and technical services that are the core functions necessary for an enterprise to securely deploy their business applications. By having a secure infrastructure it enables enterprise business plans by providing a trusted, operations-adaptable security model to appropriately protect enterprise information. A properly defined secure infrastructure:

- provides for controlled access that lets the right people into the right applications and data across the spectrum of a company's business initiatives
- builds a viable cost-effective management infrastructure that meets the objectives of manageability, scalability, performance, reliability, flexibility and security
- reduces risks to an acceptable level while ensuring access to the widest possible market

A secure infrastructure is developed through open standards and the proper balance of culture, tightly integrated processes and integrated technology solutions. Core security solutions and themes are used to achieve the desired "goal state."

Performance

While the aspect of trust is critical to ensure that business is conducted, it does not guarantee that the parties will perform as expected. An organization may have strong name recognition, great integrity in its business dealing and provide for all aspects of confidentiality and security. It does not mean, however, that it will actually execute a transaction. Daily, many trusted names in business make mistakes in transaction commerce. Their ability to "perform" more consistently and to find their mistakes and correct them is what allows them to continue to be trusted. In order to deliver on the expectation of the market, an organization must have controls and processes to ensure that they perform against these expectations. The types of controls and the issues with performance are unique, yet interrelated to those of trust.

The performance component of risk management is comprised of three main aspects:

- *payment performance*: ensuring payment is made and received
- *customer and Net Market satisfaction*: ensuring that the transactions were completed in a timely manner
- *trading partner performance*: ensuring that all parties were validated and all transactions were verified and accepted (the concept of acknowledgement is vital)

We will explore each of these components of performance.

Payment Performance

The fear that participants have when it comes to dealing with unknown parties and entities is "Will I be paid?" Sellers want to know if they will be paid from the buyer in full and within a reasonable time period. Net Markets want to know if they will be paid the insertion fee (listing fee) from the seller and the percentage of the transaction between the seller and winning bidder.

Most B2B sales are too large to be processed on credit cards, and require wire transfers, lines of credit, instant financing and escrow services. As such, an integrated network among Net Markets, payment networks and business processes of buyers and sellers is necessary to facilitate the speed of transactions over the Internet.

This allows new companies to be created to take some of the risk and friction out of the transaction process. Companies are providing real-time financing that is approved and delivered on-line and customized to each transaction such as eCredit.com. eCredit.com enables organizations to transform credit and financing into components of the business strategies that in turn helps them increase profits and strengthen their customer relationships. Further information on eCredit.com is provided in the "New Roles Emerging" section of this chapter.

Customer Satisfaction: Measuring Net Market Maker and Trading Partner Performance

Net Market participants want to be assured that the Net Market they choose to utilize will be in existence in the future. A good example of this scenario is the Paschall Truck Lines Inc. and Netfreight.com incident. The $132-million Murray, Kentucky-based transport company was the winner of an auction hosted on Netfreight.com, whose model was based on matching shippers with lowest bid carriers. The drivers from Paschall Truck Lines picked up and delivered the order, which involved a trip from Los Angeles to Florida, and later discovered that when they sent the bill it was denied, as the customer said the bill wasn't theirs. To resolve the problem and receive remuneration Paschall went back to Netfreight, which had, by then, gone bankrupt.

A new breed of ancillary service provider has been created to deal with these types of risk management issues. SGSonSite.com - SGSonSITEite, a division of SGS Société de Générale de Surveillance SA, headquartered in Geneva, Switzerland, is the world's largest verification, testing and certification group. SGSonSITE delivers a range of services that vary from on-line ordering of Inspection, Testing and Certification services to Standard On-line Service Packages and are adding tools that will address the viability concerns participants are expressing. For members who are putting themselves at higher risk levels, they can commission independent audits on the practices and procedures of the existing Net Market participants.

In an environment where collaboration between competing organizations is becoming more common, maintaining a fair and independent Net Market is crucial. In this case the concept of independence is key. Participants must be confident that there is a clear distinction between ownership and governance of the Net Market so that certain players are not unfairly advantaged. In this respect, Net Markets are attracting the attention of the Federal Trade Commission (FTC), which may in time specify new regulations for these Net Markets consistent with those already in place for the bricks-and-mortars. As Net Markets in all industries are created between collaborating competitors, one of the greatest challenges will be to set up the correct form of governance structure to protect each stockholder's interests. Solid and unbiased governance is required to enable a long-term success of the Net Market.

Specifically, multi-competitor Net Markets must:

- be flexible enough to respond to internal and external changes—structures must enable Net Markets to make quick decisions
- maintain independence from any single player or group of players
- ensure that interests and goals of the members are being met; governance processes must set performance criteria to measure management effectiveness and define approaches of improving Net Market performance

Trading Partner Performance: Guarantees

A successful Net Market is also one in which participants are confident that their counter parties will meet all their contractual obligations.

There are three areas of guarantees that all Net Market participants must address:

1. Payment
2. Quality
3. Legality

Payment

To date, few Net Markets have addressed the issue of credit support, although OTCDervnet, in the financial services industry, is a notable exception, having brought on board the London Clearing House as a central counter party, a structure which also exists at the bricks-and-mortar Net Markets.

With the growth and increasing need for B2B invoice and transaction payments over the Internet many vendors are refocusing some of their efforts and are entering the collaborative "order to cash" market. According to market research from Gartner Group, of the 14 percent of electronic invoices sent between businesses today, more than two-thirds move over EDI/VAN networks, while just five percent cross over the Internet. By 2002, surveyed businesses expect Internet invoice traffic to overtake EDI/VAN traffic by 31 percent to 28 percent of all B2B invoices transmitted. With this, vendors that started out by offering just payments (Clareon, VeriSign) are expanding their offerings (mostly via partnerships) to include functions such as credit management, invoice management, document tracking, document reconciliation and dispute processing. Other vendors offer links to logistics and financing systems by hooking up order-to-cash management services to shipping and financing companies. Still other vendors have chosen to focus on streamlining cumbersome manual processes for managing line of credit by automating line-of-credit document creation, transmittal and collaboration between buyers, sellers and financial institutions (Gartner Group: Vendors Descend on B2B "Order to Cash" Management, May 4, 2001, **www.gartner.com**).

Quality

To feel comfortable doing business through virtual Net Markets, organizations are demanding risk management services that guarantee that they get what they pay for in terms of meeting their quality standards. Testing and inspection services have been created to ensure that the goods received are the goods purchased. Some of these testing and inspection service organizations ensure the quality of a good by physically inspecting it and confirming that it adheres to various elements including safety, quality and regulatory requirements. Worldwidetesting.com is an independent third-party transaction support resource operating over the Internet. Worldwidetesting.com offers sellers the opportunity to pretest materials before listing them on the Net Market. The test results are then posted with the listing on the Net Market, giving buyers the additional information they need to make their purchases. Worldwidetesting.com allows participants to take advantage of the Internet's speed, efficiency and security without foregoing any confidence in the transaction.

Legality

Participants of Net Markets want to be assured that if they do participate that there is some type of problem prevention or resolution mechanism to call upon if transactions are not conducted as expected. Organizations such as Optika allow the right users to capture, store, access and direct the flow of documents and data supporting business transactions. When a faulty transaction occurs Optika provides buyers and sellers with all relevant transaction information and the tools and structured workflow to initiate issue resolution.

New Roles Emerging in the B2B Space

Companies are not equipped with enough information to make fully rational decisions when it comes to choosing whom they should and should not do business with on the Web.

The B2B market has not yet matured to a point where there are equivalents to the players found in the off-line world who help mitigate risk, such as:

- financial partners providing transaction credit
- agents or intermediaries who track or audit the rights, claims, and responsibilities of transacting parties so that non-repudiation protects transaction integrity, and
- Web-specific insurance partners to mitigate potential risks

As the issues of trust, performance and guarantees continue to be barriers to the rapid adoption of Net Markets, necessary new organizations have developed. These include companies that specialize in credit verification and assurance processes, guarantees or transaction completion (buyer protection), protection from liability (seller protection) and transparency for both sides of the transaction.

The level of security will determine how comfortable companies, their employees and their customers will be with the idea of integrated Net Market systems and how successful these marketplaces will be. Therefore, a Net Market's ability to measure and manage the systematic risk process will be a good indication of its potential level of success.

However, a paradox of security does exist: if the security is too lax and the Net Market is compromised, or becomes unreliable, the benefits accrued from the Net Market begin to erode and liquidity starts to dwindle. On the other hand, if the security controls are too rigid, the efficiencies derived from the Net Market become inefficiencies and the liquidity suffers as well.

A balance of security and trust is required. Companies must understand that as they move parts of their business to an open medium, they are accepting more risk, and they will need to learn to be better at managing and mitigating it.

Doing business on the Internet exposes companies to a host of new liability risks not found in the off-line world. In response, many organizations today rely on a combination of technologies that help in reducing their risk. At the same time, these organizations may benefit from new types of emerging intermediates specifically tailored to this unique environment, which can help limit their exposure in the event of a loss.

Endorsing Agencies and Rating Agencies

To help consumers discern which businesses are trustworthy and which are not, various endorsing agencies have been established. Operating in a similar manner to their counterparts in the off-line environment (where consumers depend on print references for vacation ratings, restaurant guides and movie reviews), endorsing agencies will provide this level of assessment of the trust, performance and guarantees to be expected in the Net Market. In the on-line world, the need for ratings and endorsements still exists, and some believe that their value has increased, because of the many new participants. Through the use of on-line rating and community sites, people and organizations can determine the reputations of potential trading partners by reading opinions of past users and visiting chat rooms and on-line testing sites.

Insurance Companies

Insurance companies offer endorsement by a "trusted third party" in that, if the service provider fails to deliver, the insurer will pay for the damages incurred. Traditionally, insurance companies dealt with risks that were mostly tangible and identifiable. Insurance companies are now required to deal with much more intangible risk, such as intellectual assets loss, for which standard liability insurance policies offer little or no protection.

Although insurance companies have been slow to respond, they do see value in the products and are now offering policies tailored to Internet-related businesses. Coverage being offered falls into two major categories:

- property (first-party) coverage
- liability (third-party) coverage

Property Coverage
Property coverage protects against direct losses suffered by an enterprise, stemming from insured perils. The insurance company pays the actual value of the loss of property, business interruption and expenses incurred in investigating and proving the loss. It is designed to cover the direct loss of electronic information assets, including data, electronic computer instructions, electronic data processing media and intellectual property, resulting from:

- unauthorized access
- unauthorized code
- denial of service
- denial of access (Source: Gartner Group)

Liability Coverage
Liability coverage is a type of insurance that protects against claims or suits alleging negligence or wrongdoing on the part of the enterprise. It is designed to pay defense costs and damages that an enterprise is legally obligated to pay.

Directories
In the networked economy, the flow of information is being shifted away in both time and space from the physical flows in a distribution channel. Participants have the ability to search, evaluate, negotiate, pay for and take delivery of products at different points in time and from different providers. But with this separation of flows and the ability to utilize a "best of breed" provider approach, participants are making a tradeoff between time and quality, as they must now spend

more time searching, evaluating and combing through information in order to make a decision. To right the balance and so that users can find the products and services they are interested in, directory services will be required.

Underwriters

The job of pricing the underwriting of electronic transactions will require volumes of transaction data in order to help underwriters predict loss rates. The most efficient way of gathering this data would be for underwriters to form relationships with the Net Markets themselves that gather such data. Such relationships would be beneficial to the Net Market makers as well, as by leveraging the new relationship, they will be able to offer insurance guarantees for all transactions they coordinate. When a customer receives a security assessment by an insurance company, an underwriter will assess a company's risk through a Security Certification Assessment. If approved by the underwriter, the insurance company will issue the insurance policy.

Credit Brokers

As discussed in Chapter 3, credit risk is a sub-dimension of risk efficiency and relates to the possibility that the counter party cannot buy. Participants require a trusted third party to manage the transaction settlement process, as well as a secure on-line credit and payment service, to help mitigate such risk. Third-party organizations are manually checking participants' credit and arranging and guaranteeing lines of credit. eCredit.com is an example of such an organization, and as identified in Chapter 3, using a third party is typically the most efficient solution as it limits losses to both participants which they might have been vulnerable to in the past. Through eCredit's Global Financing Network, they provide real-time credit and financing services to organizations by connecting financing to businesses to information sources around the globe. These services in turn help businesses attain faster credit and finance decisions and achieve higher approval rates. Unlike standard credit offerings, various third-party solutions are providing suppliers with payment guarantees and buyer authentication to protect them from defaults and fraud; two examples are Escrow.com and eCredible Ltd. The two companies formed a combined financial service that provides transaction settlement services, including the management of transactional elements and payment processes, through Escrow.com's TransactionPoint,^{TM} a secure settlement engine that automates all of the necessary components for completing on-line transactions, from reliable collection and disbursement of funds to tracking and confirming the performance of all transaction participants, including third parties. eCredible uses its extensive on-line credit verification system and global buyer database (supported by credit insurer NCM), authenticates prospective buyers and completes detailed credit checks to build a credit profile. If a buyer is approved for coverage, eCredible issues an on-line credit certificate to the buyer with an authorized spending limit, similar to a credit card, and backs it with the eCredible Payment Guarantee. Subsequent transactions are then covered in real-time by eCredible against payment default (Source: **www.creditman.co.uk**).

Quality Assurance Brokers

Organizations that choose to use Net Markets to purchase goods from long-distance sellers or expose themselves to greater risk by relying on Net Markets for critical components want assurance that the goods meet their quality levels and specification requirements before they are shipped. To meet these needs, quality assurance brokers have been created to help provide buyers with assurance of quality goods. But in order for these testing and inspection organizations to assure quality, it is imperative that the information used within the Net Market and for the transaction is complete, timely and current. Data quality issues such as wrong or out-of-date part numbers for supplier participants could impair the success of the Net Market.

What Is Driving This Trend?

The drivers of this trend have been reviewed extensively. Answering the six key questions surrounding risk, and ensuring that trust, performance and guarantees are created in a Net Market are the key drivers of this trend.

Market Systems

The four key drivers of the *Market system* dimension are:

- to create efficiency gains for the firm;
- to create efficiency gains for the market;
- to create productivity gains for the market;
- to allow the firm to reorient its activities to a more productive use

When we evaluate this trend against those four key drivers, it is clear that risk management services will deliver across all of them.

Through the effective delivery of risk management services, ancillary service providers can provide the Net Market, its creator and its participants with efficiency and productivity gains. It creates time, cost and risk efficiency gains for the market and for the participants by mitigating the risk of non-payment and by providing increased trust and guarantees for all parties. It also allows the member firms to reorient their time and cost in the area of risk mitigation as these services are provided by a third party that is focused on this task and will likely provide it more cost- and time-effectively than a firm could provide on its own.

With this increased information and the ability to manage trust, payment and guarantees, the firm and the market can become more efficient in providing stable prices and increasing trade.

Given this impact, we would rate the impact of the *Market system* dimension a high on this trend.

Institutions

The *Institutions* dimension has a strong influence on this trend. Risk management is a fundamental institution of business and as such the culture of business moving from traditional means to B2B Net Markets will look to manage risks in a similar fashion. Therefore, the creation of value added risk management services that provide similar, if not improved, risk efficiencies would be expected before significant liquidity can be achieved.

In effect, the institution being managed is business risk and therefore we have a paradox in that the trend is also to create a B2B institution of Net Markets. Because this institution is not currently in place for Net Markets, the impact on liquidity is that companies are less than forthcoming in using Net Markets, as they clearly do not understand how the institution of risk management operates in a B2B world. Therefore, the *Institutions* dimension drives the creation of the trend and the trend correspondingly provides the foundation for the institution.

Overall, we see the *Institutions* dimension as having a strong influence on this trend.

Demand

The fundamental premise of the *Demand* dimension is that it entails the successful completion of a buyer making a decision to actually buy. The decision is influenced by many factors including the time it takes to purchase goods, the availability of a wide range of relevant products (including information surrounding this availability) and the costs associated with executing the transaction.

With regards to risk management services, the *Demand* dimension has significant influence in driving this trend. By enabling the mitigation of risk associated with trade, this trend:

- reduces the risks and costs associated with non-payment
- reduces the risks and time associated with validating the ability of the trading partners to deliver the goods as specified
- reduces the risks of errors in information that is essential to timely delivery of the right goods and services

Ancillary service providers such as credit brokers organizations, insurance and bonding agencies and underwriters deliver services that effectively allow businesses to increase comfort and therefore increase propensity to complete a purchase. It improves the likelihood that buyers will actually buy by reducing many of the risks associated with the transaction.

For this reason, the influence of the *Demand* dimension on this trend is rated relatively high.

State Policy

State policy in the area of risk management will be a driver of this trend. Most governments have significant influence on the creation of measures in the economy to be efficient and ethical. Risks associated with non-payment, non-delivery and unscrupulous behavior are generally addressed through legislative means in most economies. There will be no difference in the Net Markets of the world and risk management services will be driven by this fundamental need in the economic fabric of business.

Technology

The *Technology* dimension is not a driver of this trend, but does have an influence in terms of the ability of the technology to actually support the trend. While many technologies to create trust, security, privacy and accuracy of data do exist, this whole field is still in its infancy. Much of the technology to secure an organization from piracy and hacker attacks has been delivered. Technology also exists to manage the security and integrity of transaction data as it moves between organizations. What has yet to be effectively tested and delivered is the real-time use of technology to validate all aspects of trading partners' integrity and return the result to a system for a decision as to whether to complete a trade or not. Most on-line trading systems today rely on a prior validation of trading partner data surrounding payment and delivery and therefore do not actually perform this validation for each trade.

The realities of a Net Market would in many cases require that this information be validated on-line, in real time, for *each and every* transaction executed on a public Net Market. While many organizations mentioned in this chapter are working toward this goal, there is not yet widespread use of this technology in a high-volume, long-term scenario.

We would rate the impact of the *Technology* driver on this trend as low, and the importance of *Technology* on delivering this trend as high.

MIDST Success Driver Framework for Risk Management Services

The impact of the five MIDST drivers are illustrated in the MIDST Success map of Figure 10.4.

Figure 10.4 MIDST SUCCESS FRAMEWORK FOR VALUE ADDED RISK MANAGEMENT SERVICES

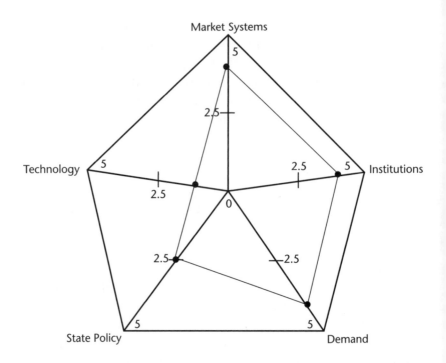

Where Is the Value?

The need for risk mitigation surrounding payment, quality and legality are fundamental to any business model. There is no difference in the underlying need for these institutions in the B2B world than in the traditional business world. Therefore, emerging service providers who can address risk management in these areas will provide real value in the B2B chain.

Applied to the MaRCoT Value Framework, this trend provides significant value along all dimensions. Ancillary service providers must consider to which dimension they can add real value.

Market Efficiency

Market efficiency (liquidity and price stability) is significantly enhanced through the existence of risk management facilitators who can mitigate payment and performance risk. As was identified in our prior discussion of risk efficiency, it is an underlying value dimension for the other dimensions of market, time and cost.

When a business can significantly reduce the risk of non-payment, or either non-delivery of ordered goods or services or delivery not meeting the agreed-upon specifications, market efficiency is greatly improved. Liquidity is enhanced since the propensity to trade (P) is encouraged through confidence in the ultimate outcome of the trade. Price stability is also enhanced as the prices generally fluctuate because of changes in overall costs to produce and deliver these goods. A component of overall cost is risk management. In the credit card industry, for example, the interest rates charged are significantly higher than those charged by banks. By collecting interest the card company attempts to recover costs associated with non-payment and passes those costs through to the consumer. The price of the service (credit card access) increases in step with increases in costs associated with managing payment risk. In many industries the costs of risk management (insurance, bad debts, bonding and other guarantees) are built into the overall cost of the goods and reflected in the market price. By providing a means of managing risk, the creation of value added risk management services aids in the creation of price stability.

Risk Efficiency

The creation of value added risk management services directly, and obviously, creates significant value along the risk efficiency dimension, as risk efficiency is directly tied to the concept of the risk flow of the primitive flows.

The risk flow influences the other flows: product, payment, information and rights. To reduce uncertainty in each of the other flows, the risk flow must mitigate the potential negative consequences of the transaction.

If an ancillary risk management service provider can reduce the uncertainty surrounding:

- the delivery of the goods (thereby positively impacting on the product flow)
- the timely receipt of payment (positively impacting the payment flow)

- timely acknowledgement of transaction being sent or received correctly, including specifications for goods or services being exchanged (positively impacting the information flow)
- the buyer's or seller's rights to use of the good or service positively impact on the rights flow (thereby positively impacting the rights flow) then it contributes significant risk efficiency value.

It is essential that ancillary service providers considering creating risk management services understand which of the primitive flows they will impact and determine the nature of the value created.

Overall, we see that the risk efficiency value created by this trend will be very high and aid in the ongoing growth of this trend.

Cost Efficiency

As suggested earlier, this trend's impact on cost efficiency is important. While the costs of insurance are not *generally* a significant component of the overall costs of a good or service, in some industries insurance costs, surrounding payment, information accuracy and rights, are substantial. The financial services industry, for example (banking, credit cards, insurance, mutual funds, brokerage), has risk management as a high component of overall costs and would therefore see the value of ancillary service providers' risk management services as very important to it in managing cost efficiencies.

While cost efficiencies can be achieved through the creation of value added risk management services, cost is not the most important or most significant value driver of this trend. We would rate its impact as moderate.

Time Efficiency

In most industries, the effort required to assess risk in a transaction is high. The costs associated with gathering information regarding a company's credit worthiness, ethics and ability to deliver on promises are quite high, yet not generally measured in a business. Site visits, meetings, market research, reference checks, credit checks and payment follow-up are all time wasters in the traditional primitive flows of an industry.

Were it possible to gather this information from a credible, independent source, quickly enabling the evaluation of risk in a particular situation, the time efficiency would be considered substantial. In industries where time is of more importance than costs (real-time trading markets), this efficiency could be still more valuable to and have more impact on the business.

We see the trend of creating service to manage this risk as having consistently higher time efficiency than cost efficiency in most industries.

MaRCoT Value Framework for Value Added Risk Management Services

Overall, we see the Value map as follows:

Figure 10.5 MaRCoT VALUE FRAMEWORK FOR VALUE ADDED RISK MANAGEMENT SERVICES

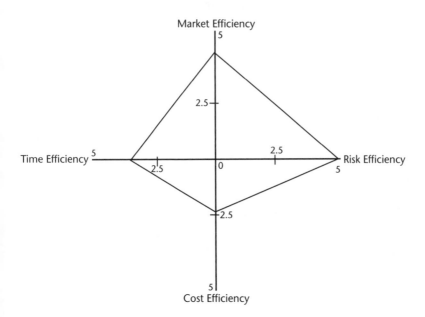

Will This Trend Survive?

While it is clear that the need for value added risk management services is a foundation to the future success of B2B, it is not clear whether the service providers will be created from the demand, or whether the service providers will, in fact, be a significant influence on demand.

Clearly, trust and risk management is necessary to the whole concept of Net Markets. As with the global stock exchange industry, ancillary service providers were created out of the needs of the first stock traders who required additional means to hedge risk and to be assured of payment on transactions. The role of the broker, dealer and other service providers in the public stock markets were not an initial part of that industry or its institutions. In a very similar way, Net Markets were not conceived with the thought of risk management organizations being a foundation for providing guarantees of performance.

Given the obvious drivers and value that have been identified for this trend, we believe that this trend will be strong and gain momentum over the next five years as Net Markets gain influence in commerce. The creation of institutions for the management of risk in the B2B world will be essential to the success of Net Markets and therefore there is a symbiotic relationship created between the success and use of Net Markets and the success and creation of ancillary service providers to manage risks in this environment.

Net Market Models and Their Security Needs

In order to effectively illustrate the concepts in this chapter, we will review the model of eBay, as one of the most successful on the market today. We will review how eBay establishes trust and manages risks for its participants.

THE eBAY BID/AUCTION MODEL

The day has arrived when you have decided to treat yourself to a new watch, but not just any watch. You choose the "avant-garde" of TAG Heuer, the Kirium, a watch you normally cannot afford as it retails for about $1,900 (US), depending on the exact model.

So, you turn on your computer, log into www.eBay.com and you type the words "TAG Heuer Kirium." On this particular day the site comes back with 39 hits and prices ranging from a measly $24.99 (US) to a whooping $1,350 (US) and the prices are rising. The question now is, which one do you choose? Who do you trust? Are you willing to risk handing over $1,300 to a person you have never conducted business with or even met? Even if the seller is honest, will the Net Market be reliable enough to submit your bid at the right time, allowing you to have a fair chance at winning the item? If these questions are hindering consumers' use of such Net Markets, imagine how businesses feel when the average B2B order is $50,000 (US) vs. $50(US)?

In Chapter 1, we looked at the business model eBay uses to remain a successful Net Market; this time we will examine the model in relation to how eBay goes about solving the trust problem with its participants: how does it get participants to hit the bid key and risk trading with a party they know nothing about, using a medium that they are unfamiliar with? In terms of transactions in 2000, $40 billion in on-line retail transactions took place. Of that, $565 million per month was transacted in auctions of all kinds (GeoTrust, July 2001). Jupiter Research estimates that 80 percent of buyers have made the extension of existing trading relationships on-line a priority, which means the other 20 percent of buyers have made it a priority to use on-line commerce to establish new relationships, where the principle of trust is the crux of the decision process.

eBay is a typical bid/ask model, which can be described as a double-sided auction where multiple buyers post their offers to acquire a good that is up for sale—the bid—and multiple sellers post their offers to sell their goods—the offer or ask. The Net Market Maker, eBay, creates the market in which buyer and seller are able to come together. In the conventional business environment, a complex system has evolved over many years and scenarios for the purpose of allocating risk. Through the use of established industry practices, various forms of insurance, financial instruments, contracts, laws and informal institutions, businesses usually can determine who will pay and how the creditor will be paid if the debtor experiences a problem.

Net Market Models and Their Business Needs

In examining the business needs requested by the auction model's participants, we will look at the following:

- viability of the Net Market
- identification

- timely process
- credit and collection mechanisms
- community of trust
- business information and creditworthiness
- qualified suppliers
- quality products and product information

Viability Risk

Users of eBay and other Net Markets want to be sure that they are not putting themselves in undue risk by choosing to use a Net Market that is bound for failure. Viability risk to individuals using a Net Market such as eBay is low as the initial investment is relatively small if not zero (depending on listing fees) compared to those made by businesses, with respect to integration costs, legal costs, time and sometimes investment costs. Finding information with respect to smaller Net Markets' viability is not an easy task, and as mentioned previously, public perception goes a long way when it comes to building and taking away trust. For Internet companies, public perception really is a double-edged sword. Companies such as eBay, Amazon and Price line were in the news daily, the creators on the cover of every magazine and the company's name a landmark. In 2000, if people were familiar with the Internet, and were asked where they would go to purchase a book, there was a very good chance they would say Amazon, a once unheard-of company. Because it was so well publicized by credible organizations, people came to trust it. The other edge of the sword was felt in March of 2000, when everything started to go downhill for the dotcoms, and people lost large amounts of wealth, and the newspapers were filled with news of failures. Trust was lost, and only a few dotcoms, such as eBay, have been able to shelter themselves from this failure and retain a large enough user community while remaining profitable.

Identification

Unlike B2B auctions where the risks are higher, eBay users want to have some type of assurance that they know whom they are trading. Due to the increases in costs and liability issues, eBay does not require a rigorous examination and verification process for its open public auctions, and works on the principle of buyer beware.

Timely Process

Bidders on eBay want to ensure that the price they agree to bid will be sent into the site and accepted real-time, therefore putting them in the lead of the auction. And at the end of the auction they want certainty that all submitted bids have been processed. Sellers want to be assured that the site is timely in that all submitted bids are processed, thereby leaving the highest bid standing. As organizations choose to use dynamic price mechanisms such as the auction in order to help them fill their spot needs for perishable and commodity goods, there is a heavy reliance on the Net Market's timeliness, efficiency and availability, especially in the case where the product is quickly decreasing in value.

Credit and Collection Mechanisms

Sellers on eBay want to be assured that if they sell something they will be paid in full (minus eBay's charges) in a reasonable time. Buyers using the site want to be assured that they will receive the product they purchased as described within a reasonable time frame. The Net Market wants to ensure that they receive all fees accruing to them (listing fees, transaction fees and, if applicable, ancillary service fees). eBay allows its users to use on-line payments, which go through BillPoint.

eBay enables sellers to accept credit cards or electronic checks from the winning bidders. Winning bidders can pay safely on-line using their credit card or electronic checks for an auction that includes eBay on-line payments as a payment method.

Community of Trust

The Internet is an open network of entities that derives value from its functionality and the number of participating parties. As more people participate in the auction, the buyer has a greater chance of finding the product they require, sellers are able to achieve a higher bid price as demand is increased, and the volume of transactions reaches a critical mass, helping the Net Markets remain profitable. To sustain this level of success, the market has witnessed the successful on-line auction models expanding to encompass communities of interest built around a number of similar or related business entities (eBay Motors, eBay Premier). Developing a self-sustaining community of interest in related products and services first requires building trust, creating a community in which participants can communicate and interact securely, without undue risk of exposure or loss of privacy. eBay uses its feedback forum to help establish a community of trust with its participants. The feedback forum:

- allows users and potential users to instantly check the "reputation" or business practices of anyone at eBay
- posts comments, organized by a rating system, made by one user about another, telling others about the trading experience

Business Information and Creditworthiness

Participants want access to information they need in order to determine both the financial health of potential trade partners and whether to use the particular Net Market for trading purposes. Companies such as GeoTrust, eCredit and long-term player Dun & Bradstreet are providing such information.

Qualified Suppliers

With such a dynamic environment, buyers face a potentially new supplier on each transaction. It will be important for the Net Market to provide a set of supplier criteria in a timely fashion, based on various elements such as ability to deliver, credit history, product quality. In the B2B environment, to help buyers accurately differentiate between potential vendors, a Net Market should enable participants to select trading partners based on multi-dimensional performance metrics. These metrics should also be used for initial and ongoing member participation in the Net Market. Participants want to deal with the "right" supplier for a given transaction, and they base their decisions on multiple attributes when determining the final transaction price and vendor selection. To make confident, well-informed purchasing decisions, buyers need instant information about suppliers' performance and financial positions. To enable this confidence, Net Markets must provide multiple levels of trust validation services to enable participants to determine the level of trust they want in their trading partners. These services must provide for:

Figure 10.6 eBAY'S AUTHENTICATION OF COMPANY IDENTITY

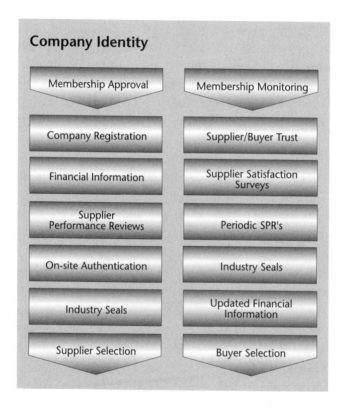

eBay ID Verify: Users' personal information is cross-checked against a consumer and business database for consistency. ID Verify uses a third party to check the information a user provides and verify that the information is accurate. After successfully completing the verification, the user will receive an ID Verify icon in their feedback profile. eBay is not verifying the information, and ID Verify does not guarantee the identity of the individual.

- an independent, on-line source of supplier/buyer performance rating, including financial strength. Rating services can provide this information
- on-line services from the NetMarket maker that allow for participants to select trading partners based on the supplier/buyer performance, financial criteria and other certifications that are available to them

- business process with supporting policies and procedures for establishing, maintaining, and renewing membership

A forum provider who claims to provide a screening of participants in the forum may be held responsible for authenticating the identity or commercial capacity of the parties. Therefore, it's important for a transaction provider to provide in its agreements that it is not responsible for authenticating the parties' identification or capacity.

Quality Products and Product Information

Participants want to be assured that the right goods have been shipped and will arrive within a specified time frame. With respect to the products sold on eBay's open, public Net Market, they generally operate on the principle of *caveat emptor* or "let the buyer beware."

Summary

There are six key issues in establishing risk and trust. These include:

1. Who am I dealing with?
2. Is the commitment they are making reasonable? Can they perform/ deliver? (Product flow risk)
3. Will the goods/services meet the specifications agreed upon? (Rights flow risk)
4. Can and will they pay? (Payment flow risk)
5. How much risk exists that the transaction will not be completed? (Information flow risk)
6. Can they be trusted to keep the business arrangement secure and confidential? (Information flow risk)

Risk is defined in five areas:

1. *Business risk*: fraud and illegal acts, data corruption, reputation or company image
2. *Technology risk*: as companies decide to go on-line, the increase in business risk is the direct result of risks associated with technology. The inability to effectively utilize technology to address the issues of risk directly correlates to the company's on-line failure. A key

issue in this area is the risk of not having your Web site provide adequate response time to the users.

3. *Process risk*: In addition to Technology Risk, processes that support B2B play a crucial role in mitigating Business Risks. Specifically, the processes that support risk-mitigating efforts include: technical processes, fulfillment processes and transaction fulfillment.

4. *Transaction risk*: The risk that the hardware and communications infrastructure provider will unintentionally become liable for the business and information transactions between the ultimate buyer and seller of goods and services who contract using the providers' products or services. Infrastructure providers and facilitators include:

   - Net Market providers such as eBay
   - e-commerce enablers such as Commerce One
   - e-commerce transaction management service providers such as Vitessa

5. *Credit risk*: The risk that a debtor will be incapable of meeting its obligations to creditors. Credit risk can be experienced from a number of sources including:

   - cash payments, goods or services owed by the debtor
   - loans, bonds, credit notes
   - supply contracts
   - derivatives

Building trust requires addressing nine key components, outlined in Table 10.1 and repeated below.

1. Authentication	• What is it?
	• Are the users who they say they are?
	• Are we dealing with the right people?
	• To what degree of certainly is identity comfirmed?
2. Access Controls and Authentication	• What are the user's rights?
	• How are the privileges implemented and maintained?
	• Is the user restricted to only authorized data/activities?

3. Application Availability	• Are application services ready when needed? • Are contingency plans in place for disruptions? • Is system performance adequate?
4. Confidentiality and Privacy	• Is stored information protected from unauthorized access? • Are messages (data in transit) protected from unauthorized read/write access?
5. Path Integrity	• Are messages routed only to intended recipients? • Is there confirmation that messages are received?
6. Non-repudiation	• Are parties to transactions accountable for their actions? • Is responsibility for transactions undeniable?
7. Audibility	• Are there appropriate records of transaction and access history?
8. Transaction Integrity	• Are transactions handled as generally or specifically intended by management? • Were authorized activities performed correctly/completely/on time?
9. Data Integrity	• Is the information reliable, accurate, complete and timely? • Do the data elements have quality attributes?

Performance is essential to managing risk. Organizations must assess the performance of the marketplace with respect to:

- payment performance
- Net Market performance
- integrity

Guarantees are essential to managing risk and organizations must assess the performance of the marketplace with respect to:

- payment
- quality
- legality

A whole new series of ancillary service providers are being created to manage risk. These include:

- insurance companies
- directory services
- underwriters
- credit brokers
- quality assurance brokers

CEO's Playbook for the Boardroom

Imagine you are about to attend a board meeting and your Chair raises the question of the security of your Web site and the risks associated with your company's participation in an industry exchange Net Market. How should you prepare for the meeting? What questions should you be prepared to ask? What answers do you need to make a measured response to the concerns raised?

Here are some points to direct to the CIO, CFO and related parties:

1. You recommend to the board that a review of enterprise risk management be performed to clearly understand the risks associated with B2B commerce that the company is currently engaged in conducting. This review should consider all aspects of business risk, technology risk, process risk and credit risk. You suggest that the CFO work with the internal audit department to assess the areas of risk surrounding trust, payment and guarantees. Specifically, you request that a review of current service providers providing underwriting, insurance, credit management and transaction settlement be undertaken to clearly understand the services they offer to Net Markets.

2. You ask the CIO to give a summary of the technology to secure the organization's Web site from hacker attacks, reviewing all aspects of security and privacy.

3. You ask the CFO and CIO to evaluate the opportunity for and ability of the organization and its key trading partners to use the services of ancillary service providers that can reduce risks and increase efficiencies related to performance guarantees. You also request that they conduct a

review of current risks associated with the specific public Net Markets the organization may be using.

4. You suggest that a review of various service providers in your industry be performed to determine the current status of their offerings in the area of B2B and to determine with which Net Markets they are working to provide risk management services. These service providers may include:

- insurance companies
- directory services
- underwriters
- credit brokers
- quality assurance brokers

11

The Maturing of Net Markets to Become Market-Efficient

OVERVIEW AND GOALS OF THE CHAPTER

In Chapter 5 we identified the maturing of Net Markets to become market-efficient as one of the seven key trends affecting the B2B marketplace. Within this chapter, to address the commonly expressed conjecture that Net Markets will evolve to become as market-efficient as organized capital markets, we first consider the basic characteristics of markets in general. This essential step permits us then to readdress what efficiency means in the context of markets. As modern capital markets are held up as the paragons of market efficiency, we briefly describe their key characteristics. Comparing and contrasting commonly cited categories of Net Markets and financial markets, we conclude the chapter with a listing of conditions that Net Markets would have to satisfy in order to qualify as market-efficient.

We seek to help the CEO become a critical evaluator of assorted claims that Net Markets will become market-efficient. The claim is often couched in reference to a B2B Net Market emulating a stock market. We seek to understand the conditions that would have to be satisfied for this to happen and for this to be desirable.

Defining the Components of Market Efficiency

The term "market efficiency" contains two distinct words, each laden with meaning. In Chapter 3 we identified market efficiency as something distinct from process or cost efficiency. We also observed that the organization of B2B Net Markets was permitting the simultaneous pursuit of both kinds of efficiency using the Internet.

Efficiency in the abstract is the ability to achieve some production aim by conserving resources. An indicator of an efficient market is a tendency toward *relatively* stable prices as the effort to accomplish exchanges is conserved by organizing a central mechanism (that is, the market). This does not mean prices would not fluctuate in an efficient market, since relevant information for the valuation of the underlying assets or commodities continuously flows. Prices of assets and commodities in an efficient market should vary less than prices of the same assets and commodities in a corresponding inefficient market. Yet, in order to appreciate what really constitutes market efficiency, we must address the bigger issue of defining not only efficiency, but the market.

What Is a Market?

Formally, a market is a device that allocates resources by enabling exchange to take place. Modern markets, in both practice and theory, are characterized as institutions that enable price formation.

Occasionally, markets do not succeed in forming prices that induce buyers and sellers to trade assets (say, money, on the one hand, and a commodity, on the other hand) or rights (for example, claims to those assets). When this happens, the price that buyers are willing to pay for some commodity or service that sellers could supply does not induce sellers to supply the commodity or service to the market. This is commonly called *market failure*. One could also view this failure as buyers being unwilling to offer their assets in the form of money, given the price at which sellers propose to supply the market. Suffice it to say that what markets do is *organize* the exchange of assets or rights.

For a market to succeed there must be inducements for players on both sides—prospective buyers and prospective sellers—to give serious consideration to vacating their asset positions or their rights in trade for positions or rights of others. Prices grease the exchange, and prices may be expressed in a variety of ways. Modern markets commonly use money prices. The money in which prices are denominated may be either private money that only a few players would accept, or it could be public money that even anonymous members of an economy would accept.

If a market is a human invention that functions to enable exchange by making it relatively easy to form prices, then what really are prices? Prices are values that players attribute to assets or rights. A price that clears the market is one that matches the values that at least one buyer and at least one seller attribute to his or her respective assets or rights. So, *market clearing prices* for any given asset can fluctuate, because the values that specific players attribute to the asset fluctuate, or because different players with different underlying preferences and requirements participate in the market at different times and places.

The reason this fluctuation is important to acknowledge is that the so-called *market price* applies only within the bounds of the market. So, what are the bounds of the market? Or, in practical terms, how does one define a market? A market is more than simply a collection of players who may have assets or rights that others among them may wish to acquire.

There are three basic requirements for organizing and sustaining any market.

Requirement 1

There must be players willing and able to engage in exchange. Exchange requires players to have symmetric intentions. At any given moment, there may be a surfeit of players eager to vacate a typical asset position. The relevant players in a market must have positions that are exchangeable. Some of the relevant players may have asset positions that are contingent positions, that is, their positions depend on the positions of at least two other players who are interested in vacating their own asset positions. We call players with contingent positions *intermediaries.*

What are the bounds of a market, and what determines who is a player and who is not? Unfortunately, there are no easy answers to these questions. Market definition is a blend of science and art.

Fundamentally, though, the way to expose the breadth of the market is to revisit the question of value.

Exchange can only take place when two parties attribute different values to the assets or rights of each other. Player A will exchange his Personal Digital Assistant (PDA) for Player B's $500 only if he thinks that $500 is more valuable to him than holding the PDA. Player B would agree to the exchange only if she thinks having the PDA is more valuable to her than holding the $500. It may seem difficult enough for one player to find another player with exactly the right asset position who would be willing to exchange it for the position he holds. Those who organize markets seek to attract players with different asset positions, betting that with enough players exchanges will occur. The more easily exchanges occur, the more liquid the market. (See Chapter 1.)

Yet, at some point, as the number of players increases, organizing exchange becomes more difficult. The values attributed to any given asset may vary significantly over the population of players. This often produces arbitrage, an interesting phenomenon that challenges the market's definition.

There are two broad reasons for arbitrage. First, prices fluctuate within the boundaries of a market if values that participants attribute to the assets exchanged fluctuate. Values will fluctuate whenever players satisfy their needs by an exchange of assets. So, the value a player may attribute to an asset of another player may be higher before an exchange than after an exchange. That is, some players become satiated: their need for the assets on offer decline after they achieve their exchange objective. When satiation can be observed, some players may have more information than other participants that would influence the attribution of value to assets.

Arbitrage can also occur because some participants move among disparate groups of players. This may suggest that an arbitrageur may have privileged information about values that players who participate in one discrete market may attribute to an asset traded in another discrete market. But privileged information may not be the *sine qua non*—it may simply be more inconvenient for some players than others to participate in two or more markets.

Requirement 2

There must be rules or conventions that govern how exchange may be organized and conducted. If two players arrive at the market with assets in identical quantities and qualities, then there must be some rule that guides the processing of equivalent positions. One rule is to have no rule at all: may the best player win! Another would be to require each to assign his or her assets for trade to an intermediary, who determines how to conduct the exchange for the assets. The intermediary's position is contingent on the positions of the principals. Rules and conventions bring at least some semblance of order to the exchange. Even in such colorful market settings as a Middle Eastern bazaar, there are unspoken rules and customs that effectively impose boundaries of acceptable behavior in the heat of intense bargaining.

In general, rules and conventions may specify processes, membership, times during which trade may or may not occur, conditions for ceasing or instigating trade, initial conditions for opening trade in any asset and the dissemination of information. An explicit example of how organized markets apply rules is the case of the New York Stock Exchange. The NYSE rules listed in Table 11.1 are intended to curb trading to foreclose wild swings in prices and index-arbitrage trading. The effectiveness of these rules was put to the test on Monday, September 17, 2001, the first trading day after the September 11 destruction of the World Trade Center. Early indications from Asian and European capital markets before the NYSE opened were not encouraging for investors seeking to vacate their positions, as indexes in Tokyo, Hong Kong, London, Sydney and Frankfurt lost more than 7% of their composite values. For the three days after trading resumed on the NYSE, the index fell relative to the previous close: 8%, 9%, 7%. After one month, however, the NYSE composite index rebounded and price variations became less pronounced even though the market did not return to the closing index level of September 10. Had the NYSE not reopened, it is doubtful that such price discipline could have been achieved as a consequence of ad hoc trades among investors.

Table 11.1 NYSE TRADING RULES

When the following thresholds in the Dow Jones industrial average are reached, trading is halted market-wide for the stated period of time.

A 1,100-point drop
- before 2 p.m. will halt trading for one hour
- between 2 p.m. and 2:30 p.m. will halt trading for 30 minutes
- at 2:30 p.m. or later will have no effect

A 2,150-point drop
- before 1 p.m. will halt trading for two hours
- between 1 p.m. and 2 p.m. will halt trading for one hour
- at 2 p.m. or later will halt trading for the rest of the day

A 3,250-point drop will halt trading for the rest of the day regardless of the time

These thresholds are recalculated quarterly and are intended to be roughly 10%, 20% and 30% of the closing levels at the end of the previous month.

Source: *New York Times*, 17 September 2001

Requirement 3

The market must have a venue where trade or exchange can take place. From Renaissance times up to the mid-1990s, the venue of most markets typically denoted a physical place like les Halles in Paris or the New York Stock Exchange on Wall Street. Since about 1995 (and the main point of this book), the market venue has typically become a logical rather than a physical form. Indeed, the Web site that presents the TDMarket Site could be on a number of mirror servers in different locations, but its appearance is logically a coherent, identifiable location on the Internet. (As we are writing this chapter, the tragedy of the World Trade Center has just burst upon us. Had market venues been only physical, certain markets organized for precious metals, bonds, commodities, real estate properties and other assets would have perished with the tenants of the World Trade Center. By and large, the venues of these markets were virtual and transactions were archived on mirror sites in remote physical locations.)

Prices Versus Valuations: An Index of Market Efficiency

In an efficient market, prices reflect without bias values of the underlying assets. This means that prices in an efficient market at any point in time would be just as likely to be somewhat higher as somewhat lower than the true underlying value of the asset. An inefficient market is one in which a pricing bias occurs, with tendencies toward either overvaluing the underlying asset (pricing too high) or undervaluing the asset (pricing too low).

Such organized capital markets as the NYSE or the London Exchange tend to stand up well to tests of market efficiency. The reasons that they perform so well exemplify the fundamental requirements: there are many players attracted to these markets who are predisposed to trade, there are clearly developed rules of exchange, and the venues are clearly identified and accessible. These markets are highly liquid—it is easy to trade on them—and the information costs associated with valuing the assets listed on these exchanges tend to be relatively low.

Can Net Markets Be as Market Efficient as Capital Markets?

There is one clear distinction between a Net Market and an organized capital market. The units of exchange on a capital market are investment instruments, such as shares of common stock. The units of exchange on Net Markets tend to be the physical assets produced and demanded for ultimate use in production or consumption activities.

Does this matter? Probably. Investment instruments, such as common stock of a firm, are in some sense products that are derived from a multitude of decisions that the management of the firm makes in the context of general economic events, competitors' actions, complementors' actions and consumers' actions. The multitude of management decisions should relate to the strategic direction the management intends for the firm to follow. Therefore, the value of the investment instrument should reduce to a proportional share of the discounted net cash flows of the firm. Net cash is measured in terms of a fungible commodity: money. That is, money can be offered in exchange for almost anything.

The physical assets exchanged on a Net Market have value that is rather more narrowly contingent on specific uses. Although a paper clip might be applied in numerous ways, a steam turbine may only be applied in one specific way.

To organize a Net Market in the physical assets probably means that the level of market efficiency commonly attributed to organized capital markets would be unattainable. The *number of players would be restricted* to those who either produce or consume the assets, or who would mediate between those who do. *The rules that would govern the exchange might have to be adapted to the underlying characteristics of the asset.* For instance, if the underlying assets of exchange were fresh seafood, then rules that addressed the declining values of perishable assets would be prominent. If the underlying asset of exchange was radioactive material, then rules that addressed the hazards of materials handling would be prominent. It is only the venue of a Net Market that might have qualities similar to those of the venue of an organized capital market.

The restrictions on players and rules that would be associated with a Net Market would seem to make it relatively easy for biased prices to evolve. Small numbers of players in the markets make it more likely for some of them to corner the market and thus drive prices high. Information costs may not be so low as those associated with organized capital markets, because some of the limited number of players might succeed in harboring inside information on either assets produced (for example, their quality) or on applications of the assets (for example, their fit for specific uses).

If a Net Market is organized with the intention of enhancing market efficiency (that is, achieving unbiased prices), then it would probably be natural for the organizers to consider introducing investment instruments that are derived from the underlying assets to be traded. This is precisely what commodities markets or futures markets are all about. The units of exchange on commodities markets are (standard) contracts for delivery or purchase of such underlying physical assets as pork bellies and cotton.

If the virtual venue of a given Net Market succeeds in attracting larger numbers of players, then it would be reasonable to expect rules to evolve that accommodate the development of investment instruments linked to the underlying physical assets. Such instruments enable players to hedge and speculate at a prospective profit.

Not all B2B Net Markets are organized as exchanges. In many cases, the driving reason for the Net Market is to secure reliable sources of supply (for example, e-procurement) or to optimize a complex array of inter-related activities to bring a product to market (for example, collaborative commerce). In these cases, the number of players would be relatively small, and market efficiency (unbiased prices) would be difficult to assure. The bounds of these kinds of B2B Net Markets are more constrained than are those of a capital market, and the motivating reasons for their organization are not simply to be market-efficient. Rather, the reasons for organizing these Net Markets are to reduce the costs of insufficient supply, on the one hand, and to assure delivery of product to destination markets, on the other hand.

Summary

In this chapter we have revisited the issue of market efficiency in response to the conjecture that Net Markets will mature to become market-efficient. We have reviewed the meaning of *market efficiency*, first by deconstructing the term. Efficiency connotes some conservation of effort in seeking to achieve some aim. The relevant aim is the purpose of a market: to allocate resources. The allocation tools of a market are prices, and markets succeed when they enable price formation. An efficient market is one that is characterized by unbiased prices, that is, prices that do not tend to be habitually higher or habitually lower than the values of the underlying assets that the market allocates.

Certain B2B Net Markets will mature to take on performance characteristics commonly associated with the paragon case: the organized capital market. These are likely to be B2B Net Markets that attract large numbers of diverse players, have well-established rules of exchange and function in virtual venues that are easily accessible. Other B2B Net Markets will likely be slower to take on key aspects of the "market-efficient" organized capital markets because they are organized for other distinct purposes. The organizers of these Net Markets may be willing to incur the costs of market inefficiency in order to secure supply from upstream sources or to assure delivery to downstream customers.

CEO Playbook for the Boardroom

Context: Your CFO informs you that your commitment to e-procurement should be re-assessed because there are other alternatives that would appear to hold more promise for market efficiency. You must ask him a few questions that will help both of you to understand how you should frame a decision. You realize that he may not have all the answers. Before either of you hires a consultant, you want to be certain that you do not give the consultant too much freedom to define the parameters of the decision-making.

Question 1: Is market efficiency really desirable?

Note: efficiency, generally, relates to conserving relevant resources in order to accomplish some goal. Your e-procurement solution may be just fine if it can demonstrate reducing certain process costs that are important to you.

Question 2: What is the relevant characterization or practical definition of the market in "market efficiency"?

Note: Markets are known to be difficult to define. It is easy to fall into a trap of defining them too narrowly, but should we be interested in reaping benefits of market efficiency because the market boundaries are changing?

Question 3: How would prices compare between the e-procurement solution we now use and some other net market alternative?

Note: Markets function to establish prices. Markets differ in terms of how easily they accomplish the establishment of prices that clear the positions of those participants who want to sell and those who want to buy.

Question 4: Would it just be a lot less complicated if we continued to use our e-procurement solution?

Note: Markets have three basic requirements: players, rules, and venues. If the rules to participate or the venues of a new net market are relatively inaccessible, no matter its promised level of market efficiency, it may be more expedient to either transact with an intermediary or to stay put with the e-procurement solution.

12
Strategies for Net Market Stakeholders

OVERVIEW AND GOALS OF THE CHAPTER

"B2B is Alive and well, it's just resting"....

In this chapter we explore the implications of the seven key trends from a business perspective on the three stakeholders in Net Markets: participants, market makers and ancillary service providers.

Throughout this book we have extensively discussed the drivers and value propositions that these trends represent. It is clear that the majority of the trends are currently having a significant impact on the future direction of B2B Net Markets. We have established the links between the drivers and the trends and have shown the implicit difficulty in creating liquidity in the marketplace.

Senior management must make business decisions with regard to Net Markets. As the three stakeholder groups have unique yet interrelated perspectives, we explore in turn the issues that each stakeholder group will face in using, building or servicing a Net Market. We will also provide some recommended "next steps" for each stakeholder group to provide some direction to management of organizations who are currently struggling with the implications on Net Market participants.

Participants include both buyers and suppliers of a Net Market and represent the single most important group in the B2B arena. Without buyers and suppliers, a Net Market cannot function. Participants must be the focal point of value and they are the essential "secret sauce" to the issue of liquidity. Senior executives who understand this and can find value in the myriad offerings of the B2B world can and should garner significant advantage for their organizations.

In a 2001 survey of 125 global corporations completed by Deloitte & Touche (*Realizing the B2B Procurement Vision*, Deloitte Research, 2001), the senior executives of those organizations provided some interesting insight into their views of the value of improving procurement operations. The findings included:

- Over 66 percent of those surveyed had created a formal e-business strategy that included specific strategies surrounding B2B.
- More than 90 percent of respondents have either implemented, are implementing or have planned an implementation of an e-procurement solution. Over 80 percent believed that e-procurement is critical or important to their organization.
- Over 66 percent of respondents expect e-procurement to deliver reductions in their spending by 5 percent or more, and 25 percent of respondents expect spending to be reduced by 15 percent or more through the use of e-procurement solutions.
- The largest challenges identified in B2B initiatives were people and process, not technology.
- While most organizations believe that supplier readiness for on-line selling is a key barrier to e-procurement success, the survey found that over 50 percent of suppliers surveyed have been able to offer their customers the ability to buy on-line. In addition, the majority (89 percent) believed that they were deriving benefits from e-procurement.

While these findings were focused on the global corporations, it is clear that the trends they embrace are
the beginning of a vast snowball effect that will have
impact upon all organizations in years to come. As solution providers see demand increase, costs of software
and hardware applications fall, thus fuelling higher demand in a wider audience of companies than can now
afford the solutions.

What is clear is that e-procurement is a mainstream
technology and appears to be the first stepping-stone
for most organizations into B2B.

Five Key Implications for Net Market Participants

When we assess the nature of the trends and information gleaned
from the survey results, a number of specific implications arise.
These implications are outlined below.

Business Objectives Drive Solutions Selection and Implementation Differences

The nature and complexity of a Net Market initiative vary widely. On
one end, a simple e-procurement project can be relatively small,
directed towards specific spending categories (indirect and administrative materials, computers, paper, and so on) and produce positive results. On the other extreme, they can be large, expensive and
complex, as is the case with building a private exchange.

One size does not fit all, and executives must consider options
and develop their overall strategy as to the needs, value and benefits
to be derived from these various solutions. CEOs must also have a
firm handle on how these solutions can be sewn together to deliver
value across the organization.

The Need to Validate Net Market Value and Performance Claims

While the hype phase of the market has passed, it is still essential for
organizations to validate the claims of Net Market makers and ancillary service providers. The creation of rating services and evaluations by major research houses such as Gartner and Forrester will

assist Net Market participants in beginning to have independent information regarding the claims of Net Market makers, but it is too early to rely solely on these sources. CEOs must obtain clear, accurate and objective information regarding the Net Market.

The information CEOs need includes:

- accurate data surrounding liquidity and transaction volumes
- a clear picture of the MaRCoT value proposition of the marketplace
- assurance that security and privacy processes and technologies are in place to manage risk
- full disclosure of the financial stability of the marketplace
- an assessment of the technology platform and the tools being used to integrate buyers, suppliers and ancillary service providers within the marketplace and to create a collaborative commerce platform

The Need to Move to a Process Relationship Management View

The impact on both internal and external processes cannot be underestimated. These process changes can be significant and result in substantial benefits to the initiative. Without these changes, it is difficult to obtain full value from any B2B initiative. In research studies by B2B software vendors and Deloitte & Touche, process redesign accounts for as much as 33 percent of the benefits to be derived. Without this component of the project being understood and implemented, value is sub-optimized.

An assessment of the organizational impact of doing business over the Web will also assist the organization in becoming process-centric and in creating a process relationship management focus. The move to collaborative commerce as discussed in Chapter 8 requires that cross-departmental processes be documented, evaluated and integrated into any Net Market B2B initiative, which also assists the organization in determining where it fits in the five primitive flows of an industry and the impact that its initiative will have on the organization and its customers and suppliers.

The Need to Significantly Increase Business Process and Technology Integration and Technical Skills in XML

Value in B2B is based on integration. The reduction of costs and time associated with data validation, data entry and error-checking procedures are significant. Substantial net benefit will be left on the table without the integration of data, transactions and technologies. Buyer and suppliers will find it essential in their organizations to commit to a level of expertise surrounding two key aspects of their business:

1. *Business process integration,* tying the organization's processes electronically to those of the Net Markets and its participants. XML is a key technology for delivering this requirement.
2. *Technology integration,* ensuring the ability to smoothly and seamlessly pass transactions, data and communications to the Net Market. The use of standardized technology platforms will greatly enhance the organization's ability to deliver on this requirement.

The Need to Understand and Manage Risk

As we discussed in Chapter 10, risk mitigation is currently a barrier to the wide adoption of Net Market transaction processing. The methods to manage the flow of risk in traditional businesses have taken hundreds, if not thousands, of years to perfect. In the digital age, these mechanisms have not yet been *created* in many circumstances, let alone been perfected. For the buyer or supplier in a Net Market, it is absolutely essential that a clear understanding of the impact on risk of using a Net Market be understood and effectively managed. While in many cases risk is relatively low (as in e-procurement or with private exchanges), it is never zero. There are a number of categories of risk that need managing, and the level of risk present in a B2B transaction is based on a complex series of circumstances. Senior management must be sure that due diligence has been performed to identify relevant risk, then determine the means of mitigation and put them into place. At the same time, the relative cost/benefit of these risk mitigation strategies must be weighed to ensure that the organization is not entering into a course of action that will lead to excessive costs in the area of risk management.

As with any insurance program, the relative costs of insurance are weighed against the amount at risk and the benefits of the insurance. In the same way, risk management in B2B is essentially a program of countermeasures set out to protect value against the overall possibility of loss.

In the years to come, we expect to see significant growth in the request of senior management and boards of directors to evaluate overall enterprise-wide risk, and expect that B2B and Net Market risk-taking will be of increasing importance in those evaluations.

Recommendations and Action Plans for Net Market Participants

Let's take a look at the types of actions that Net Market participants must consider in light of the trends in B2B.

Create a Strategy

Participants must develop an e-business strategy in general, and a Net Market strategy in particular, that takes into consideration their overall corporate objectives and the opportunities in their industries' value chain. They are advised to take a business case-based approach with clear ROI objectives that meet the challenge of the board and the shareholders, keeping in mind that these projects require people, process, technology and organizational structure to work and be successful.

Conduct a Thorough Spend Analysis

Participants must review *all* aspects of spending (any cash outflow including taxes, capital outlays, labor and related costs) to better understand actual spend levels and areas of supplier fragmentation. It is particularly important that all categories be reviewed, because Net Market initiatives can be applied to non-traditional areas such as taxation, human resource acquisition and capital spending. All business units should be covered in the analysis to ensure completeness, as should all vendors, who may be fragmented across locations and divisions. A strong sense of spending will drive decisions that are return-on-investment-based and that consider people and process issues.

Map Spending to Net Market Offerings

A clear understanding of spending will allow participants to do a focused review of the areas of opportunity and the corresponding Net Market initiatives that can service the need. Not all Net Markets are alike; the broad range of offerings from simple procurement to complex public vertical industry exchanges offer different services and different value propositions. In addition, the range of spending will directly impact the range of Net Market enablers required. Participants might consider mixing and matching the enablers to maximize value. The use of e-procurement software, a public exchange for auctioning excess inventory and a private exchange for acquiring raw materials at fixed prices may meet the specific objectives in the spend category and deliver greater value to the organization. Not all categories of spend require an auction pricing model.

Consider a Portfolio Approach

While spend analysis focuses on procurement, a portfolio approach to selling may also make sense. CEOs may want to consider connecting to their largest customers' private exchanges to drive a substantial volume of revenue, a public industry exchange to service their tier-two customers, a private Web site for their smallest customers and a specialty Net Market for discontinued or off-specification goods. The combination of solutions may offer them the flexibility to diversify risk and improve overall return. This strategy, of course, does not consider the issues and costs associated with integration to the various Net Market alternatives.

Understand Tools and Alternatives

The mass of tools and technologies available today are converging rapidly. Tools such as content management, e-procurement, Net Market and e-sourcing software continue to evolve and merge. Knowing what the genres of product can and cannot deliver and determining where the technical architecture of a solution is best derived will go a long way toward clarifying the issues associated with the technical components of an initiative. No single software vendor can provide a complete solution to all B2B needs, and participants are advised to be wary of vendors making such all-embracing claims.

Think Pilot

Finally, to build intellectual capital, manage risk and evaluate returns, participants should consider a proof-of-concept initiative as the first step in a longer-term B2B program. A pilot project, taking a full B2B initiative such as e-procurement and piloting it for a small group of spend categories (indirect materials, say) for a single division or location, can provide value while increasing awareness, building skills and creating a change agent for the organization.

Five Key Implications for Net Market Makers

Net Market makers will need to evaluate the trends in B2B differently than participants. Market makers will live and die by the value and liquidity they can create for participants, so their focus must be much more on the business model that they choose and on the unique value proposition they can create by carving out a role in the primitive flows of an industry.

The success and failure of Net Markets has been correlated to the viability of individual business models and to the value of the marketplace in driving liquidity. The CEO of a Net Market cannot ignore this fact. We have outlined the implications of the trends on this group below.

Understand Drivers

The MIDST Success Driver Framework provides a useful tool for evaluating the major drivers in an industry. It has been used extensively to assess the relative success and failure of a number of marketplaces.

We would encourage the leaders of Net Market makers to clearly understand what is driving value in their marketplace and to ensure that their organization is well positioned to support the drivers in the industry with a product and service that creates value.

We have written extensively that the MIDST Success dimensions are not always present or consistent in their influence. Influence will depend on the industry, the nature of the Net Market and its services, and the relative maturity in the use of technology. Net Market makers that can use MIDST to understand the drivers and then shape their offerings to better match the market will likely see an improvement in overall acceptance and use of the marketplace. Net Market makers that do not understand the industry drivers and that cannot carve out a role with substantial influence are likely to fail.

Focus on Value

We cannot stress enough the importance of clearly determining the MaRCoT Value Framework map for your business. It is essential in the marketing and delivery of your service offering that a clear articulation of the areas of value that are delivered is provided. As each Net Market will have a different value map depending on the service offering, the industry and its role in the five primitive flows, not all Net Markets are created equal. In fact, the use of the MaRCoT value map to define where value can be created and to shape the strategic service offering of the Net Market can provide a market differentiator. To support this value map, a detailed assessment of the five primitive flows of the marketplace and the role of the Net Market maker in those flows will be a first step in the creation of the value map and in the identification of unique services that can enhance value and create a unique value proposition for the marketplace.

Ensure the Business Model Works

At the end of the day, every business must be profitable. Profitability is variable, based on the means by which revenues are earned and costs are expended. The business model must support an ability for revenues to exceed costs on an ongoing basis at some point in time before the equity of the business is totally consumed. Extensive use of the transaction revenue model currently exists in the Net Market domain. While this model does provide for substantial profits and gross margin, it is solely dependent on liquidity. If liquidity is not robust, then this business model fails. We have seen this in many Net Markets, as discussed in Chapter 1. Other business models, including subscription fees, listing fees and agency fees, have been tried. While none has been a resounding success in the B2B space, we have seen success in the C2C space with eBay. eBay has proved that a transaction-fee business model can work, when value is created for the participants. The issue of an appropriate business model is complex and should not be taken lightly. It is tied to the MIDST Success Drivers, the MaRCoT Value Framework and the role of the Net Market in the primitive flows. Our caution to the CEO of Net Markets is that without identifying the inter-relationship of these factors on the business model, the possibility of a positive, profitable outcome drops dramatically. This is a situation most CEOs find uncomfortable and usually wish to avoid.

Independently Validate Performance Claims

As a mirror of our recommendation to Net Market participants, the requirement for Net market makers to provide some level of comfort and independent validation of their value claims, liquidity claims and financial viability will be essential to the long-term stability of the enterprise. Much the same way as ERP software vendors and ASP service providers have used independent research houses such as Gartner and Forrester to review and evaluate their products and services, Net Market makers would be wise to seek independent reviews and reports on the performance, quality, value and viability of their marketplace.

This validation could be a key strategic advantage to a marketplace that must attract and retain participants. As with the advertising industry, the Net Market business needs to use a variety of means to attract participants and then get them transacting. Verification of value, benefits and viability will provide a partial means of achieving this goal.

Become More Market-Efficient

Chapter 11 discussed the issues surrounding becoming market-efficient. It is clear that a Net Market cannot become market-efficient in the same way that the stock markets can without the broad adoption and use of the marketplace by a majority of participants and the maturing of the ancillary service providers to the market.

However, the key aspects of market efficiency will require several foundational components:

- There must be players that are willing to exchange goods or services. Liquidity is key and since liquidity is tied directly to MIDST and MaRCoT, a Net Market maker must know where it fits in the industry and how it will drive value for the participants.
- A move toward independence and effective governance. Many Net Markets do not have specific rules for governance or conduct of business. As with any efficient market, a Net Market should be able to create an environment where the participants believe that the

- market will set prices independently based on current supply and demand for a good or service
- all of the participants are operating on the same playing field of fairness and equity in the conduct of business

For Net Market makers that do not have the substance and form of independence, it will be difficult, over the long term, to create liquidity through attraction of participants. Participants must believe that they will be operating in a marketplace that is:

- not controlled or significantly influenced by a single buyer, seller or group of buyers or sellers
- not controlled or influenced by the Net Market maker
- independently run with a proper governance structure, including a duly elected board of directors that represents the stakeholders in the business. Governance, particularly in vertical marketplaces and private exchanges, is essential in building participant confidence in the marketplace.

While these items alone do not guarantee market efficiency, they create the foundation for a more independently operated market with rules and players. Over time the creation of ancillary service providers can broaden the market and allow for classic risk management and market services such as hedging to be created.

Recommendations and Action Plans for Net Market Makers

Let's take a look at the types of actions that Net Market makers must consider in light of the trends in B2B.

Strategically Define Your Value Proposition

Of all the concepts, issues and trends discussed in this book, the one of most importance and significance to Net Market makers is the definition of value and the use of the MaRCoT Value Framework to do so. Each Net Market can, and will, have a unique value proposition in the market. An organization's value and role might currently be weak on many of the MaRCoT dimensions. By knowing and understanding this, the CEO can make adjustments, create new value and move the organization along a path to building liquidity. Knowing where one is is the first step to knowing where one is going. MaRCoT can help in that journey.

Determine Your Role in the Primitive Flows

The role of the five primitive flows in business is a foundational concept that applies to all industries and all forms of business. Net Market makers, by their very nature, cause a "ripple" in the flows. In fact, Net Markets are specifically created to influence one or more of the primitive flows. Interestingly, most market makers could not clearly articulate *where* and *how* they impact the five primitive flows. Generally, they have focused on the "value propositions" of MaRCoT with most of the emphasis on *cost* and *time*.

The closest that Net Market makers come to discussing primitive flows is around disintermediation, which is an impact on primitive flows, yet a broader and more complex one. It is always assumed that disintermediation is good, yet we know that intermediation and staying in the middle of the middleman market is not always a bad idea.

It would be prudent and advisable that Net Market makers formally review, document and understand the five primitive flows that exist in their industry or market in which they wish to play, then to review, document and understand the *role* that the Net Market makers want to take in the marketplace *and* how they will influence the primitive flows. Net Market makers must clearly understand not only how they may have influence, but also whether this influence will have a positive or negative impact on MaRCoT and MIDST. Finally, it is essential to the ultimate success of the Net Market to determine the degree of shift that might need to be made in the service offering to line up MaRCoT value, MIDST drivers and the influence on the primitive flows.

Understand Business Process Needs of Participants

Tied directly to the primitive flows, part of the external world for participants, will be the internal processes and control points that a participant requires inside the four walls of their business. Clearly, an understanding of the challenges participants face every day in delivering their own value to the market will allow the Net Market maker to see potential areas for value creation. Focusing on the internal processes of the participants will provide a key source of ideas and allow the Net Market maker to better understand what products and services can satisfy a latent need in the industry.

Since all businesses have real issues with internal processes, they will have even larger issues with external process management. A Net Market maker that can leverage this potential pain and integrate more and more business process management into their offering will drive a higher value proposition to participants. By becoming an industry process hub that not only manages the data and the transaction, but manages the effective execution of all of the intermediate processes for all participants, a Net Market maker can reduce or eliminate the time-consuming and costly exercise outlined in Chapter 8 for all of its participants. Now we are talking value!

Micro thinking about participant processes is just as important as macro thinking about the industry processes.

Validate Your Business Model

We continue to see failure in the market due to poor business models. If one thing is clear, most Net Market makers ignored basic business concepts of revenue and cost when they got started. The whole concept of the "network effect" and the potential exponential growth in transaction volumes certainly supported the idea that "making it up on volume" was the way in which profits would be generated. Clearly, a business must be able to support its costs with revenues based on some form of revenue model that is directly related not only to costs, but also to market volume. Many businesses can scale their operations and costs to meet demand. Many businesses grow costs *only* when revenues support that need. Net Market makers must face the economic reality of revenues, costs and investment and be realistic regarding the likelihood of sufficient gross margin being generated to support the business.

If the model does not work at some reasonably low level of volume (as was the case with Chemed and Bisbee), Net Market makers need to change the model of how revenues are generated or get out of the business. Though directly linked to the liquidity issues, this is a different issue. A business model based on transaction revenues may not be the right model for the industry. A business model based on being the middleman and making a margin may be right (but not likely if it is at a six percent gross margin). Whatever the model, it must be realistic and supportable by the industry.

eBay has found a model that works, and it is based on transaction fees. However, not every industry wants an eBay or has the MIDST and MaRCoT dimensions to support one. Just because eBay's business model is successful in their industry and market, does not mean it will work for somebody else.

Think About Connecting

Of the seven trends in B2B discussed, the trend with the greatest short-term benefit and impact to Net Market makers is the formation of exchange-to-exchange Net Markets. For all of the reasons outlined in Chapter 7, there is potential for a Net Market maker to quickly and relatively easily increase reach, value and liquidity through collaboration with other Net Markets in the industry. As part of their overall strategic review and assessment of MaRCoT value, Net Market makers should take a larger view of how other Net Markets in the industry provide value and identify where connections can be made.

A second component of connection is the integration of transactional data for suppliers and buyers. The single greatest value for participants is found in the benefits derived from integration of transaction data from their suppliers and their customers. Integrating is complex, time-consuming and costly. The Net Market makers that can make this process easier, faster, and cheaper will be able to position themselves for real value delivery. Once again, this area has been either avoided or forgotten by Net Market makers as a key issue and source of value. While it is a difficult area due to the issues outlined in Chapter 9, the ongoing maturity of the XML standards and their adoption by major suppliers and buyers in many industries will help to solve the problem.

Address Risk

On-line buying and selling has risk associated with it. Risk is generally the most ignored of the MaRCoT dimensions, though risk mitigation has the potential to provide the most value to *and* the highest resonance with participants. When Net Market makers evaluate their role in the market, the MIDST drivers and where value may emanate, they need to think of risk—not only in terms of delivering value on the risk dimension, but of providing sufficient information in marketing literature, white papers and third-party evaluations to clearly address risk in the industry and on how their Net Market deals with and provides value in the area of risk.

Five Key Implications for Net Market Ancillary Service Providers

Know Where You Fit

This comment applies to all Net Market participants but most importantly to ancillary service providers. Knowing where their organizations fit in the five primitive flows is as or more important for them as it is for Net Market makers. By knowing where they currently fit, they can move their organization to where they need to be in order to satisfy a specific unmet need of the industry.

A more difficult challenge for ancillary service providers is to understand where they fit with Net Market makers and how to work alongside them to increase the overall value proposition of the offering. Their challenge is in dancing the fine line between collaboration and competition with the marketplace.

Create a Compelling Value Proposition

Everything we said for Net Market makers applies equally to ancillary service providers.

Pick Your Partners Well

A unique issue for ancillary service providers is created by their ability to offer services to a wide variety of Net Markets. Those in the insurance, credit check and logistics areas could find themselves with the opportunity to connect with many types of horizontal, vertical and specialized marketplaces. While this abundance of choice can be appealing, it can also be fraught with business risk landmines. As we have seen, not all Net Markets are created equal with regards to value and liquidity. Association with Net Markets that fail to deliver participants can and will have a direct impact on business and success. Therefore, the ancillary service provider is urged to review the Net Market partners' value propositions, roles in the primitive flows and the overall drivers in the industry they serve. Steering clear of potential failures will obviously limit risk and ensures that focus is trained on those Net Markets that can deliver customers for their services.

Market Directly to Participants

The symbiotic relationship between Net Market makers and ancillary service providers may lead many to believe that the right partnership will reduce the overall costs of marketing. Ancillary service providers should not leave the delivery of the message surrounding their services or value to Net Market makers. Ancillary service providers *must* be front and center to all participants with their messages. In this regard, private labeling of services may not be the best approach to the market for ancillary service providers. If this is the route chosen, they need to ensure that sufficient marketing of the specific value is directed to the participants.

Reduce Participant Risk

Ancillary service providers, too, may look at the risk dimension as an opportunity to provide value. Ancillary service providers have the opportunity to provide unique services that currently do not exist in the B2B world. Looking at the organized capital markets and attempting to correlate their maturity and offerings to equivalent offerings required in the B2B space could yield some interesting business opportunities.

Recommendations and Action Plans for Net Market Ancillary Service Providers

Let's take a look at the types of actions that Net Market ancillary service providers must consider in light of the trends in B2B.

Determine Role in Primitive Flows

Again, knowing one's role in the primitive flows is essential for an ancillary service provider. In addition to the comments we have directed to Net Market makers above, we would add that ancillary service providers need to know the role their organizations play *and* the role played by the Net Markets in which they will be offering their services.

Evaluate and Articulate Value

The comments to Net Market makers apply equally to ancillary service providers. A clear understanding of both primitive flows and the value proposition of the Net Market maker is essential to success.

Enable Liquidity

For the foreseeable future liquidity will continue to be the challenge for all Net Market makers. A real opportunity for ancillary service providers will be to assist in the creation of liquidity. Services that build, enhance or drive liquidity for a Net Market are sure to be winners in the next few years.

Create a Net Market

If their organizations can service broad, horizontal sets of Net Markets, ancillary service providers might think about creating their own Net Markets and linking to other exchanges as service providers with their own identities and controls. Some services such as XML translation, bank clearing and process management could be offered through a central Net Market that is connected to other ancillary service providers.

The concepts of MIDST, MaRCoT and primitive flows apply in this case as well.

Summary

The value and benefits of Net Markets will take years to gel and solidify. As with any new, discontinuous improvement in business and technology, the impact and adoption take substantially longer than anyone expects. Unexpected shifts happen that take a technology or trend in a different direction. We will briefly explore how unexpected events might impact B2B in the next, and concluding, chapter.

Conclusion

September 11, 2001

At the time of writing this book, the future of B2B was not clear. We had prepared an assessment of possible outcomes and future directions of B2B based on current trends and several possible scenarios in the changing landscape.

Unfortunately, the events of September 11, 2001, had a direct impact on us, our firm, the economy and the B2B industry. The impacts of these events are much more significant and dramatic on humankind and our quest for peace and the creation of a more civilized world than on B2B. However, September 11 created a real-life case study on which to test the concepts of B2B outlined in this book and to allow for the application of the MIDST Success framework upon a situation filled with potential challenges to the B2B model. From this analysis, we can, at the very least, glimpse the potential values that Net Markets may deliver in a world filled with pervasive change.

A Validation of MIDST

The new B2B models and systems have demonstrated a remarkable resiliency in the face of the September 11 tragedy. Indeed, had the destruction of the World Trade Center towers happened before 1990, would the disruptions in business-to-business market systems have been significantly more pronounced?

We have assessed the impact through the use of the MIDST framework.

Technology

The technology supporting the B2B domain is fundamentally the Internet. As a public infrastructure—a network of networks—there is redundancy engineered into the technology: data and information may be archived at minimal incremental cost in multiple locations and transactions may be conducted on different servers at different physical locations or mirror sites for any given enterprise. Hence, destruction of one or a small number of nodes would probably not bring the system down. While the New York Stock Exchange was closed for several days after September 11, it is generally reported that its closure was due to the damage to the surrounding area, which restricted access to the streets for most employees of the exchange. Security had to be put in place and structural damage to buildings in the area had to be reviewed. It was not reported that technology damage had caused the NYSE to shut down.

Many of the organizations located in the World Trade Center were also able to relatively quickly get "back to work" including many of those directly related to providing ancillary services to the NYSE.

The ability for future enterprises to conduct business over the redundant infrastructure of the Internet on a Net Market could provide significant benefits in protecting the viability of business operations in times of crisis.

The use of technology in the conduct of business will be accelerated by this event. On a simple level, the use of voice mail, e-mail and video conferencing will grow in response to the new challenges surrounding air travel.

This event provided a real-life lens through which to view again the reason the Internet was created. In war times, it could provide a means of communication that would be very difficult, if not impossible, to knock out. Mission accomplished.

Institutions

Exploiting the potential of the technology, the business models (one example of the institutions) have supported redundancy—hence resiliency. That is, it has become customary to build the business systems on top of technology standards such as TCP/IP, to create mirror sites, and in many cases, to realize revenues away from money centers such as New York City for tax reasons. While tax reasons were one of the top reasons for separation of technology (Web servers, and so on) from actual business market and operations, there is now a second, more profound and real, reason.

Additionally, various formal institutions associated with the organizing of markets, such as the NYSE, chose to halt trading temporarily to permit the reinstatement of an orderly conduct of exchange.

The implications on Institutions of September 11 will be significant as CEOs and business leaders look to protect their businesses and make contingency plans for their people and organizations. There will be a direct challenge to institutions such as air travel and face-to-face meetings that are woven into the fabric of such industries as consulting.

We, as a firm, have been challenged to change our institutions surrounding travel and the way in which consulting projects are conducted. These institutions in the consulting industry will change, and will lead to new applications of technology and B2B for our industry and our clients.

We challenge you to look at your industry and challenge time tested institutions, which may be altered by the events of September 11.

State Policy

Given the significance of the markets affected by the September 11 tragedy, Federal, State and the New York municipal governments responded by creating protections, providing insurance and infusing capital into affected elements of the market system. We will see increased injection of state policy into a number of industries that have been economically impacted by the tragedy. In such an event, the increase in the influence of state is expected and necessary. The downstream effect will be, at least for a period of time, an increase in the influence of *State policy* on the economy and, by conjecture, on the B2B marketplace.

Demand

Demand throughout most market systems was seriously affected by the events of September 11. The uncertainty of market outcomes over even a relatively short planning horizon encouraged buyers at all levels to consider deferring purchases. The tragedy exacerbated a contraction of the economy that was apparently already in motion. The standard mechanism of responding to declining demand is for suppliers ultimately to reduce prices so that demand might be re-stimulated. Net Markets offer the ability for *Demand* to be stimulated much more quickly than through traditional means. Over time, as they become more efficient (as with stock markets), it is possible that Net Markets could react and respond much like the capital markets, thus providing a real value to the economy.

Market Systems

At the time of writing, there is evidence that market prices across a broad spectrum of industries are declining. Notwithstanding the decline in share prices on the organized capital markets, trading volume was extremely robust after September 11—that is, the markets continued to function despite the scale of the devastation. Indeed, not only have markets continued to function, they appear to be responding quickly to information that in previous eras was processed more slowly. Price declines are an indication of a functioning market system under the twin circumstances of a contracting economy and the devastation of the September 11 tragedy. The tragedy supports the influence of the *Market systems* dimension as a key driver of both B2B and the economy more broadly. For Net Market participants, the effectiveness of the market system supports the fact that B2B Net Markets have a place and value in the economy and can provide significant value in time of uncertainty.

An Accelerator of the Trends in Net Markets?

Will the events of September 11, 2001, be a stimulus to the trends outlined in this book? We are not able to tell. Our MIDST Success Driver Framework and the dimensions of it are supported as a means of evaluating these events and their impact on B2B Net Markets. Net Markets will be impacted by these events because the MIDST drivers will be affected.

The economy and technology's role in it will continue. Net Markets, as a way of ensuring that the economy can function efficiently and ensure that supply and demand are matched, as quickly and efficiently as possible, in any circumstance, seem to be able to play a key role. We can only wait and see what the future will hold for B2B.

Keep your eyes and mind open.

Glossary

Accessibility: An intermediation service produced for the benefit of both the upstream and downstream players, relating to ease of entering market exchange.

Adverse Selection: When one party to a transaction cannot ascertain relevant characteristics of a counter party before the transaction.

Aggregation of Demand: An intermediation service produced for the benefit of upstream players, relating to economies stemming from the grouping of potential buyers.

Aggregation of Supply: An intermediation service produced for the benefit of downstream players, measured in terms of the breadth and depth of the assortment of products available at a supply point in the market system.

Ambiance: The environment created, such as comforts or trappings, for the point at which exchange occurs between transacting parties.

Assurance of Product Delivery: An intermediation service that may provide either the downstream player, the upstream player, or both with assurance that a product desired by the downstream player will be delivered within the time desired by either the upstream or downstream player or in the form desired by the upstream or downstream player.

Availability of Information: Availability of information represents the degree to which each firm within a market system is in a position to inform upstream players of the characteristics of demand and downstream players of the characteristics of supply.

Back-End Integration: A real frontier in future B2B space. Taking the automation of individual company systems and raising it an order of magnitude. What is to prevent a purchase order from rippling back down a company's IT chain to inventory management, accounting, and God-knows-what-all? Nothing. Dell already does this. When you buy a computer on Dell's Web site, all the specifications are sent to manufacturing, which assembles the customized product and immediately updates all company inventory systems.

Broker: A market intermediary, a broker is an agent for buyers and sellers. The role of a broker is to reduce the overall search costs in the market and to provide the facilities to execute orders.

Business Failure: Evidence that an enterprise has not delivered an intended value proposition in a way that produces the intended economic return.

Business Model: An idea, a concept for one to earn an economic return from an activity that provides value for someone else.

Collaborative Commerce: A means of leveraging new technologies to enable a set of complex, cross-enterprise business processes to share decision-making, workflow and other information with each other to create a unique value proposition in the marketplace through the value chain.

Contingent Contract: A contract that ties the seller's compensation to the performance of the product in use after the transaction.

Co-opetition: Combines cooperative strategies with competitive strategies. Enterprises who are co-opetitive cooperate to enlarge the pie and then compete to divide it up. This approach is supported by the notion that a business's opponents need not fail for the business to succeed.

Customer Relations Management (CRM): CRM generally refers to information systems that help sales and marketing functions, as opposed to ERP (Enterprise Resource Planning), which is for back-end integration.

Dealer: A market intermediary who acts as a principal, taking positions for his own account.

Disintermediation: This occurs when one or more player in a value chain is bypassed by at least two transacting parties.

Downstream Player: A buyer of some kind, who purchases or acquires the rights to goods or services to be used or resold; one who consumes a produced good.

Electronic Bill Presentment (EBP): Improves customer review, develops structured ways to handle payments, creates more efficient payment processing by streamlining accounts receivable and accounts payable functions.

Enterprise Application Integration (EAI): EAI ties together business processes between companies so that they can operate more cost effectively, collaborate more effectively with partners and capture value together.

e-Procurement: A market that is established for the benefit of the buyer so that its purchasing can be simplified and more efficient by occurring in a single location.

Functionality: A specification or characteristic of software or of a software platform that performs a function. The most rudimentary functionality is informational: directories, product databases, content, search, editorial content, discussion forums and job markets. More advanced functionality moves toward facilitation: RFQ (Request For Quotation) posting, auctions, negotiation and collaboration. Cutting-edge functionality includes transactional support, such as shipment integration, accounts receivable integration, renegotiated terms and pricing, back-end integration, support of workflow and OLAP (OnLine Analytical Processing) capability.

Fungible: Being of such a nature that one part or quantity may be replaced by another equal part or quantity in the satisfaction of an obligation. For example, legal tender in most national economies [$CDN, $US, Euro, etc.] is a fungible instrument as it can be exchanged for almost anything of value.

Hedge: Taking of a position to reduce one's exposure to risk.

Infomediary: An agent who works as a go-between, in regards to information, for parties that have an interest in transactions dealing with the subject matter.

Information Asymmetries: When different parties to a transaction have different levels of information.

Intermediaries: Players that exist because they perform activities organizing exchange or transactions that others players value.

Legal Tender: Money the state accepts in payment of its claims against its citizens.

Leverage: Analogous to the principle of physics, leverage is the intended advantage gained by asking something small and applying it to achieve some grander purpose. Can be financial or technological.

Liquid: When an asset is liquid, the owner can find another party who would be willing to exchange cash or a money instrument either for the asset or for some instrument secured by the asset.

Liquidity: Strictly speaking, liquidity is the ease with which prices are set to achieve exchange. A liquid market is one that clears easily.

Market System: The market system comprises the mix of supply and demand chains associated with any firm or collection of firms of interest, as well as the firms that enable desired exchanges by providing such ancillary services as credit, advertising and consulting. The key distinguishing element of a market system is the interaction of players through market exchange.

Middleware: A suite of "packaged" software tools that connects various business applications together to allow them to exchange data.

Moral Hazard: Moral hazard exists when one party to a transaction cannot observe the performance or behavior of the counter party after the transaction.

Net Market Makers: The organization that creates a marketplace or hub as the primary "clearing house" for transactions.

Notional Money: A weak form of money that requires an accounting of cumulative positions that parties claim against each other such that periodic net resolution of claims may be recorded.

Operational Efficiency: The benefits derived from improving upon the processes used to create a good or service. These efficiencies could include reduced effort to produce or deliver a good or service. It does not include efficiencies in time or cost associated with changing production processes.

Physicals: In an organized commodities market, these are the actual products being bought and delivered, as opposed to the future or forward purchase or delivery contracts that are traded.

Principal Based System: A trading system in which one party participates as the buyer or seller on each transaction.

Private Marketplace: A marketplace established by an industry player that is solely accessible to its supply chain partners.

Process Relationship Management: The refining of business processes by analyzing the individual steps to ensure efficiency and understanding of the responsibilities of those involved.

Promise to Produce: To create a product, for a specified price, which has features not already available on the market.

Promise to Purchase: A conditional position to buy a product at a certain price.

Public Infrastructure: The backbone network accessible to almost anyone with a common protocol supporting the World Wide Web.

Public Net Market: A market created to be accessed by any party wishing to participate.

Reverse Auction: Auctions with one buyer and many suppliers bidding. Bizbuyer.com, SupplyMarkets.com and FreeMarkets.com are classic examples of a buyer putting out an RFQ and many suppliers bidding against it.

Scalability: How quickly and efficiently can a supplier meet demand? Perhaps the key component of a successful B2B business model. The economies of scale require achieving a threshold level of operations before revenues growth can outstrip the rise in cost of operations.

Space: "Space" in B2B connotes a marketplace, as in "vertical space."

Speculate: To speculate is to take a position for the purpose of attempting to profit from increasing one's exposure to risk.

Supply Chain Management (SCM): Likely to become a key competitive advantage of selected e-marketplaces. Similar concept to Back-End Integration, but with greater emphasis on the moving of goods and services.

Taxonomy: Classification by business types or models.

Translation Hubs: Act as central registries that allow companies to store and retrieve information about trading partner's capabilities, transaction processing requirements and unique integration requirements. With translation hubs, an organization can interface with a trading partner on data and process levels.

Upstream Player: One who produces goods or services for end use or for re-sale.

Value Added Resellers (VARs): Players in the market system who add services to a product that a buyer values.

Value Proposition: What does the net market offer to members? To be effective, the value proposition has to be two-sided, providing benefit to buyers and sellers.

Vertical Hub: A net market serving one specific industry.

Vertical Net Market: A market that is established to serve the upstream and downstream players of a specific industry.

X2X Net Market: A network of Net Markets that have connected to each other to provide benefits to the participants of those connected Net Markets.

XML (Extensible Markup Language): XML is a kind of meta-language allowing businesses to talk to each other.

Index